THE NEGRO

THE NEGRO

W.E.B. DU BOIS

Afterword by Robert Gregg

PENN

University of Pennsylvania Press

Philadelphia

Originally published 1915 by Henry Holt and Company
Afterword copyright © 2001
University of Pennsylvania Press
10 9 8 7 6 5 4 3 2 1

Published by
University of Pennsylvania Press
Philadelphia, Pennsylvania 19104-4011

ISBN 0-8122-1775-6

Library of Congress Cataloging-in-Publication Data

Du Bois, W.E.B. (William Edward Burghardt), 1868-1963.
    The Negro : W.E.B. DuBois ; afterword by Robert Gregg.
        p.   cm.
    ISBN 0-8122-1775-6 (pbk. : alk. paper)
    (Originally published: New York : Holt, 1915).
    Includes bibliographical references and index.
    Black race.   Africa—History. I. Title
HT1581.D8   2001
305'.896.073—dc21   2001027383

TO

A FAITHFUL HELPER

M. G. A.

PREFACE

THE time has not yet come for a complete history of the Negro peoples. Archæological research in Africa has just begun, and many sources of information in Arabian, Portuguese, and other tongues are not fully at our command ; and, too, it must frankly be confessed, racial prejudice against darker peoples is still too strong in so-called civilized centers for judicial appraisement of the peoples of Africa. Much intensive monographic work in history and science is needed to clear mooted points and quiet the controversialist who mistakes present personal desire for scientific proof.

Nevertheless, I have not been able to withstand the temptation to essay such short general statement of the main known facts and their fair interpretation as shall enable the general reader to know as men a sixth or more of the human race. Manifestly so short a story must be mainly conclusions and generalizations with but meager indication of authorities and underlying arguments. Possibly, if the Public will, a later and larger book may be more satisfactory on these points.

W. E. BURGHARDT Du BOIS.

NEW YORK CITY, Feb. 1, 1915.

CONTENTS

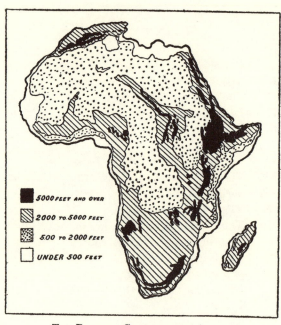

THE PHYSICAL GEOGRAPHY OF AFRICA

THE NEGRO

CHAPTER I

AFRICA

> "Behold!
> The Sphinx is Africa. The bond
> Of Silence is upon her. Old
> And white with tombs, and rent and shorn;
> With raiment wet with tears and torn,
> And trampled on, yet all untamed."
>
> MILLER

AFRICA is at once the most romantic and the
most tragic of continents. Its very names
reveal its mystery and wide-reaching influence.
It is the "Ethiopia" of the Greek, the "Kush"
and "Punt" of the Egyptian, and the Arabian
"Land of the Blacks." To modern Europe it
is the "Dark Continent" and "Land of Contrasts"; in literature it is the seat of the Sphinx
and the lotus eaters, the home of the dwarfs,
gnomes, and pixies, and the refuge of the gods;
in commerce it is the slave mart and the source
of ivory, ebony, rubber, gold, and diamonds.
What other continent can rival in interest this
Ancient of Days?

There are those, nevertheless, who would write
universal history and leave out Africa. But how,
asks Ratzel, can one leave out the land of Egypt

and Carthage? and Frobenius declares that in future Africa must more and more be regarded as an integral part of the great movement of world history. Yet it is true that the history of Africa is unusual, and its strangeness is due in no small degree to the physical peculiarities of the continent. With three times the area of Europe it has a coast line a fifth shorter. Like Europe it is a peninsula of Asia, curving southwestward around the Indian Sea. It has few gulfs, bays, capes, or islands. Even the rivers, though large and long, are not means of communication with the outer world, because from the central high plateau they plunge in rapids and cataracts to the narrow coastlands and the sea.

The general physical contour of Africa has been likened to an inverted plate with one or more rows of mountains at the edge and a low coastal belt. In the south the central plateau is three thousand or more feet above the sea, while in the north it is a little over one thousand feet. Thus two main divisions of the continent are easily distinguished: the broad northern rectangle, reaching down as far as the Gulf of Guinea and Cape Guardafui, with seven million square miles; and the peninsula which tapers toward the south, with five million square miles.

Four great rivers and many lesser streams water the continent. The greatest is the Congo in the center, with its vast curving and endless estuaries; then the Nile, draining the cluster of the Great Lakes and flowing northward "like some grave,

mighty thought, threading a dream"; the Niger
in the northwest, watering the Sudan below the
Sahara; and, finally, the Zambesi, with its greater
Niagara in the southeast. Even these waters
leave room for deserts both south and north, but
the greater ones are the three million square
miles of sand wastes in the north.

More than any other land, Africa lies in the
tropics, with a warm, dry climate, save in the
central Congo region, where rain at all seasons
brings tropical luxuriance. The flora is rich but
not wide in variety, including the gum acacia,
ebony, several dye woods, the kola nut, and probably tobacco and millet. To these many plants
have been added in historic times. The fauna is
rich in mammals, and here, too, many from other
continents have been widely introduced and
used.

Primarily Africa is the Land of the Blacks.
The world has always been familiar with black
men, who represent one of the most ancient of
human stocks. Of the ancient world gathered
about the Mediterranean, they formed a part and
were viewed with no surprise or dislike, because
this world saw them come and go and play their
part with other men. Was Clitus the brother-
in-law of Alexander the Great less to be honored
because he happened to be black? Was Terence
less famous? The medieval European world,
developing under the favorable physical conditions of the north temperate zone, knew the black
man chiefly as a legend or occasional curiosity,

but still as a fellow man — an Othello or a Prester John or an Antar.

The modern world, in contrast, knows the Negro chiefly as a bond slave in the West Indies and America. Add to this the fact that the darker races in other parts of the world have, in the last four centuries, lagged behind the flying and even feverish footsteps of Europe, and we face to-day a widespread assumption throughout the dominant world that color is a mark of inferiority.

The result is that in writing of this, one of the most ancient, persistent, and widespread stocks of mankind, one faces astounding prejudice. That which may be assumed as true of white men must be proven beyond peradventure if it relates to Negroes. One who writes of the development of the Negro race must continually insist that he is writing of a normal human stock, and that whatever it is fair to predicate of the mass of human beings may be predicated of the Negro. It is the silent refusal to do this which has led to so much false writing on Africa and of its inhabitants. Take, for instance, the answer to the apparently simple question "What is a Negro?" We find the most extraordinary confusion of thought and difference of opinion. There is a certain type in the minds of most people which, as David Livingstone said, can be found only in caricature and not in real life. When scientists have tried to find an extreme type of black, ugly, and woolly-haired Negro, they have been compelled more and more to limit his home even in Africa. At least nine-tenths of the African people do not at all conform to this type, and the typical Negro, after being denied a dwelling place in the Sudan, along the Nile, in East Central Africa, and in South Africa, was finally given a very small country between the Senegal and the Niger, and even there was found to give trace of many stocks. As Winwood Reade says, "The typical Negro is a rare variety even among Negroes."

As a matter of fact we cannot take such extreme and largely fanciful stock as typifying that which we may fairly call the Negro race. In the case of no other race is so narrow a definition attempted. A "white" man may be of any color, size, or facial conformation and have endless variety of cranial measurement and physical characteristics. A "yellow" man is perhaps an even vaguer conception.

In fact it is generally recognized to-day that no scientific definition of race is possible. Differences, and striking differences, there are between men and groups of men, but they fade into each other so insensibly that we can only indicate the main divisions of men in broad outlines. As Von Luschan says, "The question of the number of human races has quite lost its *raison d'être* and has become a subject rather of philosophic speculation than of scientific research. It is of no more importance now to know how many human races there are than to know how

many angels can dance on the point of a needle.
Our aim now is to find out how ancient and primitive races developed from others and how races
changed or evolved through migration and in-
ter-breeding." [1]

The mulatto (using the term loosely to indicate either an intermediate type between white
and black or a mingling of the two) is as typically
African as the black man and cannot logically
be included in the "white" race, especially when
American usage includes the mulatto in the Negro
race.

It is reasonable, according to fact and historic
usage, to include under the word "Negro" the
darker peoples of Africa characterized by a brown
skin, curled or "frizzled" hair, full and sometimes everted lips, a tendency to a development
of the maxillary parts of the face, and a doli-
chocephalic head. This type is not fixed or
definite. The color varies widely; it is never
black or bluish, as some say, and it becomes
often light brown or yellow. The hair varies from
curly to a wool-like mass, and the facial angle and
cranial form show wide variation.

It is as impossible in Africa as elsewhere to
fix with any certainty the limits of racial variation due to climate and the variation due to intermingling. In the past, when scientists assumed
one unvarying Negro type, every variation from
that type was interpreted as meaning mixture

[1] Von Luschan: in *Inter-Racial Problems,* p. 16.

of blood. To-day we recognize a broader normal African type which, as Palgrave says, may best be studied "among the statues of the Egyptian rooms of the British Museum; the larger gentle eye, the full but not over-protruding lips, the rounded contour, and the good-natured, easy, sensuous expression. This is the genuine African model." To this race Africa in the main and parts of Asia have belonged since prehistoric times.

The color of this variety of man, as the color of other varieties, is due to climate. Conditions of heat, cold, and moisture, working for thousands of years through the skin and other organs, have given men their differences of color. This color pigment is a protection against sunlight and consequently varies with the intensity of the sunlight. Thus in Africa we find the blackest men in the fierce sunlight of the desert, red pygmies in the forest, and yellow Bushmen on the cooler southern plateau.

Next to the color, the hair is the most distinguishing characteristic. of the Negro, but the two characteristics do not vary with each other. Some of the blackest of the Negroes have curly rather than woolly hair, while the crispest, most closely curled hair is found among the yellow Hottentots and Bushmen. The difference between the hair of the lighter and darker races is a difference of degree, not of kind, and can be easily measured. If the hair follicles of a Chinaman, a European, and a Negro are cut across

transversely, it will be found that the diameter of
the first is 100 by 77 to 85, the second 100 by 62
to 72, while that of the Negro is 100 by 40 to 60.
This elliptical form of the Negro's hair causes it
to curl more or less tightly.

There have been repeated efforts to discover,
by measurements of various kinds, further and
more decisive differences which would serve as
really scientific determinants of race. Gradually
these efforts have been given up. To-day we
realize that there are no hard and fast racial
types among men. Race is a dynamic and not a
static conception, and the typical races are continually changing and developing, amalgamating
and differentiating. In this little book, then, we
are studying the history of the darker part of the
human family, which is separated from the rest
of mankind by no absolute physical line, but which
nevertheless forms, as a mass, a social group distinct in history, appearance, and to some extent
in spiritual gift.

We cannot study Africa without, however,
noting some of the other races concerned in its
history, particularly the Asiatic Semites. The
intercourse of Africa with Arabia and other parts
of Asia has been so close and long-continued that
it is impossible to-day to disentangle the blood
relationships. Negro blood certainly appears in
strong strain among the Semites, and the obvious
mulatto groups in Africa, arising from ancient
and modern mingling of Semite and Negro, has
given rise to the term "Hamite," under cover of

which millions of Negroids have been characteristically transferred to the "white" race by some eager scientists.

The earliest Semites came to Africa across the Red Sea. The Phœnicians came along the northern coasts a thousand years before Christ and began settlements which culminated in Carthage and extended down the Atlantic shores of North Africa nearly to the Gulf of Guinea.

From the earliest times the Greeks have been in contact with Africa as visitors, traders, and colonists, and the Persian influence came with Cambyses and others. Roman Africa was bounded by the desert, but at times came into contact with the blacks across the Sahara and in the valley of the Nile. After the breaking up of the Roman Empire the Greek and Latin Christians filtered through Africa, followed finally by a Germanic invasion in 429 A.D.

In the seventh century the All-Mother, Asia, claimed Africa again for her own and blew a cloud of Semitic Mohammedanism all across North Africa, veiling the dark continent from Europe for a thousand years and converting vast masses of the blacks to Islam. The Portuguese began to raise the veil in the fifteenth century, sailing down the Atlantic coast and initiating the modern slave trade. The Spanish, French, Dutch, and English followed them, but as traders in men rather than explorers.

The Portuguese explored the coasts of the Gulf of Guinea, visiting the interior kingdoms, and then passing by the mouth of the Congo proceeded southward. Eventually they rounded the Cape of Good Hope and pursued their explorations as far as the mountains of Abyssinia. This began the modern exploration of Africa, which is a curious fairy tale, and recalls to us the great names of Livingstone, Burton, Speke, Stanley, Barth, Schweinfurth, and many others. In this way Africa has been made known to the modern world.

The difficulty of this modern lifting of the veil of centuries emphasizes two physical facts that underlie all African history: the peculiar inaccessibility of the continent to peoples from without, which made it so easily possible for the great human drama played here to hide itself from the ears of other worlds; and, on the other hand, the absence of interior barriers — the great stretch of that central plateau which placed practically every budding center of culture at the mercy of barbarism, sweeping a thousand miles, with no Alps or Himalayas or Appalachians to hinder.

With this peculiarly uninviting coast line and the difficulties in interior segregation must be considered the climate of Africa. While there is much diversity and many salubrious tracts along with vast barren wastes, yet, as Sir Harry Johnston well remarks, "Africa is the chief stronghold of the real Devil — the reactionary forces of Nature hostile to the uprise of Humanity. Here Beelzebub, King of the Flies, marshals his vermiform and arthropod hosts — insects, ticks, and nematode worms — which more than in other continents (excepting Negroid Asia) convey to the skin, veins, intestines, and spinal marrow of men and other vertebrates the micro-organisms which cause deadly, disfiguring, or debilitating diseases, or themselves create the morbid condition of the persecuted human being, beasts, bird, reptile, frog, or fish." [1] The inhabitants of this land have had a sheer fight for physical survival comparable with that in no other great continent, and this must not be forgotten when we consider their history.

[1] Johnston: *Negro in the New World*, pp. 14–15.

CHAPTER II

THE movements of prehistoric man can be seen as yet but dimly in the uncertain mists of time. This is the story that to-day seems most probable: from some center in southern Asia primitive human beings began to differentiate in two directions. Toward the south appeared the primitive Negro, long-headed and with flattened hair follicle. He spread along southern Asia and passed over into Africa, where he survives to-day as the reddish dwarfs of the center and the Bushmen of South Africa.

Northward and eastward primitive man became broader headed and straight-haired and spread over eastern Asia, forming the Mongolian type. Either through the intermingling of these two types or, as some prefer to think, by the direct prolongation of the original primitive man, a third intermediate type of human being appeared with hair and cranial measurement intermediate between the primitive Negro and Mongolian. All these three types of men intermingled their blood freely and developed variations according to climate and environment.

Other and older theories and legends of the origin and spread of mankind are of interest now only because so many human beings have believed them in the past. The biblical story of Shem, Ham, and Japheth retains the interest of a primitive myth with its measure of allegorical truth,[1] but has, of course, no historic basis.

The older "Aryan" theory assumed the migration into Europe of one dominant Asiatic race of civilized conquerors, to whose blood and influence all modern culture was due. To this "white" race Semitic Asia, a large part of black Africa, and all Europe was supposed to belong. This "Aryan" theory has been practically abandoned in the light of recent research, and it seems probable now that from the primitive Negroid stock evolved in Asia the Semites either by local variation or intermingling with other stocks; later there developed the Mediterranean race, with Negroid characteristics, and the modern Negroes. The blue-eyed, light-haired Germanic people may have arisen as a modern variation of the mixed peoples produced by the mingling of Asiatic and African elements. The last word on this development has not yet been said, and there is still much

---

[1] Ham is probably the Egyptian word "Khem" (black), the native name of Egypt. In the original myth Canaan and not Ham was Noah's third son.

The biblical story of the "curse of Canaan" (Genesis IX, 24–25) has been the basis of an astonishing literature which has to-day only a psychological interest. It is sufficient to remember that for several centuries leaders of the Christian Church gravely defended Negro slavery and oppression as the rightful curse of God upon the descendants of a son who had been disrespectful to his drunken father! Cf. Bishop Hopkins: *Bible Views of Slavery*, p. 7.

to learn and explain; but it is certainly proved to-day beyond doubt that the so-called Hamites of Africa, the brown and black curly and frizzly-haired inhabitants of North and East Africa, are not "white" men if we draw the line between white and black in any logical way.

The primitive Negroid race of men developed in Asia wandered eastward as well as westward. They entered on the one hand Burmah and the South Sea Islands, and on the other hand they came through Mesopotamia and gave curly hair and a Negroid type to Jew, Syrian, and Assyrian. Ancient statues of Indian divinities show the Negro type with black face and close-curled hair, and early Babylonian culture was Negroid. In Arabia the Negroes may have divided, and one stream perhaps wandered into Europe by way of Syria. Traces of these Negroes are manifest not only in skeletons, but in the brunette type of all South Europe. The other branch proceeded to Egypt and tropical Africa. Another, but perhaps less probable, theory is that ancient Negroes may have entered Africa from Europe, since the most ancient skulls of Algeria are Negroid.

The primitive African was not an extreme type. One may judge from modern pygmy and Bushmen that his color was reddish or yellow, and his skull was sometimes round like the Mongolian. He entered Africa not less than fifty thousand years ago and settled eventually in the broad region between Lake Chad and the

Great Lakes and remained there long stretches of years.

After a lapse of perhaps thirty thousand years there entered Africa a further migration of Asiatic people, Negroid in many characteristics, but lighter and straighter haired than the primitive Negroes. From this Mediterranean race was developed the modern inhabitants of the shores of the Mediterranean in Europe, Asia, and Africa and, by mingling with the primitive Negroes, the ancient Egyptians and modern Negroid races of Africa.

As we near historic times the migrations of men became more frequent from Asia and from Europe, and in Africa came movements and minglings which give to the whole of Africa a distinct mulatto character. The primitive Negro stock was "mulatto" in the sense of being not widely differentiated from the dark, original Australoid stock. As the earlier yellow Negro developed in the African tropics to the bigger, blacker type, he was continually mingling his blood with similar types developed in temperate climes to sallower color and straighter hair.

We find therefore, in Africa to-day, every degree of development in Negroid stocks and every degree of intermingling of these developments, both among African peoples and between Africans, Europeans, and Asiatics. The mistake is continually made of considering these types as transitions between absolute Caucasians and absolute Negroes. No such absolute type

ever existed on either side. Both were slowly
differentiated from a common ancestry and continually remingled their blood while the differentiating was progressing. From prehistoric
times down to to-day Africa is, in this sense,
primarily the land of the mulatto. So, too, was
earlier Europe and Asia; only in these countries
the mulatto was early bleached by the climate,
while in Africa he was darkened.

It is not easy to summarize the history of
these dark African peoples, because so little is
known and so much is still in dispute. Yet, by
avoiding the real controversies and being unafraid
of mere questions of definition, we may trace a
great human movement with considerable defi-
niteness.

Three main Negro types early made their
appearance: the lighter and smaller primitive
stock; the larger forest Negro in the center and
on the west coast, and the tall, black Nilotic
Negro in the eastern Sudan. In the earliest
times we find the Negroes in the valley of the
Nile, pressing downward from the interior. Here
they mingled with Semitic types, and after a
lapse of millenniums there arose from this mingling the culture of Ethiopia and Egypt, probably
the first of higher human cultures.

To the west of the Nile the Negroes expanded
straight across the continent to the Atlantic.
Centers of higher culture appeared very early
along the Gulf of Guinea and curling backward
met Egyptian, Ethiopian, and even European

and Asiatic influences about Lake Chad. To the
southeast, nearer the primitive seats of the earliest African immigrants and open to Egyptian
and East Indian influences, the Negro culture
which culminated at Zymbabwe arose, and one
may trace throughout South Africa its wide ramifications.

All these movements gradually aroused the
central tribes to unrest. They beat against the
barriers north, northeast, and west, but gradually settled into a great southeastward migration. Calling themselves proudly La Bantu
(The People), they grew by agglomeration into
a warlike nation, speaking one language. They
eventually conquered all Africa south of the Gulf
of Guinea and spread their influence to the
northward.

While these great movements were slowly
transforming Africa, she was also receiving influences from beyond her shores and sending
influences out. With mulatto Egypt black
Africa was always in closest touch, so much so
that to some all evidences of Negro uplift seem
Egyptian in origin. The truth is, rather, that
Egypt was herself always palpably Negroid, and
from her vantage ground as almost the only
African gateway received and transmitted Negro
ideals.

Phœnician, Greek, and Roman came into
touch more or less with black Africa. Carthage,
that North African city of a million men, had a
large caravan trade with Negroland in ivory,

metals, cloth, precious stones, and slaves. Black men served in the Carthaginian armies and marched with Hannibal on Rome. In some of the North African kingdoms the infiltration of Negro blood was very large and kings like Massinissa and Jugurtha were Negroid. By way of the Atlantic the Carthaginians reached the African west coast. Greek and Roman influences came through the desert, and the Byzantine Empire and Persia came into communication with Negroland by way of the valley of the Nile. The influence of these trade routes, added to those of Egypt, Ethiopia, Benin, and Yoruba, stimulated centers of culture in the central and western Sudan, and European and African trade early reached large volume.

Negro soldiers were used largely in the armies that enabled the Mohammedans to conquer North Africa and Spain. Beginning in the tenth century and slowly creeping across the desert into Negroland, the new religion found an already existent culture and came, not a conqueror, but as an adapter and inspirer. Civilization received new impetus and a wave of Mohammedanism swept eastward, erecting the great kingdoms of Melle, the Songhay, Bornu, and the Hausa states. The older Negro culture was not overthrown, but, like a great wedge, pushed upward and inward from Yoruba, and gave stubborn battle to the newer culture for seven or eight centuries.

Then it was, in the fifteenth century, that the

heart disease of Africa developed in its most
virulent form. There is a modern theory that
black men are and always have been naturally
slaves. Nothing is further from the truth. In
the ancient world Africa was no more a slave
hunting ground than Europe or Asia, and both
Greece and Rome had much larger numbers of
white slaves than of black. It was natural that
a stream of black slaves should have poured into
Egypt, because the chief line of Egyptian conquest and defense lay toward the heart of Africa.
Moreover, the Egyptians, themselves of Negro
descent, had not only Negro slaves but Negroes
among their highest nobility and even among
their Pharaohs. Mohammedan conquerors enslaved peoples of all colors in Europe, Asia, and
Africa, but eventually their empire centered in
Asia and Africa and their slaves came principally from these countries. Asia submitted to
Islam except in the Far East, which was self-
protecting. Negro Africa submitted only partially, and the remaining heathen were in small
states which could not effectively protect themselves against the Mohammedan slave trade.
In this wise the slave trade gradually began to
center in Africa, for religious and political rather
than for racial reasons.

The typical African culture was the culture of
family, town, and small tribe. Hence domestic
slavery easily developed a slave trade through
war and commerce. Only the integrating force
of state building could have stopped this slave

trade. Was this failure to develop the great state a racial characteristic? This does not seem a fair conclusion. In four great centers state building began in Africa. In Ethiopia several large states were built up, but they tottered before the onslaughts of Egypt, Persia, Rome, and Byzantium, on the one hand, and finally fell before the turbulent Bantu warriors from the interior. The second attempt at empire building began in the southeast, but the same Bantu hordes, pressing now slowly, now fiercely, from the congested center of the continent, gradually overthrew this state and erected on its ruins a series of smaller and more transient kingdoms.

The third attempt at state building arose on the Guinea coast in Benin and Yoruba. It never got much beyond a federation of large industrial cities. Its expansion toward the Congo valley was probably a prime cause of the original Bantu movements to the southeast. Toward the north and northeast, on the other hand, these city-states met the Sudanese armed with the new imperial Mohammedan idea. Just as Latin Rome gave the imperial idea to the Nordic races, so Islam brought this idea to the Sudan.

In the consequent attempts at imperialism in the western Sudan there arose the largest of the African empires. Two circumstances, however, militated against this empire building: first, the fierce resistance of the heathen south made war continuous and slaves one of the articles of systematic commerce. Secondly, the highways of legitimate African commerce had for millenniums lain to the northward. These were suddenly closed by the Moors in the sixteenth century, and the Negro empires were thrown into the turmoil of internal war.

It was then that the European slave traders came from the southwest. They found partially disrupted Negro states on the west coast and falling empires in the Sudan, together with the old unrest of over-population and migration in the valley of the Congo. They not only offered a demand for the usual slave trade, but they increased it to an enormous degree, until their demand, added to the demand of the Mohammedan in Africa and Asia, made human beings the highest priced article of commerce in Africa. Under such circumstances there could be but one end: the virtual uprooting of ancient African culture, leaving only misty reminders of the ruin in the customs and work of the people. To complete this disaster came the partition of the continent among European nations and the modern attempt to exploit the country and the natives for the economic benefit of the white world, together with the transplanting of black nations to the new western world and their rise and self-assertion there.

CHAPTER III

HAVING viewed now the land and movements of African people in main outline, let us scan more narrowly the history of five main centers of activity and culture, namely: the valleys of the Nile and of the Congo, the borders of the great Gulf of Guinea, the Sudan, and South Africa. These divisions do not cover all of Negro Africa, but they take in the main areas and the main lines in development.

First, we turn to the valley of the Nile, perhaps the most ancient of known seats of civilization in the world, and certainly the oldest in Africa, with a culture reaching back six or eight thousand years. Like all civilizations it drew largely from without and undoubtedly arose in the valley of the Nile, because that valley was so easily made a center for the meeting of men of all types and from all parts of the world. At the same time Egyptian civilization seems to have been African in its beginnings and in its main line of development, despite strong influences from all parts of Asia. Of what race, then, were the Egyptians? They certainly were not white in any sense of the modern use of that word — neither in color nor physical measurement, in hair nor countenance, in language nor social customs. They stood in relationship nearest the Negro race in earliest times, and then gradually through the infiltration of Mediterranean and Semitic elements became what would be described in America as a light mulatto stock of Octoroons or Quadroons. This stock was varied continually: now by new infiltration of Negro blood from the south, now by Negroid and Semitic blood from the east, now by Berber types from the north and west.

Egyptian monuments show distinctly Negro and mulatto faces. Herodotus, in an incontrovertible passage, alludes to the Egyptians as "black and curly-haired" [1] — a peculiarly significant statement from one used to the brunette Mediterranean type; in another passage, concerning the fable of the Dodonian Oracle, he again alludes to the swarthy color of the Egyptians as exceedingly dark and even black. Æschylus, mentioning a boat seen from the shore, declares that its crew are Egyptians, because of their black complexions.

Modern measurements, with all their admitted limitations, show that in the Thebaid from oneseventh to one-third of the Egyptian population were Negroes, and that of the predynastic Egyptians less than half could be classed as nonNegroid. Judging from measurements in the tombs of nobles as late as the eighteenth dynasty,

---

[1] "αὐτός δὲ εἴκασα τῇδε καὶ ὅτε μελάγχροές εἰσι καὶ οὐλότριχες." Liber II, Cap. 104.

Negroes form at least one-sixth of the higher class.[1]

Such measurements are by no means conclusive, but they are apt to be under rather than over statements of the prevalence of Negro blood. Head measurements of Negro Americans would probably place most of them in the category of whites. The evidence of language also connects Egypt with Africa and the Negro race rather than with Asia, while religious ceremonies and social customs all go to strengthen this evidence.

The ethnic history of Northeast Africa would seem, therefore, to have been this: predynastic Egypt was settled by Negroes from Ethiopia. They were of varied types: the broad-nosed, woolly-haired type to which the word "Negro" is sometimes confined; the black, curly-haired, sharper featured type, which must be considered an equally Negroid variation. These Negroes met and mingled with the invading Mediterranean race from North Africa and Asia. Thus the blood of the sallower race spread south and that of the darker race north. Black priests appear in Crete three thousand years before Christ, and Arabia is to this day thoroughly permeated with Negro blood. Perhaps, as Chamberlain says, "one of the prime reasons why no civilization of the type of that of the Nile arose in other parts of the continent, if such a thing were at all possible, was that Egypt acted as a sort of channel by which the genius of Negro-

[1] Cf. Maciver and Thompson: *Ancient Races of the Thebaid.*

land was drafted off into the service of Mediterranean and Asiatic culture." [1]

To one familiar with the striking and beautiful types arising from the mingling of Negro with Latin and Germanic types in America, the puzzle of the Egyptian type is easily solved. It was unlike any of its neighbors and a unique type until one views the modern mulatto; then the faces of Rahotep and Nefert, of Khafra and Amenemhat I, of Aahmes and Nefertari, and even of the great Ramessu II, become curiously familiar.

The history, of Egypt is a science in itself. Before the reign of the first recorded king, five thousand years or more before Christ, there had already existed in Egypt a culture and art arising by long evolution from the days of paleolithic man, among a distinctly Negroid people. About 4777 B.C. Aha-Mena began the first of three successive Egyptian empires. This lasted two thousand years, with many Pharaohs, like Khafra of the Fourth Dynasty, of a strongly Negroid cast of countenance.

At the end of the period the empire fell apart into Egyptian and Ethiopian halves, and a silence of three centuries ensued. It is quite possible that an incursion of conquering black men from the south poured over the land in these years and dotted Egypt in the next centuries with monuments on which the full-blooded Negro type is strongly and trium-

[1] *Journal of Race Development*, I, 484.

phantly impressed. The great Sphinx at Gizeh, so familiar to all the world, the Sphinxes of Tanis, the statue from the Fayum, the statue of the Esquiline at Rome, and the Colossi of Bubastis all represent black, full-blooded Negroes and are described by Petrie as "having high cheek bones, flat cheeks, both in one plane, a massive nose, firm projecting lips, and thick hair, with an austere and almost savage expression of power." [1]

Blyden, the great modern black leader of West Africa, said of the Sphinx at Gizeh: "Her features are decidedly of the African or Negro type, with 'expanded nostrils.' If, then, the Sphinx was placed here — looking out in majestic and mysterious silence over the empty plain where once stood the great city of Memphis in all its pride and glory, as an 'emblematic representation of the king' — is not the inference clear as to the peculiar type or race to which that king belonged?" [2]

The middle empire arose 3064 B.C. and lasted nearly twenty-four centuries. Under Pharaohs whose Negro descent is plainly evident, like Amenemhat I and III and Usertesen I, the ancient glories of Egypt were restored and surpassed. At the same time there is strong continuous pressure from the wild and unruly Negro tribes of the upper Nile valley, and we get some idea of the fear which they inspired throughout Egypt

[1] Petrie: *History of Egypt*, I, 51, 237.
[2] *From West Africa to Palestine*, p. 114.

when we read of the great national rejoicing which followed the triumph of Usertesen III (c. 2660–22) over these hordes. He drove them back and attempted to confine them to the edge of the Nubian Desert above the Second Cataract. Hemmed in here, they set up a state about this time and founded Nepata.

Notwithstanding this repulse of black men, less than one hundred years later a full-blooded Negro from the south, Ra Nehesi, was seated on the throne of the Pharaohs and was called "The king's eldest son." This may mean that an incursion from the far south had placed a black conqueror on the throne. At any rate, the whole empire was in some way shaken, and two hundred years later the invasion of the Hyksos began. The domination of Hyksos kings who may have been Negroids from Asia [1] lasted for five hundred years.

The redemption of Egypt from these barbarians came from Upper Egypt, led by the mulatto Aahmes. He founded in 1703 B.C. the new empire, which lasted fifteen hundred years. His queen, Nefertari, "the most venerated figure of Egyptian history," [2] was a Negress of great beauty, strong personality, and of unusual administrative force. She was for many years

[1] Depending partly on whether the so-called Hyksos sphinxes belong to the period of the Hyksos kings or to an earlier period (cf. Petrie, I, 52–53, 237). That Negroids largely dominated in the early history of western Asia is proven by the monuments.

[2] Petrie: *History of Egypt*, II, 337.

joint ruler with her son, Amenhotep I, who succeeded his father.[1]

The new empire was a period of foreign conquest and internal splendor and finally of
religious dispute and overthrow. Syria was conquered in these reigns and Asiatic civilization
and influences poured in upon Egypt. The great
Tahutmes III, whose reign was "one of the
grandest and most eventful in Egyptian history,"[2]
had a strong Negroid countenance, as had also
Queen Hatshepsut, who sent the celebrated expedition to reopen ancient trade with the Hottentots of Punt. A new strain of Negro blood
came to the royal line through Queen Mutemua
about 1420 B.C., whose son, Amenhotep III,
built a great temple at Luqsor and the Colossi
at Memnon.

The whole of the period in a sense culminated
in the great Ramessu II, the oppressor of the
Hebrews, who with his Egyptian, Libyan, and
Negro armies fought half the world. His reign,
however, was the beginning of decline, and foes
began to press Egypt from the white north and
the black south. The priests transferred their
power at Thebes, while the Assyrians under
Nimrod overran Lower Egypt. The center of
interest is now transferred to Ethiopia, and
we pass to the more shadowy history of that
land.

The most perfect example of Egyptian poetry

[1] Chamberlain: *Journal of Race Development*, April, 1911.
[2] Petrie: *History of Egypt*, II, 337.

left to us is a celebration of the prowess of Usertesen III in confining the turbulent Negro tribes to the territory below the Second Cataract of the Nile. The Egyptians called this territory Kush, and in the farthest confines of Kush lay Punt, the cradle of their race. To the ancient Mediterranean world Ethiopia (i.e., the Land of the Black-faced) was a region of gods and fairies. Zeus and Poseidon feasted each year among the "blameless Ethiopians," and Black Memnon, King of Ethiopia, was one of the greatest of heroes.

"The Ethiopians conceive themselves," says Diodorus Siculus (Lib. III), "to be of greater antiquity than any other nation; and it is probable that, born under the sun's path, its warmth may have ripened them earlier than other men. They suppose themselves also to be the inventors of divine worship, of festivals, of solemn assemblies, of sacrifices, and every religious practice. They affirm that the Egyptians are one of their colonies."

The Egyptians themselves, in later days, affirmed that they and their civilization came from the south and from the black tribes of Punt, and certainly "at the earliest period in which human remains have been recovered Egypt and Lower Nubia appear to have formed culturally and racially one land." [1]

The forging ahead of Egypt in culture was mainly from economic causes. Ethiopia, living

[1] Reisner: *Archeological Survey of Nubia*, I, 319.

in a much poorer land with limited agricultural facilities, held to the old arts and customs, and at the same time lost the best elements of its population to Egypt, absorbing meantime the oncoming and wilder Negro tribes from the south and west. Under the old empire, therefore, Ethiopia remained in comparative poverty, except as some of its tribes invaded Egypt with their handicrafts.

As soon as the civilization below the Second Cataract reached a height noticeably above that of Ethiopia, there was continued effort to protect that civilization against the incursion of barbarians. Hundreds of campaigns through thousands of years repeatedly subdued or checked the blacks and brought them in as captives to mingle their blood with the Egyptian nation; but the Egyptian frontier was not advanced.

A separate and independent Ethiopian culture finally began to arise during the middle empire of Egypt and centered at Nepata and Meroe. Widespread trade in gold, ivory, precious stones, skins, wood, and works of handicraft arose.[1] The Negro began to figure as the great trader of Egypt.

This new wealth of Ethiopia excited the cupidity of the Pharaohs and led to aggression and larger intercourse, until at last, when the dread Hyksos appeared, Ethiopia became both a physical and cultural refuge for conquered Egypt. The legitimate Pharaohs moved to Thebes, nearer the

---

[1] Hoskins declares that the arch had its origin in Ethiopia.

boundaries of Ethiopia, and from here, under Negroid rulers, Lower Egypt was redeemed.

The ensuing new empire witnessed the gradual incorporation of Ethiopia into Egypt, although the darker kingdom continued to resist. Both mulatto Pharaohs, Aahmes and Amenhotep I, sent expeditions into Ethiopia, and in the latter's day sons of the reigning Pharaoh began to assume the title of "Royal Son of Kush" in some such way as the son of the King of England becomes the Prince of Wales.

Trade relations were renewed with Punt under circumstances which lead us to place that land in the region of the African lakes. The Sudanese tribes were aroused by these and other incursions, until the revolts became formidable in the fourteenth century before Christ.

Egyptian culture, however, gradually conquered Ethiopia where her armies could not, and Egyptian religion and civil rule began to center in the darker kingdom. When, therefore, Shesheng I, the Libyan, usurped the throne of the Pharaohs in the tenth century b.c., the Egyptian legitimate dynasty went to Nepata as king priests and established a theocratic monarchy. Gathering strength, the Ethiopian kingdom under this dynasty expanded north about 750 b.c. and for a century ruled all Egypt.

The first king, Pankhy, was Egyptian bred and not noticeably Negroid, but his successors showed more and more evidence of Negro blood — Kashta the Kushite, Shabaka, Tarharqa, and

Tanutamen. During the century of Ethiopian rule a royal son was appointed to rule Egypt, just as formerly a royal Egyptian had ruled Kush. In many ways this Ethiopian kingdom showed its Negro peculiarities: first, in its worship of distinctly Sudanese gods; secondly, in the rigid custom of female succession in the kingdom, and thirdly, by the election of kings from the various royal claimants to the throne. "It was the heyday of the Negro. For the greater part of the century. . . . Egypt itself was subject to the blacks, just as in the new empire the Sudan had been subject to Egypt."[1]

Egypt now began to fall into the hands of Asia and was conquered first by the Assyrians and then by the Persians, but the Ethiopian kings kept their independence. Aspeluta, whose mother and sister are represented as full-blooded Negroes, ruled from 630 to 600 B.C. Horsiatef (560–525 B.C.) made nine expeditions against the warlike tribes south of Meroe, and his successor, Nastosenen (525–500 B.C.) was the one who repelled Cambyses. He also removed the capital from Nepata to Meroe, although Nepata continued to be the religious capital and the Ethiopian kings were still crowned on its golden throne.

From the fifth to the second century B.C. we find the wild Sudanese tribes pressing in from the west and Greek culture penetrating from the east. King Arg-Amen (Ergamenes) showed

[1] Maciver and Wooley: *Areika*, p. 2.

strong Greek influences and at the same time
began to employ the Ethiopian speech in writing
and used a new Ethiopian alphabet.

While the Ethiopian kings were still crowned
at Nepata, Meroe gradually became the real
capital and supported at one time four thousand
artisans and two hundred thousand soldiers. It
was here that the famous Candaces reigned as
queens. Pliny tells us that one Candace of the
time of Nero had had forty-four predecessors on
the throne, while another Candace figures in the
New Testament.[1]

It was probably this latter Candace who
warred against Rome at the time of Augustus
and received unusual consideration from her
formidable foe. The prestige of Ethiopia at
this time was considerable throughout the
world. Pseudo-Callisthenes tells an evidently
fabulous story of the visit of Alexander the
Great to Candace, Queen of Meroe, which nevertheless illustrates her fame: Candace will not
let him enter Ethiopia and says he is not to
scorn her people because they are black, for they
are whiter in soul than his white folk. She sent
him gold, maidens, parrots, sphinxes, and a crown
of emeralds and pearls. She ruled eighty tribes,
who were ready to punish those who attacked her.

The Romans continued to have so much
trouble with their Ethiopian frontier that finally,
when Semitic mulattoes appeared in the east,
the Emperor Diocletian invited the wild Sudanese

[1] Acts VIII, 27.

tribe of Nubians (Nobadæ) from the west to repel them. These Nubians eventually embraced Christianity, and northern Ethiopia came to be known in time as Nubia.

The Semitic mulattoes from the east came from the highlands bordering the Red Sea and Asia. On both sides this sea Negro blood is strongly in evidence, predominant in Africa and influential in Asia. Ludolphus, writing in the seventeenth century, says that the Abyssinians "are generally black, which [color] they most admire." Trade and war united the two shores, and merchants have passed to and fro for thirty centuries.

In this way Arabian, Jewish, Egyptian, Greek, and Roman influences spread slowly upon the Negro foundation. Early legendary history declares' that a queen, Maqueda, or Nikaula of Sheba, a state of Central Abyssinia, visited Solomon in 1050 B.C. and had her son Menelik educated in Jerusalem. This was the supposed beginning of the Axumite kingdom, the capital of which, Axume, was a flourishing center of trade. Ptolemy Evergetes and his successors did much to open Abyssinia to the world, but most of the population of that day was nomadic. In the fourth century Byzantine influences began to be felt, and in 330 St. Athanasius of Alexandria consecrated Fromentius as Bishop of Ethiopia. He tutored the heir to the Abyssinian kingdom and began its gradual christianization. By the early part of the sixth century Abyssinia was trading with India and Byzantium and was so far recognized as a Christian country that the Emperor Justinian appealed to King Kaleb to protect the Christians in southwestern Arabia. Kaleb conquered Yemen in 525 and held it fifty years.

Eventually a Jewish princess, Judith, usurped the Axumite throne; the Abyssinians were expelled from Arabia, and a long period begins when as Gibbon says, "encompassed by the enemies of their religion, the Ethiopians slept for nearly a thousand years, forgetful of the world by whom they were forgotten." Throughout the middle ages, however, the legend of a great Christian kingdom hidden away in Africa persisted, and the search for Prester John became one of the world quests.

It was the expanding power of Abyssinia that led Rome to call in the Nubians from the western desert. The Nubians had formed a strong league of tribes, and as the ancient kingdom of Ethiopia declined they drove back the Abyssinians, who had already established themselves at Meroe.

In the sixth century the Nubians were converted to Christianity by a Byzantine priest, and they immediately began to develop. A new capital, Dongola, replaced Nepata and Meroe, and by the twelfth century churches and brick dwellings had appeared. As the Mohammedan flood pressed up the Nile valley it was the Nubians that held it back for two centuries.

Farther south other wild tribes pushed out of the Sudan and began a similar development. Chief among these were the Fung, who fixed their capital at Senaar, at the junction of the White and Blue Nile. When the Mohammedan flood finally passed over Nubia, the Fung diverted it by declaring themselves Moslems. This left the Fung as the dominant power in the fifteenth century from the Three Cataracts to Fazogli and from the Red Sea at Suakin to the White Nile. Islam then swept on south in a great circle, skirted the Great Lakes, and then curled back to Somaliland, completely isolating Abyssinia.

Between the thirteenth and sixteenth centuries the Egyptian Sudan became a congeries of Mohammedan kingdoms with Arab, mulatto, and Negro kings. Far to the west, near Lake Chad, arose in 1520 the sultanate of Baghirmi, which reached its highest power in the seventh century. This dynasty was overthrown by the Negroid Mabas, who established Wadai to the eastward about 1640. South of Wadai lay the heathen and cannibals of the Congo valley, against which Islam never prevailed. East of Wadai and nearer the Nile lay the kindred state of Darfur, a Nubian nation whose sultans reigned over two hundred years and which reached great prosperity in the early seventeenth century under Soliman Solon.

Before the Mohammedan power reached Abyssinia the Portuguese pioneers had entered the country from the east and begun to open the country again to European knowledge. Without doubt, in the centuries of silence, a civilization of some height had flourished in Abyssinia, but all authentic records were destroyed by fire in the tenth century. When the Portuguese came, the older Axumite kingdom had fallen and had been succeeded by a number of petty states.

The Sudanese kingdoms of the Sudan resisted the power of the Mameluke beys in Egypt, and later the power of the Turks until the nineteenth century, when the Sudan was made nominally a part of Egypt. Continuous upheaval, war, and conquest had by this time done their work, and little of ancient Ethiopian culture survived except the slave trade.

The entrance of England into Egypt, after the building of the Suez Canal, stirred up eventually revolt in the Sudan, for political, economic, and religious reasons. Led by a Sudanese Negro, Mohammed Ahmad, who claimed to be the Messiah (Mahdi), the Sudan arose in revolt in 1881, determined to resist a hated religion, foreign rule, and interference with their chief commerce, the trade in slaves. The Sudan was soon aflame, and the able mulatto general, Osman Digna, aided by revolt among the heathen Dinka, drove Egypt and England out of the Sudan for sixteen years. It was not until 1898 that England reëntered the Sudan and in petty revenge desecrated the bones of the brave, even if misguided, prophet.

Meantime this Mahdist revolt had delayed England's designs on Abyssinia, and the Italians, replacing her, attempted a protectorate. Menelik of Shoa, one of the smaller kingdoms of Abyssinia, was a shrewd man of predominantly Negro blood, and had been induced to make a treaty with the Italians after King John had been killed by the Mahdists. The exact terms of the treaty were disputed, but undoubtedly the Italians tried by this means to reduce Menelik to vassalage. Menelik stoutly resisted, and at the great battle of Adua, one of the decisive battles of the modern world, the Abyssinians on March 1, 1896, inflicted a crushing defeat on the Italians, killing four thousand of them and capturing two thousand prisoners. The empress, Taitou, a full-blooded Negress, led some of the charges. By this battle Abyssinia became independent.

Such in vague and general outline is the strange story of the valley of the Nile — of Egypt, the motherland of human culture and

> "That starr'd Ethiop Queen that strove
> To set her beauty's praise above
> The sea nymphs."

CHAPTER IV

THE NIGER AND ISLAM

THE Arabian expression "Bilad es Sudan" (Land of the Blacks) was applied to the whole region south of the Sahara, from the Atlantic to the Nile. It is a territory some thirty-five hundred miles by six hundred miles, containing two million square miles, and has to-day a population of perhaps eighty million. It is thus two-thirds the size of the United States and quite as thickly settled. In the western Sudan the Niger plays the same role as the Nile in the east. In this chapter we follow the history of the Niger.

The history of this part of Africa was probably something as follows: primitive man, entering Africa from Arabia, found the Great Lakes, spread in the Nile valley, and wandered westward to the Niger. Herodotus tells of certain youths who penetrated the desert to the Niger and found there a city of black dwarfs. Succeeding migrations of Negroes and Negroids pushed the dwarfs gradually into the inhospitable forests and occupied the Sudan, pushing on to the Atlantic. Here the newcomers, curling northward, met the Mediterranean race coming down across the western desert, while to the southward the Negro came to the Gulf of Guinea and the thick forests of the Congo valley. Indigenous civilizations arose on the west coast in Yoruba and Benin, and contact of these with the Mediterranean race in the desert, and with Egyptian and Arab from the east, gave rise to centers of Negro culture in the Sudan at Ghana and Melle and in Songhay, Nupe, the Hausa states, and Bornu.

The history of the Sudan thus leads us back again to Ethiopia, that strange and ancient center of world civilization whose inhabitants in the ancient world were considered to be the most pious and the oldest of men. From this center the black originators of African culture, and to a large degree of world culture, wandered not simply down the Nile, but also westward. These Negroes developed the original substratum of culture which later influences modified but never displaced.

We know that Egyptian Pharaohs in several cases ventured into the western Sudan and that Egyptian influences are distinctly traceable. Greek and Byzantine culture and Phœnician and Carthaginian trade also penetrated, while Islam finally made this whole land her own. Behind all these influences, however, stood from the first an indigenous Negro culture. The stone figures of Sherbro, the megaliths of Gambia, the art and industry of the west coast are all too deep and original evidences of civilization to be merely importations from abroad.

Nor was the Sudan the inert recipient of foreign influence when it came. According to credible legend, the "Great King" at Byzantium imported glass, tin, silver, bronze, cut stones, and other treasure from the Sudan. Embassies were sent and states like Nupe recognized the suzerainty of the Byzantine emperor. The people of Nupe especially were filled with pride when the Byzantine people learned certain kinds of work in bronze and glass from them, and this intercourse was only interrupted by the Mohammedan conquest.

To this ancient culture, modified somewhat by Byzantine and Christian influences, came Islam. It approached from the northwest, coming stealthily and slowly and being handed on particularly by the Mandingo Negroes. About 1000–1200 A.D. the situation was this: Ghana was on the edge of the desert in the north, Mandingoland between the Niger and the Senegal in the south and the western Sahara, Djolof was in the west on the Senegal, and the Songhay on the Niger in the center. The Mohammedans came chiefly as traders and found a trade already established. Here and there in the great cities were districts set aside for these new merchants, and the Mohammedans gave frequent evidence of their respect for these black nations.

Islam did not found new states, but modified and united Negro states already ancient; it did not initiate new commerce, but developed a widespread trade already established. It is, as Frobenius says, "easily proved from chronicles written in Arabic that Islam was only effective in fact as a fertilizer and stimulant. The essential point is the resuscitative and invigorative concentration of Negro power in the service of a new era and a Moslem propaganda, as well as the reaction thereby produced." [1]

Early in the eighth century Islam had conquered North Africa and converted the Berbers. Aided by black soldiers, the Moslems crossed into Spain; in the following century Berber and Arab armies crossed the west end of the Sahara and came to Negroland. Later in the eleventh century Arabs penetrated the Sudan and Central Africa from the east, filtering through the Negro tribes of Darfur, Kanem, and neighboring regions. The Arabs were too nearly akin to Negroes to draw an absolute color line. Antar, one of the great pre-Islamic poets of Arabia, was the son of a black woman, and one of the great poets at the court of Haroun al Raschid was black. In the twelfth century a learned Negro poet resided at Seville, and Sidjilmessa, the last town in Lower Morocco toward the desert, was founded in 757 by a Negro who ruled over the Berber inhabitants. Indeed, many towns in the Sudan and the desert were thus ruled, and felt no incongruity in this arrangement. They say, to be sure, that the Moors destroyed Audhoghast because it paid tribute to the black town of Ghana, but this was because the town was hea-

[1] Frobenius: *Voice of Africa*, II, 359-360.

then and not because it was black. On the other hand, there is a story that a Berber king overthrew one of the cities of the Sudan and all the black women committed suicide, being too proud to allow themselves to fall into the hands of white men.

In the west the Moslems first came into touch with the Negro kingdom of Ghana. Here large quantities of gold were gathered in early days, and we have names of seventy-four rulers before 300 A.D. running through twenty-one generations. This would take us back approximately a thousand years to 700 B.C., or about the time that Pharaoh Necho of Egypt sent out the Phœnician expedition which circumnavigated Africa, and possibly before the time when Hanno, the Carthaginian, explored the west coast of Africa.

By the middle of the eleventh century Ghana was the principal kingdom in the western Sudan. Already the town had a native and a Mussulman quarter, and was built of wood and stone with surrounding gardens. The king had an army of two hundred thousand and the wealth of the country was great. A century later the king had become Mohammedan in faith and had a palace with sculptures and glass windows. The great reason for this development was the desert trade. Gold, skins, ivory, kola nuts, gums, honey, wheat, and cotton were exported, and the whole Mediterranean coast traded in the Sudan. Other and lesser black kingdoms like Tekrou, Silla, and Masina surrounded Ghana.

In the early part of the thirteenth century the prestige of Ghana began to fall before the rising Mandingan kingdom to the west. Melle, as it was called, was founded in 1235 and formed an open door for Moslem and Moorish traders. The new kingdom, helped by its expanding trade, began to grow, and Islam slowly surrounded the older Negro culture west, north, and east. However, a great mass of the older heathen culture, pushing itself upward from the Guinea coast, stood firmly against Islam down to the nineteenth century.

Steadily Mohammedanism triumphed in the growing states which almost encircled the protagonists of ancient Atlantic culture. Mandingan Melle eventually supplanted Ghana in prestige and power, after Ghana had been overthrown by the heathen Su Su from the south.

The territory of Melle lay southeast of Ghana and some five hundred miles north of the Gulf of Guinea. Its kings were known by the title of Mansa, and from the middle of the thirteenth century to the middle of the fourteenth the Mellestine, as its dominion was called, was the leading power in the land of the blacks. Its greatest king, Mari Jalak (Mansa Musa), made his pilgrimage to Mecca in 1324, with a caravan of sixty thousand persons, including twelve thousand young slaves gowned in figured cotton and Persian silk. He took eighty camel loads of gold dust (worth about five million dollars) to defray his expenses, and greatly impressed the people of the East with his magnificence.

On his return he found that Timbuktu had been sacked by the Mossi, but he rebuilt the town and filled the new mosque with learned blacks from the University of Fez. Mansa Musa reigned twenty-five years and "was distinguished by his ability and by the holiness of his life. The justice of his administration was such that the memory of it still lives." [1] The Mellestine preserved its preëminence until the beginning of the sixteenth century, when the rod of Sudanese empire passed to Songhay, the largest and most famous of the black empires.

The known history of Songhay covers a thousand years and three dynasties and centers in the great bend of the Niger. There were thirty kings of the First Dynasty, reigning from 700 to 1335. During the reign of one of these the Songhay kingdom became the vassal kingdom of Melle, then at the height of its glory. In addition to this the Mossi crossed the valley, plundered Timbuktu in 1339, and separated Jenne, the original seat of the Songhay, from the main empire. The sixteenth king was converted to Mohammedanism in 1009, and after that all the Songhay princes were Mohammedans. Mansa Musa took two young Songhay princes to the court of Melle to be educated in 1326. These boys when grown ran away and founded a new dynasty in Songhay, that of the Sonnis, in 1355. Seventeen of these kings reigned, the last and greatest being Sonni Ali, who ascended

[1] Ibn Khaldun, quoted in Lugard, p. 128.

the throne in 1464. Melle was at this time
declining, other cities like Jenne, with its seven
thousand villages, were rising, and the Tuaregs
(Berbers with Negro blood) had captured Timbuktu.

Sonni Ali was a soldier and began his career
with the conquest of Timbuktu in 1469. He
also succeeded in capturing Jenne and attacked
the Mossi and other enemies on all sides. Finally
he concentrated his forces for the destruction of
Melle and subdued nearly the whole empire on
the west bend of the Niger. In summing up Sonni
Ali's military career the chronicle says of him,
"He surpassed all his predecessors in the numbers and valor of his soldiery. His conquests
were many and his renown extended from the
rising to the setting of the sun. If it is the will
of God, he will be long spoken of." [1]

Sonni Ali was a Songhay Negro whose father
was a Berber. He was succeeded by a full-
blooded black, Mohammed Abou Bekr, who had
been his prime minister. Mohammed was hailed
as "Askia" (usurper) and is best known as
Mohammed Askia. He was strictly orthodox
where Ali was rather a scoffer, and an organizer
where Ali was a warrior. On his pilgrimage to
Mecca in 1495 there was nothing of the barbaric
splendor of Mansa Musa, but a brilliant group
of scholars and holy men with a small escort of
fifteen hundred soldiers and nine hundred thousand dollars in gold. He stopped and consulted

[1] Quoted in Lugard, p. 180.

with scholars and politicians and studied matters of taxation, weights and measures, trade, religious tolerance, and manners.   In Cairo, where he was invested by the reigning caliph of Egypt, he may have heard of the struggle of Europe for the trade of the Indies, and perhaps of the parceling of the new world between Portugal and Spain. He returned to the Sudan in 1497, instituted a standing army of slaves, undertook a holy war against the indomitable Mossi, and finally marched against the Hausa.   He subdued these cities and even imposed the rule of black men on the Berber town of Agades, a rich city of merchants and artificers with stately mansions. In fine Askia, during his reign, conquered and consolidated an empire two thousand miles long by one thousand wide at its greatest diameters; a territory as large as all Europe.   The territory was divided into four vice royalties, and the system of Melle, with its semi-independent native dynasties, was carried out.   His empire extended from the Atlantic to Lake Chad and from the salt mines of Tegazza and the town of Augila in the north to the 10th degree of north latitude toward the south.

It was a six months' journey across the empire and, it is said, "he was obeyed with as much docility on the farthest limits of the empire as he was in his own palace, and there reigned everywhere great plenty and absolute peace." [1]   The University of Sankore became a center of learn-

[1] Es-Sa'di, quoted by Lugard, p. 199.

ing in correspondence with Egypt and North
Africa and had a swarm of black Sudanese students. Law, literature, grammar, geography,
and surgery were studied. Askia the Great
reigned thirty-six years, and his dynasty continued on the throne until after the Moorish
conquest in 1591.

Meanwhile, to the eastward, two powerful
states appeared. They never disputed the military supremacy of Songhay, but their industrial
development was marvelous. The Hausa states
were formed by seven original cities, of which
Kano was the oldest and Katsena the most
famous. Their greatest leaders, Mohammed
Rimpa and Ahmadu Kesoke, arose in the fifteenth
and early sixteenth centuries. The land was
subject to the Songhay, but the cities became
industrious centers of smelting, weaving, and
dyeing. Katsena especially, in the middle of
the sixteenth century, is described as a place
thirteen or fourteen miles in circumference,
divided into quarters for strangers, for visitors
from various other states, and for the different
trades and industries, as saddlers, shoemakers,
dyers, etc.

Beyond the Hausa states and bordering on
Lake Chad was Bornu. The people of Bornu had
a large infiltration of Berber blood, but were
predominantly Negro. Berber mulattoes had
been kings in early days, but they were soon
replaced by black men. Under the early kings,
who can be traced back to the third century,

these people had ruled nearly all the territory
between the Nile and Lake Chad. The country
was known as Kánem, and the pagan dynasty of
Dugu reigned there from the middle of the ninth
to the end of the eleventh century. Mohammedanism was introduced from Egypt at the end of
the eleventh century, and under the Mohammedan kings Kanem became one of the first powers
of the Sudan. By the end of the twelfth century
the armies of Kanem were very powerful and its
rulers were known as "Kings of Kanem and
Lords of Bornu." In the thirteenth century the
kings even dared to invade the southern country
down toward the valley of the Congo.

Meantime great things were happening in the
world beyond the desert, the ocean, and the
Nile. Arabian Mohammedanism had succumbed
to the wild fanaticism of the Seljukian Turks.
These new conquerors were not only firmly
planted at the gates of Vienna, but had swept
the shores of the Mediterranean and sent all
Europe scouring the seas for their lost trade
connections with the riches of India. Religious
zeal, fear of conquest, and commercial greed in-
flamed Europe against the Mohammedan and
led to the discovery of a new world, the riches of
which poured first on Spain. Oppression of the
Moors followed, and in 1502 they were driven
back into Africa, despoiled and humbled. Here
the Spaniards followed and harassed them and
here the Turks, fighting the Christians, captured
the Mediterranean ports and cut the Moors off

permanently from Europe. In the slow years that followed, huddled in Northwest Africa, they became a decadent people and finally cast their eyes toward Negroland.

The Moors in Morocco had come to look upon the Sudan as a gold mine, and knew that the Sudan was especially dependent upon salt. In 1545 Morocco claimed the principal salt mines at Tegazza, but the reigning Askia refused to recognize the claim.

When the Sultan Elmansour came to the throne of Morocco, he increased the efficiency of his army by supplying it with fire arms and cannon. Elmansour determined to attack the Sudan and sent four hundred men under Pasha Djouder, who left Morocco in 1590. The Songhay, with their bows and arrows, were helpless against powder and shot, and they were defeated at Tenkadibou April 12, 1591. Askia Ishak, the king, offered terms, and Djouder Pasha referred them to Morocco. The sultan, angry with his general's delay, deposed him and sent another, who crushed and treacherously murdered the king and set up a puppet. Thereafter there were two Askias, one under the Moors at Timbuktu and one who maintained himself in the Hausa states, which the Moors could not subdue. Anarchy reigned in Songhay. The Moors tried to put down disorder with a high hand, drove out and murdered the distinguished men of Timbuktu, and as a result let loose a riot of robbery and decadence throughout the Sudan.

Pasha now succeeded pasha with revolt and misrule until in 1612 the soldiers elected their own pasha and deliberately shut themselves up in the Sudan by cutting off approach from the north.

Hausaland and Bornu were still open to Turkish and Mohammedan influence from the east, and the Gulf of Guinea to the slave trade from the south, but the face of the finest Negro civilization the modern world had ever produced was veiled from Europe and given to the defilement of wild Moorish soldiers. In 1623 it is written "excesses of every kind are now committed unchecked by the soldiery," and "the country is profoundly convulsed and oppressed." [1] The Tuaregs marched down from the desert and deprived the Moors of many of the principal towns. The rest of the empire of the Songhay was by the end of the eighteenth century divided among separate Moorish chiefs, who bought supplies from the Negro peasantry and were "at once the vainest, proudest, and perhaps the most bigoted, ferocious, and intolerant of all the nations of the south." [2] They lived a nomadic life, plundering the Negroes. To such depths did the mighty Songhay fall.

As the Songhay declined a new power arose in the nineteenth century, the Fula. The Fula, who vary in race from Berber mulattoes to full-blooded Negroes, may be the result of a westward migration of some people like the

[1] Lugard, p. 373.
[2] Mungo Park, quoted in Lugard, p. 374.

"Leukoæthiopi" of Pliny, or they may have arisen from the migration of Berber mulattoes in the western oases, driven south by Romàns and Arabs.

These wandering herdsmen lived on the Senegal River and the ocean in very early times and were not heard of until the nineteenth century. By this time they had changed to a Negro or dark mulatto people and lived scattered in small communities between the Atlantic and Darfur. They were without political union or national sentiment, but were all Mohammedans. Then came a sudden change, and led by a religious fanatic, these despised and persecuted people became masters of the central Sudan. They were the ones who at last broke down that great wedge of resisting Atlantic culture, after it had been undermined and disintegrated by the American slave trade.

Thus Islam finally triumphed in the Sudan and the ancient culture combined with the new. In the Sudan to-day one may find evidences of the union of two classes of people. The representatives of the older civilization dwell as peasants in small communities, carrying on industries and speaking a large number of different languages. With them or above them is the ruling Mohammedan caste, speaking four main languages: Mandingo, Hausa, Fula, and Arabic. These latter form the state builders. Negro blood predominates among both classes, but naturally there is more Berber blood among the Mohammedan invaders.

Europe during the middle ages had some knowledge of these movements in the Sudan and Africa. Melle and Songhay appear on medieval maps. In literature we have many allusions: the mulatto king, Feirifis, was one of Wolfram von Eschenbach's heroes; Prester John furnished endless lore; Othello, the warrior, and the black king represented by medieval art as among the three wise men, and the various black Virgin Marys' all show legendary knowledge of what African civilization was at that time doing.

It is a curious commentary on modern prejudice that most of this splendid history of civilization and uplift is unknown to-day, and men confidently assert that Negroes have no history.

CHAPTER V

GUINEA AND CONGO

ONE of the great cities of the Sudan was Jenne.
The chronicle says "that its markets are held
every day of the week and its populations are very
enormous. Its seven thousand villages are so
near to one another that the chief of Jenne has
no need of messengers. If he wishes to send a
note to Lake Dibo, for instance, it is cried from
the gate of the town and repeated from village to
village, by which means it reaches its destination
almost instantly." [1]

From the name of this city we get the modern
name Guinea, which is used to-day to designate
the country contiguous to the great gulf of that
name — a territory often referred to in general as
West Africa. Here, reaching from the mouth of
the Gambia to the mouth of the Niger, is a coast
of six hundred miles, where a marvelous drama of
world history has been enacted. The coast and
its hinterland comprehends many well-known
names. First comes ancient Guinea, then, modern Sierra Leone and Liberia; then follow the
various "coasts" of ancient traffic — the grain,
ivory, gold, and slave coasts — with the adjoining

[1] Quoted in DuBois: *Timbuktu*.

territories of Ashanti, Dahomey, Lagos, and
Benin, and farther back such tribal and territorial names as those of the Mandingoes, Yorubas,
the Mossi, Nupe, Borgu, and others.

Recent investigation makes it certain that an
ancient civilization existed on this coast which
may have gone back as far as three thousand
years before Christ. Frobenius, perhaps fanci-
fully, identified this African coast with the Atlan-
tis of the Greeks and as part of that great western
movement in human culture, "beyond the pillars
of Hercules," which thirteen centuries before
Christ strove with Egypt and the East. It is, at
any rate, clear that ancient commerce reached
down the west coast. The Phœnicians, 600 B.C.,
and the Carthaginians, a century or more later,
record voyages, and these may have been attempted revivals of still more ancient intercourse.

These coasts at some unknown prehistoric
period were peopled from the Niger plateau
toward the north and west by the black West
African type of Negro, while along the west end
of the desert these Negroes mingled with the
Berbers, forming various Negroid races.

Movement and migration is evident along this
coast in ancient and modern times. The Yoruba-
Benin-Dahomey peoples were among the earliest
arrivals, with their remarkable art and industry,
which places them in some lines of technique
abreast with the modern world. Behind them
came the Mossi from the north, and many other

peoples in recent days have filtered through, like the Limba and Temni of Sierra Leone and the Agni-Ashanti, who moved from Borgu some two thousand years ago to the Gold and Ivory coasts.

We have already noted in the main the history of black men along the wonderful Niger and seen how, pushing up from the Gulf of Guinea, a powerful wedge of ancient culture held back Islam for a thousand years, now victorious, now stubbornly disputing every inch of retreat. The center of this culture lay probably, in oldest time, above the Bight of Benin, along the Slave Coast, and reached east, west, and north. We trace it to-day not only in the remarkable tradition of the natives, but in stone monuments, architecture, industrial and social organization, and works of art in bronze, glass, and terra cotta.

Benin art has been practiced without interruption for centuries, and Von Luschan says that it is "of extraordinary significance that by the sixteenth and seventeenth centuries a local and monumental art had been learned in Benin which in many respects equaled European art and developed a technique of the very highest accomplishment." [1]

Summing up Yoruban civilization, Frobenius concluded that "the technical summit of that civilization was reached in the terra-cotta industry, and that the most important achieve-

[1] Von Luschan: *Verhandlungen der berliner Gesellschaft für Anthropologie*, etc., 1898.

ments in art were not expressed in stone, but in fine clay baked in the furnace; that hollow casting was thoroughly known, too, and practiced by these people; that iron was mainly used for decoration; that, whatever their purpose, they kept their glass beads in stoneware urns within their own locality, and that they manufactured both earthen and glass ware; that the art of weaving was highly developed among them; that the stone monuments, it is true, show some dexterity in handling and are so far instructive, but in other respects evidence a cultural condition insufficiently matured to grasp the utility of stone monumental material; and, above all, that the then great and significant idea of the universe as imaged in the Templum was current in those days." [1]

Effort has naturally been made to ascribe this civilization to white people. First it was ascribed to Portuguese influence, but much of it is evidently older than the Portuguese discovery. Egypt and India have been evoked and Greece and Carthage. But all these explanations are far-fetched. If ever a people exhibited unanswerable evidence of indigenous civilization, it is the west-coast Africans. Undoubtedly they adapted much that came to them, utilized new ideas, and grew from contact. But their art and culture is Negro through and through.

Yoruba forms one of the three city groups of West Africa; another is around Timbuktu, and a

[1] Frobenius: *Voice of Africa*, Vol. I.

third in the Hausa states. The Timbuktu cities have from five to fifteen hundred towns, while the Yoruba cities have one hundred and fifty thousand inhabitants and more. The Hausa cities are many of them important, but few are as large as the Yoruba cities and they lie farther apart. All three centers, however, are connected with the Niger, and the group nearest the coast — that is, the Yoruba cities — has the greatest numbers of towns, the most developed architectural styles, and the oldest institutions.

The Yoruba cities are not only different from the Sudanese in population, but in their social relations. The Sudanese cities were influenced from the desert and the Mediterranean, and form nuclei of larger surrounding monarchial states. The Yoruba cities, on the other hand, remained comparatively autonomous organizations down to modern times, and their relative importance changed from time to time without developing an imperialistic idea or subordinating the group to one overpowering city.

This social and industrial state of the Yorubas formerly spread and wielded great influence. We find Yoruba reaching out and subduing states like Nupe toward the northward. But the industrial democracy and city autonomy of Yoruba lent itself indifferently to conquest, and the state fell eventually a victim to the fanatical Fula Mohammedans and was made a part of the modern sultanate of Gando.

West of Yoruba on the lower courses of the

Niger is Benin, an ancient state which in 1897 traced its twenty-three kings back one thousand years; some legends even named a line of sixty kings. It seems probable that Benin developed the imperial idea and once extended its rule into the Congo valley. Later and also to the west of the Yoruba come two states showing a fiercer and ruder culture, Dahomey and Ashanti. The state of Dahomey was founded by Tacondomi early in the seventeenth century, and developed into a fierce and bloody tyranny with wholesale murder. The king had a body of two thousand to five thousand Amazons renowned for their bravery and armed with rifles. The kingdom was overthrown by the French in 1892–93. Under Sai Tutu, Ashanti arose to power in the seventeenth century. A military aristocracy with cruel blood sacrifices was formed. By 1816 the king had at his disposal two hundred thousand soldiers. The Ashanti power was crushed by the English in the war of 1873–74.

In these states and in later years in Benin the whole character of west-coast culture seems to change. In place of the Yoruban culture, with its city democracy, its elevated religious ideas, its finely organized industry, and its noble art, came Ashanti and Dahomey. What was it that changed the character of the west coast from this to the orgies of war and blood sacrifice which we read of later in these lands?

There can be but one answer: the slave trade. Not simply the sale of men, but an organized traffic of such proportions and widely organized ramifications as to turn the attention and energies of men from nearly all other industries, encourage war and all the cruelest passions of war, and concentrate this traffic in precisely that part of Africa farthest from the ancient Mediterranean lines of trade.

We need not assume that the cultural change was sudden or absolute. Ancient Yoruba had the cruelty of a semi-civilized land, but it was not dominant or tyrannical. Modern Benin and Dahomey showed traces of skill, culture, and industry along with inexplicable cruelty and bloodthirstiness. But it was the slave trade that turned the balance and set these lands backward. Dahomey was the last word in a series of human disasters which began with the defeat of the Askias at Tenkadibou.[1]

From the middle of the fifteenth to the last half of the nineteenth centuries the American slave trade centered in Guinea and devastated the coast morally, socially, and physically. European rum and fire arms were traded for human beings, and it was not until 1787 that any measures were taken to counteract this terrible scourge. In that year the idea arose of repatriating stolen Negroes on that coast and establishing civilized centers to supplant the slave trade. About four hundred Negroes from England were sent to Sierra Leone, to whom the promoters considerately added sixty white prosti-

[1] Cf. p. 58.

tutes as wives. The climate on the low coast, however, was so deadly that new recruits were soon needed. An American Negro, Thomas Peters, who had served as sergeant under Sir Henry Clinton in the British army in America, went to England seeking an allotment of land for his fellows. The Sierra Leone Company welcomed him and offered free passage and land in Sierra Leone to the Negroes of Nova Scotia. As a result fifteen vessels sailed with eleven hundred and ninety Negroes in 1792. Arriving in Africa, they found the chief white man in control there so drunk that he soon died of delirium tremens. John Clarkson, however, brother of Thomas Clarkson, the abolitionist, eventually took the lead, founded Freetown, and the colony began its checkered career. In 1896 the colony was saved from insurrection by the exiled Maroon Negroes from Jamaica. After 1833, when emancipation in English colonies took place, severer measures against the slave trade was possible and the colony began to grow. To-day its imports and exports amount to fifteen million dollars a year.

Liberia was a similar American experiment. In 1816 American philanthropists decided that slavery was bound to die out, but that the problem lay in getting rid of the freed Negroes, of which there were then two hundred thousand in the United States. Accordingly the American Colonization Society was proposed this year and founded January 1, 1817, with Bushrod

Washington as President. It was first thought to encourage migration to Sierra Leone, and eighty-eight Negroes were sent, but they were not welcomed. As a result territory was bought in the present confines of Liberia, December 15, 1821, and colonists began to arrive. A little later an African depot for recaptured slaves taken in the contraband slave trade, provided for in the Act of 1819, was established and an agent was sent to Africa to form a settlement. Gradually this settlement was merged with the settlement of the Colonization Society, and from this union Liberia was finally evolved.

The last white governor of Liberia died in 1841 and was succeeded by the first colored governor, Joseph J. Roberts, a Virginian. The total population in 1843 was about twenty-seven hundred and ninety, and with this as a beginning in 1847 Governor Roberts declared the independence of the state. The recognition of Liberian independence by all countries except the United States followed in 1849. The United States, not wishing to receive a Negro minister, did not recognize Liberia until 1862.

No sooner was the independence of Liberia announced than England and France began a long series of aggressions to limit her territory and sovereignty. Considerable territory was lost by treaty, and in the effort to get capital to develop the rest, Liberia was saddled with a debt of four hundred thousand dollars, of which she received less than one hundred thousand dollars in actual cash. Finally the Liberians turned to the United States for capital and protection. As a result the Liberian customs have been put under international control and Major Charles Young, the ranking Negro officer in the United States army, with several colored assistants, has been put in charge of the making of roads and drilling a constabulary to keep order in the interior.

To-day Liberia has an area of forty thousand square miles, about three hundred and fifty miles of coast line, and an estimated total population of two million of which fifty thousand are civilized. The revenue amounted in 1913 to $531,500. The imports in 1912 were $1,667,857 and the exports $1,199,152. The latter consisted chiefly of rubber, palm oil and kernels, coffee, piassava fiber, ivory, ginger, camwood, and arnotto.

Perhaps Liberia's greatest citizen was the late Edward Wilmot Blyden, who migrated in early life from the Danish West Indies and became a prophet of the renaissance of the Negro race.

Turning now from Guinea we pass down the west coast. In 1482 Diego Cam of Portugal, sailing this coast, set a stone at the mouth of a great river which he called "The Mighty," but which eventually came to be known by the name of the powerful Negro kingdom through which it flowed — the Congo.

We must think of the valley of the Congo with its intricate interlacing of water routes and jungle

of forests as a vast caldron shut away at first
from the African world by known and unknown
physical hindrances. Then it was penetrated by
the tiny red dwarfs and afterward horde after
horde of tall black men swirled into the valley
like a maelstrom, moving usually from north to
east and from south to west.

The Congo valley became, therefore, the center
of the making of what we know to-day as the
Bantu nations. They are not a unified people,
but a congeries of tribes of considerable physical
diversity, united by the compelling bond of
language and other customs imposed on the
conquered by invading conquerors.

The history of these invasions we must to-day
largely imagine. Between two and three thousand years ago the wilder tribes of Negroes began
to move out of the region south or southeast of
Lake Chad. This was always a land of shadows
and legends, where fearful cannibals dwelt and
where no Egyptian or Ethiopian or Sudanese
armies dared to go. It is possible, however,
that pressure from civilization in the Nile valley
and rising culture around Lake Chad was at this
time reënforced by expansion of the Yoruba-
Benin culture on the west coast. Perhaps, too,
developing culture around the Great Lakes in
the east beckoned or the riotous fertility of the
Congo valleys became known. At any rate the
movement commenced, now by slow stages, now
in wild forays. There may have been a preliminary movement from east to west to the Gulf

of Guinea. The main movement, however, was eastward, skirting the Congo forests and passing down by the Victoria Nyanza and Lake Tanganyika. Here two paths beckoned: the lakes and the sea to the east, the Congo to the west. A great stream of men swept toward the ocean and, dividing, turned northward and fought its way down the Nile valley and into the Abyssinian highlands; another branch turned south and approached the Zambesi, where we shall meet it again.

Another horde of invaders turned westward and entered the valley of the Congo in three columns. The northern column moved along the Lualaba and Congo rivers to the Cameroons; the second column became the industrial and state-building Luba and Lunda peoples in the southern Congo valley and Angola; while the third column moved into Damaraland and mingled with Bushman and Hottentot.

In the Congo valley the invaders settled in village and plain, absorbed such indigenous inhabitants as they found or drove them deeper into the forest, and immediately began to develop industry and political organization. They became skilled agriculturists, raising in some localities a profusion of cereals, fruit, and vegetables such as manioc, maize, yams, sweet potatoes, ground nuts, sorghum, gourds, beans, peas, bananas, and plantains. Everywhere they showed skill in mining and the welding of iron, copper, and other metals. They made weapons, wire and ingots, cloth, and pottery, and a widespread system of trade arose. Some tribes extracted rubber from the talamba root; others had remarkable breeds of fowl and cattle, and still others divided their people by crafts into farmers, smiths, boat builders, warriors, cabinet makers, armorers, and speakers. Women here and there took part in public assemblies and were rulers in some cases. Large towns were built, some of which required hours to traverse from end to end.

Many tribes developed intelligence of a high order. Wissmann called the Ba Luba "a nation of thinkers." Bateman found them "thoroughly and unimpeachably honest, brave to foolhardiness, and faithful to each other and to their superiors." One of their kings, Calemba, "a really princely prince," Bateman says would "amongst any people be a remarkable and indeed in many respects a magnificent man." [1]

These beginnings of human culture were, however, peculiarly vulnerable to invading hosts of later comers. There were no natural protecting barriers like the narrow Nile valley or the Kong mountains or the forests below Lake Chad. Once the pathways to the valleys were open and for hundreds of years the newcomers kept arriving, especially from the welter of tribes south of the Sudan and west of the Nile, which rising culture beyond kept in unrest and turmoil.

Against these intruders there was but one defense, the State. State building was thus forced

[1] Keane: *Africa*, II, 117–118.

on the Congo valley. How early it started we cannot say, but when the Portuguese arrived in the fifteenth century, there had existed for centuries a large state among the Ba-Congo, with its capital at the city now known as San Salvador.

The Negro Mfumu, or emperor, was eventually induced to accept Christianity. His sons and many young Negroes of high birth were taken to Portugal to be educated. There several were raised to the Catholic priesthood and one became bishop; others distinguished themselves at the universities. Thus suddenly there arose a Catholic kingdom south of the valley of the Congo, which lasted three centuries, but was partially overthrown by invading barbarians from the interior in the seventeenth century. A king of Congo still reigns as pensioner of Portugal, and on the coast to-day are the remains of the kingdom in the civilized blacks and mulattoes, who are intelligent traders and boat builders.

Meantime the Luba-Lunda people to the eastward founded Kantanga and other states, and in the sixteenth century the larger and more ambitious realm of the Mwata Yanvo. The last of the fourteen rulers of this line was feudal lord of about three hundred chiefs, who paid him tribute in ivory, skins, corn, cloth, and salt. His territory included about one hundred thousand square miles and two million or more inhabitants. Eventually this state became torn by internal strife and revolt, especially by attacks from the south across the Congo-Zambesi divide.

Farther north, among the Ba-Lolo and the Ba-Songo, the village policy persisted and the cannibals of the northeast pressed down on the more settled tribes. The result was a curious blending of war and industry, artistic tastes and savage customs.

The organized slave trade of the Arabs penetrated the Congo valley in the sixteenth century and soon was aiding all the forces of unrest and turmoil. Industry was deranged and many tribes forced to take refuge in caves and other hiding places.

Here, as on the west coast, disintegration and retrogression followed, for as the American traffic lessened, the Arabian traffic increased. When, therefore, Stanley opened the Congo valley to modern knowledge, Leopold II of Belgium conceived the idea of founding here a free international state which was to bring civilization to the heart of Africa. Consequently there was formed in 1878 an international committee to study the region. Stanley was finally commissioned to inquire as to the best way of introducing European trade and culture. "I am charged," he said, "to open and keep open, if possible, all such districts and countries as I may explore, for the benefit of the commercial world. The mission is supported by a philanthropic society, which numbers nobleminded men of several nations. It is not a religious society, but my instructions are entirely of that spirit. No violence must be used, and wherever rejected, the mission must withdraw to seek another field."[1]

The Bula Matadi or Stone Breaker, as the natives called Stanley, threw himself energetically into the work and had by 1881 built a road past the falls to the plateau, where thousands of miles of river navigation were thus opened. Stations were established, and by 1884 Stanley returned armed with four hundred and fifty "treaties" with the native chiefs, and the new "State" appealed to the world for recognition.

The United States first recognized the "Congo Free State," which was at last made a sovereign power under international guarantees by the Congress of Berlin in the year 1885, and Leopold II was chosen its king. The state had an area of about nine hundred thousand square miles, with a population of about thirty million.

One of the first tasks before the new state was to check the Arab slave traders. The Arabs had hitherto acted as traders and middlemen along the upper Congo, and when the English and Congo state overthrew Mzidi, the reigning king in the Kantanga country, a general revolt of the Arabs and mulattoes took place. For a time, 1892–93, the whites were driven out, but in a year or two the Arabs and their allies were subdued.

Humanity and commerce, however, did not

[1] *The Congo*, I, Chap. III.

replace the Arab slave traders. Rather European greed and serfdom were substituted. The land was confiscated by the state and farmed out to private Belgian corporations. The wilder cannibal tribes were formed into a militia to prey on the industrious, who were taxed with specific amounts of ivory and rubber, and scourged and mutilated if they failed to pay. Harris declares that King Leopold's regime meant the death of twelve million natives.

"Europe was staggered at the Leopoldian atrocities, and they were terrible indeed; but what we, who were behind the scenes, felt most keenly was the fact that the real catastrophe in the Congo was desolation and murder in the larger sense. The invasion of family life, the ruthless destruction of every social barrier, the shattering of every tribal law, the introduction of criminal practices which struck the chiefs of the people dumb with horror — in a word, a veritable avalanche of filth and immorality overwhelmed the Congo tribes." [1]

So notorious did the exploitation and misrule become that Leopold was forced to take measures toward reform, and finally in 1909 the Free State became a Belgian colony. Some reforms have been inaugurated and others may follow, but the valley of the Congo will long stand as a monument of shame to Christianity and European civilization.

---

[1] Harris: *Dawn in Africa.*

CHAPTER VI

THE GREAT LAKES AND ZYMBABWE

WE have already seen how a branch of the conquering Bantus turned eastward by the Great Lakes and thus reached the sea and eventually both the Nile and South Africa.

This brought them into the ancient and mysterious land far up the Nile, south of Ethiopia. Here lay the ancient Punt of the Egyptians (whether we place it in Somaliland or, as seems far more likely, around the Great Lakes) and here, as the Egyptians thought, their civilization began. The earliest inhabitants of the land were apparently of the Bushman or Hottentot type of Negro. These were gradually pushed southward and westward by the intrusion of the Nilotic Negroes. Five thousand years before Christ the mulatto Egyptians were in the Nile valley below the First Cataract. The Negroes were in the Nile valley down as far as the Second Cataract and between the First and Second Cataracts were Negroes into whose veins Semitic blood had penetrated more or less. These mixed elements became the ancestors of the modern Somali, Gala, Bishari, and Beja and spread Negro blood into Arabia beyond the Red Sea. The Nilotic

Negroes to the south early became great traders in ivory, gold, leopard skins, gums, beasts, birds, and slaves, and they opened up systematic trade between Egypt and the Great Lakes.

The result was endless movement and migration both in ancient and modern days, which makes the cultural history of the Great Lakes region very difficult to understand. Three great elements are, however, clear: first, the Egyptian element, by the northward migration of the Negro ancestors of predynastic Egypt and the southern conquests and trade of dynastic Egypt; second, the Semitic influence from Arabia and Persia; third, the Negro influences from western and central Africa.

The migration of the Bantu is the first clearly defined movement of modern times. As we have shown, they began to move southward at least a thousand years before .Christ, skirting the Congo forests and wandering along the Great Lakes and down to the Zambesi. What did they find in this land?

We do not know certainly, but from what we do know we may reconstruct the situation in this way: the primitive culture of the Hottentots of Punt had been further developed by them and by other stronger Negro stocks until it reached a highly developed culture. Widespread agriculture, and mining of gold, silver, and precious stones started a trade that penetrated to Asia and North Africa. This may have been the source of the gold of the Ophir.

The state that thus arose became in time strongly organized; it employed slave labor in crushing the hard quartz, sinking pits, and carrying underground galleries; it carried out a system of irrigation and built stone buildings and fortifications. There exists to-day many remains of these building operations in the Kalahari desert and in northern Rhodesia. Five hundred groups, covering over an area of one hundred and fifty thousand square miles, lie between the Limpopo and Zambesi rivers. Mining operations have been carried on in these plains for generations, and one estimate is that at least three hundred and seventy-five million dollars' worth of gold had been extracted. Some have thought that the older workings must date back to one or even three thousand years before the Christian era.

"There are other mines," writes De Barros in the seventeenth century,[1] "in a district called Toroa, which is otherwise known as the kingdom of Butua, whose ruler is a prince, by name Burrow, a vassal of Benomotapa. This land is near the other which we said consisted of extensive plains, and those ruins are the oldest that are known in that region. They are all in a plain, in the middle of which stands a square fortress, all of dressed stones within and without, well wrought and of marvelous size, without any lime showing the joinings, the walls of which are over twenty-five hands thick, but the height is not so great com-

[1] Quoted in Bent: *Ruined Cities of Mashonaland*, pp. 203 ff.

pared to the thickness. And above the gateway of that edifice is an inscription which some Moorish [Arab] traders who were there could not read, nor say what writing it was. All these structures the people of this country call Symbaoe [Zymbabwe], which with them means a court, for every place where Benomotapa stays is so called."

Later investigation has shown that these buildings were in many cases carefully planned and built fortifications. At Niekerk, for instance, nine or ten hills are fortified on concentric walls thirty to fifty feet in number, with a place for the village at the top. The buildings are forts, miniature citadels, and also workshops and cattle kraals. Iron implements and handsome pottery were found here, and close to the Zambesi there are extraordinary fortifications. Farther south at Inyanga there is less strong defense, and at Umtali there are no fortifications, showing that builders feared invasion from the north.

These people worked in gold, silver, tin, copper, and bronze and made beautiful pottery. There is evidence of religious significance in the buildings, and what is called the temple was the royal residence and served as a sort of acropolis. The surrounding residences in the valley were evidently occupied by wealthy traders and were not fortified. Here the gold was received from surrounding districts and bartered with traders.

As usual there have been repeated attempts

to find an external and especially an Asiatic origin for this culture. So far, however, archeological research seems to confirm its African origin. The implements, weapons, and art are characteristically African and there is no evident connection with outside sources. How far back this civilization dates it is difficult to say, a great deal depending upon the dating of the iron age in South Africa. If it was the same as in the Mediterranean regions, the earliest limit was 1000 B.C.; it might, however, have been much earlier, especially if, as seems probable, the use of iron originated in Africa. On the other hand the culmination of this culture has been placed by some as late as the modern middle ages.

What was it that overthrew this civilization? Undoubtedly the same sort of raids of barbarous warriors that we have known in our day. For instance, in 1570 there came upon the country of Mozambique, farther up the coast, "such an inundation of pagans that they could not be numbered. They came from that part of Monomotapa where is the great lake from which spring these great rivers. They left no other signs of the towns they passed but the heaps of ruins and the bones of inhabitants." So, too, it is told how the Zimbas came, "a strange people never before seen there, who, leaving their own country, traversed a great part of this Ethiopia like a scourge of God, destroying every living thing they came across. They were twenty thousand strong and marched without children or women," just as four hundred years later the Zulu impi marched. Again in 1602 a horde of people came from the interior called the Cabires, or cannibals. They entered the kingdom of Monomotapa, and the reigning king, being weak, was in great terror. Thus gradually the Monomotapa fell, and its power was scattered until the Kaffir-Zulu raids of our day.[1]

The Arab writer, Macoudi, in the tenth century visited the East African coast somewhere north of the equator. He found the Indian Sea at that time frequented by Arab and Persian vessels, but there were no Asiatic settlements on the African shore. The Bantu, or as he calls them, Zenji, inhabited the country as far south as Sofala, where they bordered upon the Bushmen. These Bantus were under a ruler with the dynastic title of Waklimi. He was paramount over all the other tribes of the north and could put three hundred thousand men in the field. They used oxen as beasts of burden and the country produced gold in abundance, while panther skin was largely used for clothing. Ivory was sold to Asia and the Bantu used iron for personal adornment instead of gold or silver. They rode on their oxen, which ran with great speed, and they ate millet and honey and the flesh of animals.

Inland among the Bantu arose later the line of rulers called the Monomotapa among the gifted Makalanga. Their state was very ex-

[1] Cf. "Ethiopia Oriental," by J. Dos Santos, in Theal's *Records of South Africa*, Vol. VII.

tensive, ranging from the coast far into the interior and from Mozambique down to the Limpopo. It was strongly organized, with feudatory allied states, and carried on an extensive commerce by means of the traders on the coast. The kings were converted to nominal Christianity by the Portuguese.

There are indications of trade between Nupe in West Africa and Sofala on the east coast, and certainly trade between Asia and East Africa is earlier than the beginning of the Christian era. The Asiatic traders settled on the coast and by means of mulatto and Negro merchants brought Central Africa into contact with Arabia, India, China, and Malaysia.

The coming of the Asiatics was in this wise: Zaide, great-grandson of Ali, nephew and son-in-law of Mohammed, was banished from Arabia as a heretic. He passed over to Africa and formed temporary settlements. His people mingled with the blacks, and the resulting mulatto traders, known as the Emoxaidi, seem to have wandered as far south as the equator. Soon other Arabian families came over on account of oppression and founded the towns of Magadosho and Brava, both not far north of the equator. The first town became a place of importance and other settlements were made. The Emoxaidi, whom the later immigrants regarded as heretics, were driven inland and became the interpreting traders between the coast and the Bantu. Some wanderers from Magadosho came into the Port of Sofala and there learned that gold could be obtained. This led to a small Arab settlement at that place.

Seventy years later, and about fifty years before the Norman conquest of England, certain Persians settled at Kilwa in East Africa, led by Ali, who had been despised in his land because he was the son of a black Abyssinian slave mother. Kilwa, because of this, eventually became the most important commercial station on the East African coast, and in this and all these settlements a very large mulatto population grew up, so that very soon the whole settlement was indistinguishable in color from the Bantu.

In 1330 Ibn Batuta visited Kilwa. He found an abundance of ivory and some gold and heard that the inhabitants of Kilwa had gained victories over the Zenji or Bantu. Kilwa had at that time three hundred mosques and was "built of handsome houses of stone and lime, and very lofty, with their windows like those of the Christians; in the same way it has streets, and these houses have got terraces, and the woodwork is with the masonry, with plenty of gardens, in which there are many fruit trees and much water." [1] Kilwa after a time captured Sofala, seizing it from Magadosho. Eventually Kilwa became mistress of the island of Zanzibar, of Mozambique, and of much other territory. The forty-third ruler of Kilwa after Ali was named Abraham, and he was ruling when the Portuguese arrived. The latter reported that

[1] Barbosa, quoted in Keane, II, 482.

these people cultivated rice and cocoa, built ships, and had considerable commerce with Asia. All the people, of whatever color, were Mohammedans, and the richer were clothed in gorgeous robes of silk and velvet. They traded with the inland Bantus and met numerous tribes, receiving gold, ivory, millet, rice, cattle, poultry, and honey.

On the islands the Asiatics were independent, but on the main lands south of Kilwa the sheiks ruled only their own people, under the over-lordship of the Bantus, to whom they were compelled to pay large tribute each year.

Vasco da Gama doubled the Cape of Good Hope in 1497 and went north on the east coast as far as India. In the next ten years the Portuguese had occupied more than six different points on that coast, including Sofala.[1]

Thus civilization waxed and waned in East Africa among prehistoric Negroes, Arab and Persian mulattoes on the coast, in the Zend or Zeng empire of Bantu Negroes, and later in the Bantu rule of the Monomotapa. And thus, too, among later throngs of the fiercer, warlike Bantu, the ancient culture of the land largely died. Yet something survived, and in the modern Bantu state, language, and industry can be found

[1] It was called Sofala, from an Arabic word, and may be associated with the Ophir of Solomon. So, too, the river Sabi, a little off Sofala, may be associated with the name of the Queen of Sheba, whose lineage was supposed to be perpetuated in the powerful Monomotapa as well as the Abyssinians.

clear links that establish the essential identity
of the absorbed peoples with the builders of
Zymbabwe.

So far we have traced the history of the lands
into which the southward stream of invading
Bantus turned, and have followed them to the
Limpopo River. We turn now to the lands north
from Lake Nyassa.

The aboriginal Negroes sustained in prehistoric time invasions from the northeast by
Negroids of a type like the ancient Egyptians
and like the modern Gallas, Masai, and Somalis.
To these migrations were added attacks from
the Nile Negroes to the north and the Bantu
invaders from the south. This has led to great
differences among the groups of the population
and in their customs. Some are fierce moun-
taineers, occupying hilly plateaus six thousand
feet above the sea level; others, like the Wa
Swahili, are traders on the coast. There are the
Masai, chocolate-colored and frizzly-haired, organized for war and cattle lifting; and Negroids
like the Gallas, who, blending with the Bantus,
have produced the race of modern Uganda.

It was in this region that the kingdom of Kit-
wara was founded by the Galla chief, Kintu.
About the beginning of the nineteenth century
the empire was dismembered, the largest share
falling to Uganda. The ensuing history of
Uganda is of great interest. When King Mutesa
came to the throne in 1862, he found Mohammedan influences in his land and was induced to

admit English Protestants and French Catholics. Uganda thereupon became an extraordinary religious battlefield between these three beliefs. Mutesa's successor, Mwanga, caused an English bishop to be killed in 1885, believing (as has since proven quite true) that the religion he offered would be used as a cloak for conquest. The final result was that, after open war between the religions, Uganda was made an English protectorate in 1894.

The Negroes of Uganda are an intelligent people who had organized a complex feudal state. At the head stood the king, and under him twelve feudal lords. The present king, Daudi Chua, is the young grandson of Mutesa and rules under the overlordship of England.

Many things show the connection between Egypt and this part of Africa. The same glass beads are found in Uganda and Upper Egypt, and similar canoes are built. Harps and other instruments bear great resemblance. Finally the Bahima, as the Galla invaders are called, are startlingly Egyptian in type; at the same time they are undoubtedly Negro in hair and color. Perhaps we have here the best racial picture of what ancient Egyptian and upper Nile regions were in predynastic times and later.

Thus in outline was seen the mission of The People — La Bantu as they called themselves. They migrated, they settled, they tore down, and they learned, and they in turn were often overthrown by succeeding tribes of their own folk.

They rule with their tongue and their power all Africa south of the equator, save where the Europeans have entered. They have never been conquered, although the gold and diamond traders have sought to debauch them, and the ivory and rubber capitalists have cruelly wronged their weaker groups. They are the Africans with whom the world of to-morrow must reckon, just as the world of yesterday knew them to its cost.

CHAPTER VII

THE WAR OF RACES AT LAND'S END

PRIMITIVE man in Africa is found in the interior jungles and down at Land's End in South Africa. The Pygmy people in the jungles represent to-day a small survival from the past, but a survival of curious interest, pushed aside by the torrent of conquest. Also pushed on by these waves of Bantu conquest, moved the ancient Abatwa or Bushmen. They are small in stature, yellow in color, with crisp-curled hair. The traditions of the Bushmen say that they came southward from the regions of the Great Lakes, and indeed the king and queen of Punt, as depicted by the Egyptians, were Bushmen or Hottentots.

Their tribes may be divided, in accordance with their noticeable artistic talents, into the painters and the sculptors. The sculptors entered South Africa by moving southward through the more central portions of the country, crossing the Zambesi, and coming down to the Cape. The painters, on the other hand, came through Damaraland on the west coast; when they came to the great mountain regions, they turned eastward and can be traced as far as the mountains

opposite Delagoa Bay. The mass of them settled down in the lower part of the Cape and in the
Kalahari desert. The painters were true cave
dwellers, but the sculptors lived in large communities on the stony hills, which they marked
with their carvings.

These Bushmen believed in an ancient race of
people who preceded them in South Africa.
They attributed magic power to these unknown
folk, and said that some of them had been
translated as stars to the sky. Before their
groups were dispersed the Bushmen had regular
government. Tribes with their chiefs occupied
well-defined tracts of country and were sub-
divided into branch tribes under subsidiary
chiefs. The great cave represented the dignity
and glory of the entire tribe.

The Bushmen suffered most cruelly in the succeeding migrations and conquests of South
Africa. They fought desperately in self-defense;
they saw their women and children carried into
bondage and they themselves hunted like wild
beasts. Both savage and civilized men appropriated their land. Still they were brave people.
"In this struggle for existence their bitterest
enemies, of whatever shade of color they might
be, were forced to make an unqualified acknowledgment of the courage and daring they so in-
variably exhibited." [1]

Here, to a remote corner of the world, where,
as one of their number said, they had supposed

[1] Stowe: *Native Races of South Africa*, pp. 215–216.

that the only beings in the world were Bushmen and lions, came a series of invaders. It was the outer ripples of civilization starting far away, the indigenous and external civilizations of Africa beating with great impulse among the Ethiopians and the Egyptian mulattoes and Sudanese Negroes and Yorubans, and driving the Bantu race southward. The Bantus crowded more and more upon the primitive Bushmen, and probably a mingling of the Bushmen and the Bantus gave rise to the Hottentots.

The Hottentots, or as they called themselves, Khoi Khoin (Men of Men), were physically a stronger race than the Abatwa and gave many evidences of degeneration from a high culture, especially in the "phenomenal perfection" of a language which "is so highly developed, both in its rich phonetic system, as represented by a very delicately graduated series of vowels and diphthongs, and in its varied grammatical structure, that Lepsius sought for its affinities in the Egyptian at the other end of the continent."

When South Africa was first discovered there were two distinct types of Hottentot. The more savage Hottentots were simply large, strong Bushmen, using weapons superior to the Bushmen, without domestic cattle or sheep. Other tribes nearer the center of South Africa were handsomer in appearance and raised an Egyptian breed of cattle which they rode.

In general the Hottentots were yellow, with close-curled hair, high cheek bones, and somewhat oblique eyes. Their migration commenced about the end of the fourteenth century and was, as is usual in such cases, a scattered, straggling movement. The traditions of the Hottentots point to the lake country of Central Africa as their place of origin, whence they were driven by the Bechuana tribes of the Bantu. They fled westward to the ocean and then turned south and came upon the Bushmen, whom they had only partially subdued when the Dutch arrived as settlers in 1652.

The Dutch "Boers" began by purchasing land from the Hottentots and then, as they grew more powerful, they dispossessed the dark men and tried to enslave them. There grew up a large Dutch-Hottentot class. Indeed the filtration of Negro blood noticeable in modern Boers accounts for much curious history. Soon after the advent of the Dutch some of the Hottentots, of whom there were not more than thirty or forty thousand, led by the Korana clans, began slowly to retreat northward, followed by the invading Dutch and fighting the Dutch, each other, and the wretched Bushmen. In the latter part of the eighteenth century the Hottentots had reached the great interior plain and met the on-coming outposts of the Bantu nations.

The Bechuana, whom the Hottentots first met, were the most advanced of the Negro tribes of Central Africa. They had crossed the Zambesi in the fourteenth or fifteenth century; their government was a sort of feudal system with

hereditary chiefs and vassals; they were careful
agriculturists, laid out large towns with great
regularity, and were the most skilled of smiths.
They used stone in building, carved on wood, and
many of them, too, were keen traders. These
tribes, coming southward, occupied the east-
central part of South Africa comprising modern
Bechuanaland. Apparently they had started
from the central lake country somewhere late
in the fifteenth century, and by the middle of
the eighteenth century one of their great chiefs,
Tao, met the on-coming Hottentots.

The Hottentots compelled Tao to retreat, but
the mulatto Gricquas arrived from the south,
and, allying themselves with the Bechuana,
stopped the rout. The Gricquas sprang from
and took their name from an old Hottentot
tribe. They were led by Kok and Barends, and
by adding other elements they became, partly
through their own efforts and partly through the
efforts of the missionaries, a community of fairly
well civilized people. In Gricqualand West the
mulatto Gricquas, under their chiefs Kok and
Waterboer, lived until the discovery of diamonds.

The Gricquas and Bechuana tribes were thus
gradually checking the Hottentots when, in the
nineteenth century, there came two new developments: first, the English took possession of Cape
Colony, and the Dutch began to move in larger
numbers toward the interior; secondly, a
newer and fiercer element of the Bantu tribes,
the Zulu-Kaffirs, appeared. The Kaffirs, or as

they called themselves, the Amazosas, claimed descent from Zuide, a great chief of the fifteenth century in the lake country. They are among the tallest people in the world, averaging five feet ten inches, and are slim, well-proportioned, and muscular. The more warlike tribes were usually clothed in leopard or ox skins. Cattle formed their chief wealth, stock breeding and hunting and fighting their main pursuits. Mentally they were men of tact and intelligence, with a national religion based upon ancestor worship, while their government was a patriarchal monarchy limited by an aristocracy and almost feudal in character. The common law which had grown up from the decisions of the chiefs made the head of the family responsible for the conduct of its branches, a village for all its residents, and the clan for all its villages. Finally there was a paramount chief, who was the civil and military father of his people. These people laid waste to the coast regions and in 1779 came in contact with the Dutch. A series of Dutch-Kaffir wars ensued between 1779 and 1795 in which the Dutch were hard pressed.

In 1806 the English took final possession of Cape Colony. At that time there were twenty-five thousand Boers, twenty-five thousand pure and mixed Hottentots, and twenty-five thousand slaves secured from the east coast. Between 1811 and 1877 there were six Kaffir-English wars. One of these in 1818 grew out of the ignorant interference of the English with the Kaffir tribal system; then there came a terrible war between 1834 and 1835, followed by the annexation of all the country as far as the Kei River. The war of the Axe (1846–48) led to further annexation by the British.

Hostilities broke out again in 1856 and 1863. In the former year, despairing of resistance to invading England, a prophet arose who advised the wholesale destruction of all Kaffir property except weapons, in order that this faith might bring back their dead heroes. The result was that almost a third of the nation perished from hunger. Fresh troubles occurred in 1877, when the Ama-Xosa confederacy was finally broken up, and to-day gradually these tribes are passing from independence to a state of mild vassalage to the British.

Meantime the more formidable part of the Zulu-Kaffirs had been united under the terrible Chief Chaka. He had organized a military system, not a new one by any means, but one of which we hear rumors back in the lake regions in the fourteenth and fifteenth centuries. McDonald says, "There has probably never been a more perfect system of discipline than that by which Chaka ruled his army and kingdom. At a review an order might be given in the most unexpected manner, which meant death to hundreds. If the regiment hesitated or dared to remonstrate, so perfect was the discipline and so great the jealousy that another was ready to cut them down. A warrior returning from battle without his arms was put to death without trial. A general returning unsuccessful in the main purpose of his expedition shared the same fate. Whoever displeased the king was immediately executed. The traditional courts practically ceased to exist so far as the will and action of the tyrant was concerned." With this army Chaka fell on tribe after tribe. The Bechuana fled before him and some tribes of them were entirely destroyed. The Hottentots suffered severely and one of his rival Zulu tribes under Umsilikatsi fled into Matabililand, pushing back the Bechuana. By the time the English came to Port Natal, Chaka was ruling over the whole southeastern seaboard, from the Limpopo River to Cape Colony, including the Orange and Transvaal states and the whole of Natal. Chaka was killed in 1828 and was eventually succeeded by his brother Dingan, who reigned twelve years. It was during Dingan's reign that England tried to abolish slavery in Cape Colony, but did not pay promptly for the slaves, as she had promised; the result was the so-called "Great Trek," about 1834, when thousands of Boers went into the interior across the Orange and Vaal rivers.

Dingan and these Boers were soon engaged in a death struggle in which the Zulus were repulsed and Dingan replaced by Panda. Under this chief there was something like repose for sixteen years, but in 1856 civil war broke out between his sons, one of whom, Cetewayo, succeeded his father in 1882. He fell into border disputes with the

English, and the result was one of the fiercest
clashes of Europe and Africa in modern days.
The Zulus fought desperately, annihilating at
one time a whole detachment and killing the
young prince Napoleon. But after all it was
assagais against machine guns, and the Zulus
were finally defeated at Ulundi, July 4, 1879.
Thereupon Zululand was divided among thirteen
semi-independent chiefs and became a British
protectorate.

Since then the best lands have been gradually
reoccupied by a large number of tribes — Kaffirs
from the south and Zulus from the north. The
tribal organization, without being actually broken
up, has been deprived of its dangerous features
by appointing paid village headmen and transforming the hereditary chief into a British government official. In Natal there are about one hundred and seventy tribal chiefs, and nearly half
of these have been appointed by the governor.

Umsilikatsi, who had been driven into Matabililand by the terrible Chaka in 1828 and defeated by the Dutch in 1837, had finally reëstablished his headquarters in Rhodesia in 1838.
Here he introduced the Zulu military system and
terrorized the peaceful and industrious Bechuana
populations. Lobengula succeeded Umsilikatsi
in 1870 and, realizing that his power was waning,
began to retreat northward toward the Zambesi.
He was finally defeated by the British and native
forces in 1893 and the land was incorporated into
South Central Africa.

The result of all these movements was to break the inhabitants of Bechuanaland into numerous fragments. There were small numbers of mulatto Gricquas in the southwest and similar Bastaards in the northwest. The Hottentots and Bushmen were dispersed into groups and seem doomed to extinction, the last Hottentot chief being deposed in 1810 and replaced by an English magistrate. Partially civilized Hottentots still live grouped together in their kraals and are members of Christian churches. The Bechuana hold their own in several centers; one is in Basutoland, west of Natal, where a number of tribes were welded together under the far-sighted Moshesh into a modern and fairly well civilized nation. In the north part of Bechuanaland are the self-governing Bamangwato and the Batwana, the former ruled by Khama, one of the canniest of modern rulers in Africa.

Meantime, in Portuguese térritory south of the Zambesi, there arose Gaza, a contemporary and rival of Chaka. His son, Manikus, was deputed by Dingan, Chaka's successor, to drive out the Portuguese. This Manikus failed to do, and to escape vengeance he migrated north of the Limpopo. Here he established his military kraal in a district thirty-six hundred and fifty feet above the sea and one hundred and twenty miles inland from Sofala. From this place his soldiery nearly succeeded in driving the Portuguese out of East Africa. He was succeeded by his son, Umzila, and Umzila's brother, Guzana (better known as Gungunyana), who exercised for a time joint authority. Gungunyana was finally overthrown in November, 1895, captured, and removed to the Azores.

North of the Zambesi, in British territory, the chief role in recent times has been played by the Bechuana, the first of the Bantu to return northward after the South African migration. Livingstone found there the Makolo, who with other tribes had moved northward on account of the pressure of the Dutch and Zulus below, and by conquering various tribes in the Zambesi region had established a strong power. This kingdom was nearly overthrown by the rebellion of the Barotse, and in 1875 the Barotse kingdom comprised a large territory. To-day their king, Newaneika, rules directly and indirectly fifty thousand square miles, with a population between one and two and a half million. They are under a protectorate of the British.

In Southwest Africa, Hottentot mulattoes crossing from the Cape caused widespread change. They were strong men and daring fighters and soon became dominant in what is now German Southwest Africa, where they fought fiercely with the Bantu Ova-Hereros. Armed with fire arms, these Namakwa Hottentots threatened Portuguese West Africa, but Germany intervened, ostensibly to protect missionaries. By spending millions of dollars and thousands of soldiers Germany has nearly exterminated these brave men.

Thus we have between the years 1400 and 1900 a great period of migration up to 1750, when Bushmen, Hottentot, Bantu, and Dutch appeared in succession at Land's End. In the latter part of the eighteenth century we have the clash of the Hottentots and Bechuana, followed in the nineteenth century by the terrible wars of Chaka, the Kaffirs, and Matabili. Finally, in the latter half of the nineteenth century, we see the gradual subjection of the Kaffir-Zulus and the Bechuana under the English and the final conquest of the Dutch. The resulting racial problem in South Africa is one of great intricacy.

To the racial problem has been added the tremendous problems of modern capital brought by the discovery of gold and diamond mines, so that the future of the Negro race is peculiarly bound up in developments here at Land's End, where the ship of the Flying Dutchman beats back and forth on its endless quest.

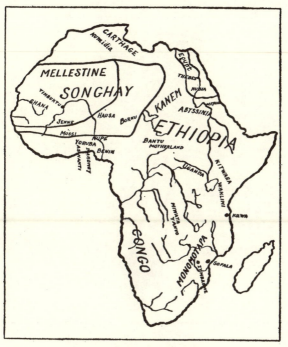

ANCIENT KINGDOMS OF AFRICA

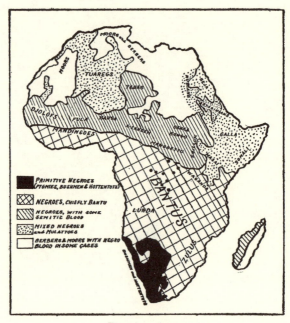

RACES IN AFRICA

Legend:

- **PRIMITIVE NEGROES** (PYGMIES, BUSHMEN & HOTTENTOTS)
- **NEGROES, CHIEFLY BANTU**
- **NEGROES, WITH SOME SEMITIC BLOOD**
- **MIXED NEGROES and MULATTOES**
- **BERBERS & MOORS WITH NEGRO BLOOD IN SOME CASES**

Map labels: MOORS and BERBERS, MOORS, TUAREGS, TIBBU, DIOLOFS, FULA, HAUSA, MANDINGOES, N. SUDAN, NILO-HAMITIC, GALLA, BANTU, LUNDA, ZULUS, BUSHMEN & HOTTENTOTS

CHAPTER VIII

WE have followed the history of mankind in Africa down the valley of the Nile, past Ethiopia to Egypt; we have seen kingdoms arise along the great bend of the Niger and strive with the ancient culture at its mouth. We have seen the remnants of mankind at Land's End, the ancient culture at Punt and Zymbabwe, and followed the invading Bantu east, south, and west to their greatest center in the vast jungle of the Congo valleys.

We must now gather these threads together and ask what manner of men these were and how far and in what way they progressed on the road of human culture.

That Negro peoples were the beginners of civilization along the Ganges, the Euphrates, and the Nile seems proven. Early Babylon was founded by a Negroid race. Hammurabi's code, the most ancient known, says "Anna and Bel called me, Hammurabi the exalted prince, the worshiper of the gods; to cause justice to prevail in the land, to destroy the wicked, to prevent the strong from oppressing the weak, to go forth like the sun over the black-head race, to enlighten

103

the land, and to further the welfare of the people." The Assyrians show a distinct Negroid strain and early Egypt was predominantly Negro. These earliest of cultures were crude and primitive, but they represented the highest attainment of mankind after tens of thousands of years in unawakened savagery.

It has often been assumed that the Negro is physically inferior to other races and markedly distinguishable from them; modern science gives no authority for such an assumption. The supposed inferiority cannot rest on color,[1] for that is "due to the combined influences of a great number of factors of environment working through physiological processes," and "however marked the contrasts may be, there is no corresponding difference in anatomical structure discoverable."[2] So, too, difference in texture of hair is a matter of degree, not kind, and is caused by heat, moisture, exposure, and the like.

The bony skeleton presents no distinctly racial lines of variation. Prognathism "presents too many individual varieties to be taken as a distinctive character of race."[3] Difference in physical measurements does not show the Negro to be a more primitive evolutionary form. Comparative ethnology to-day affords "no support to the view which sees in the so-called lower

[1] "Some authors write that the Ethiopians paint the devil white, in disdain of our complexions." — Ludolf: *History of Ethiopia*, p. 72.

[2] Ripley: *Races of Europe*, pp. 58, 62.

[3] Denniker: *Races of Men*, p. 63.

drinks from grain, or the manufacture of cotton, are widely known and sedulously fostered." [1]

Bücher reminds us of the deep impression made upon travelers when they sight suddenly the well-attended fields of the natives on emerging from the primeval forests. "In the more thickly populated parts of Africa these fields often stretch for many a mile, and the assiduous care of the Negro women shines in all the brighter light when we consider the insecurity of life, the constant feuds and pillages, in which no one knows whether he will in the end be able to harvest what he has sown. Livingstone gives somewhere a graphic description of the devastations wrought by slave hunts; the people were lying about slain, the dwellings were demolished; in the fields, however, the grain was ripening and there was none to harvest it." [2]

Sheep, goat, and chickens are domestic animals all over Africa, and Von Franzius considers Africa the home of the house cattle and the Negro as the original tamer. Northeastern Africa especially is noted for agriculture, cattle raising, and fruit culture. In the eastern Sudan, and among the great Bantu tribes extending from the Sudan down toward the south, cattle are evidences of wealth; one tribe, for instance, having so many oxen that each village had ten or twelve thousand head. Lenz (1884), Bouet-Williaumez (1848), Hecquard (1854), Bosman (1805), and

[1] Ratzel: *History of Mankind*, II, 380 ff.
[2] *Industrial Evolution*, p. 47.

races of mankind a transition stage from beast to man." [1]

Much has been made of the supposed smaller brain of the Negro race; but this is as yet an unproved assumption, based on the uncritical measurement of less than a thousand Negro brains as compared with eleven thousand or more European brains. Even if future measurement prove the average Negro brain lighter, the vast majority of Negro brain weights fall within the same limits as the whites; and finally, "neither size nor weight of the brain seems to be of importance" as an index of mental capacity. We may, therefore, say with Ratzel, "There is only one species of man. The variations are numerous, but do not go deep." [2]

To this we may add the word of the Secretary of the First Races Congress: "We are, then, under the necessity of concluding that an impartial investigator would be inclined to look upon the various important peoples of the world as to all intents and purposes essentially equal in intellect, enterprise, morality, and physique." [3]

If these conclusions are true, we should expect to see in Africa the human drama play itself out much as in other lands, and such has actually been the fact. At the same time we must expect peculiarities arising from the physiography of

[1] G. Finot: *Race Prejudice*. F. Herz: *Moderne Rassentheorien*.
[2] Ratzel: quoted in Spiller: *Inter-Racial Problems*, p. 31.
[3] Spiller: *Inter-Racial Problems*, p. 35.

the land — its climate, its rainfall, its deserts, and the peculiar inaccessibility of the coast.

Three principal zones of habitation appear: first, the steppes and deserts around the Sahara in the north and the Kalahari desert in the south; secondly, the grassy highlands bordering the Great Lakes and connecting these two regions; thirdly, the forests and rivers of Central and West Africa. In the deserts are the nomads, and the Pygmies are in the forest fastnesses. Herdsmen and their cattle cover the steppes and highlands, save where the tsetse fly prevents. In the open forests and grassy highlands are the agriculturists.

Among the forest farmers the village is the center of life, while in the open steppes political life tends to spread into larger political units. Political integration is, however, hindered by an ease of internal communication almost as great as the difficulty of reaching outer worlds beyond the continent. The narrow Nile valley alone presented physical barriers formidable enough to keep back the invading barbarians of the south, and even then with difficulty. Elsewhere communication was all too easy. For a while the Congo forests fended away the restless, but this only temporarily.

On the whole Africa from the Sahara to the Cape offered no great physical barrier to the invader, and we continually have whirlwinds of invading hosts rushing now southward, now northward, from the interior to the coast and

from the coast inland, and hurling their force against states, kingdoms, and cities. Some resisted for generations, some for centuries, some but a few years. It is, then, this sudden change and the fear of it that marks African culture, particularly in its political aspects, and which makes it so difficult to trace this changing past. Nevertheless beneath all change rests the strong substructure of custom, religion, industry, and art well worth the attention of students.

Starting with agriculture, we learn that "among all the great groups of the 'natural' races, the Negroes are the best and keenest tillers of the ground. A minority despise agriculture and breed cattle; many combine both occupations. Among the genuine tillers the whole life of the family is taken up in agriculture, and hence the months are by preference called after the operations which they demand. Constant clearings change forests to fields, and the ground is manured with the ashes of the burnt thicket. In the middle of the fields rise the light watch-towers, from which a watchman scares grain-eating birds and other thieves. An African cultivated landscape is incomplete without barns. The rapidity with which, when newly imported, the most various forms of cultivation spread in Africa says much for the attention which is devoted to this branch of economy. Industries, again, which may be called agricultural, like the preparation of meal from millet and other crops, also from cassava, the fabrication of fermented

Baker (1868) all bear witness to this, and Schweinfurth (1878) tells us of great cattle parks with two to three thousand head and of numerous agricultural and cattle-raising tribes. Von der Decken (1859–61) described the paradise of the dwellers about Kilimanjaro — the bananas, fruit, beans and peas, cattle raising with stall feed, the fertilizing of the fields, and irrigation. The Negroid Gallas have seven or eight cattle to each inhabitant. Livingstone bears witness to the busy cattle raising of the Bantus and Kaffirs. Hulub (1881) and Chapman (1868) tell of agriculture and fruit raising in South Africa. Shutt (1884) found the tribes in the southwestern basin of the Congo with sheep, swine, goats, and cattle. On this agricultural and cattle-raising economic foundation has arisen the organized industry of the artisan, the trader, and the manufacturer.

While the Pygmies, still living in the age of wood, make no iron or stone implements, they seem to know how to make bark cloth and fiber baskets and simple outfits for hunting and fishing. Among the Bushmen the art of making weapons and working in hides is quite common. The Hottentots are further advanced in the industrial arts, being well versed in the manufacture of clothing, weapons, and utensils. In the dressing of skins and furs, as well as in the plaiting of cords and the weaving of mats, we find evidences of their workmanship. In addition they are good workers in iron and copper, using the sheepskin bellows for this purpose. The Ashantis of the Gold Coast know how to make "cotton fabrics, turn and glaze earthenware, forge iron, fabricate instruments and arms, embroider rugs and carpets, and set gold and precious stones."[1] Among the people of the banana zone we find rough basket work, coarse pottery, grass cloth, and spoons made of wood and ivory. The people of the millet zone, because of uncertain agricultural resources, quite generally turn to manufacturing. Charcoal is prepared by the smiths, iron is smelted, and numerous implements are manufactured. Among them we find axes, hatchets, hoes, knives, nails, scythes, and other hardware. Cloaks, shoes, sandals, shields, and water and oil vessels are made from leather which the natives have dressed. Soap is manufactured in the Bautschi district, glass is made, formed, and colored by the people of Nupeland, and in almost every city cotton is spun and woven and dyed. Barth tells us that the weaving of cotton was known in the Sudan as early as the eleventh century. There is also extensive manufacture of wooden ware, tools, implements, and utensils.

In describing particular tribes, Baker and Felkin tell of smiths of wonderful adroitness, goatskins prepared better than a European tanner could do, drinking cups and kegs of remarkable symmetry, and polished clay floors. Schwein-

[1] These and other references in this chapter are from Schneider: *Cultur-fähigkeit des Negers.*

furth says, "The arrow and the spear heads are of the finest and most artistic work; their bristle-like barbs and points are baffling when one knows how few tools these smiths have." Excellent wood carving is found among the Bongo, Ovambo, and Makololo. Pottery and basketry and careful hut building distinguish many tribes. Cameron (1877) tells of villages so clean, with huts so artistic, that, save in book knowledge, the people occupied no low plane of civilization. The Mangbettu work both iron and copper. "The masterpieces of the Monbutto [Mangbettu] smiths are the fine chains worn as ornaments, and which in perfection of form and fineness compare well with our best steel chains." Shubotz in 1911 called the Mangbettu "a highly cultivated people" in architecture and handicraft. Barth found copper exported from Central Africa in competition with European copper at Kano.

Nor is the iron industry confined to the Sudan. About the Great Lakes and other parts of Central Africa it is widely distributed. Thornton says, "This iron industry proves that the East Africans stand by no means on so low a plane of culture as many travelers would have us think. It is unnecessary to be reminded what a people without instruction, and with the rudest tools to do such skilled work, could do if furnished with steel tools." Arrows made east of Lake Nyanza were found to be nearly as good as the best Swedish iron in Birmingham. From Egypt to the

Cape, Livingstone assures us that the mortar and pestle, the long-handled axe, the goatskin bellows, etc., have the same form, size, etc., pointing to a migration southwestward. Holub (1879), on the Zambesi, found fine workers in iron and bronze. The Bantu huts contain spoons, wooden dishes, milk pails, calabashes. handmills, and axes.

Kaffirs and Zulus, in the extreme south, are good smiths, and the latter melt copper and tin together and draw wire from it, according to Kranz (1880). West of the Great Lakes, Stanley (1878) found wonderful examples of smith work: figures worked out of brass and much work in copper. Cameron (1878) saw vases made near Lake Tanganyika which reminded him of the amphoræ in the Villa of Diomedes, Pompeii. Horn (1882) praises tribes here for iron and copper work. Livingstone (1871) passed thirty smelting houses in one journey, and Cameron came across bellows with valves, and tribes who used knives in eating. He found tribes which no Europeans had ever visited, who made ingots of copper in the form of the St. Andrew's cross, which circulated even to the coast. In the southern Congo basin iron and copper are worked; also wood and ivory carving and pottery making are pursued. In equatorial West Africa, Lenz and Du Chaillu (1861) found iron workers with charcoal, and also carvers of bone and ivory. Near Cape Lopez, Hübbe-Schleiden found tribes making ivory needles inlaid with ebony, while the arms and dishes of the Osaka are found among many tribes even as far as the Atlantic Ocean. Wilson (1856) found natives in West Africa who could repair American watches.

Gold Coast Negroes make gold rings and chains, forming the metal into all kinds of forms. Soyaux says, "The works in relief which natives of Lower Guinea carve with their own knives out of ivory and hippopotamus teeth are really entitled to be called works of art, and many wooden figures of fetishes in the Ethnographical Museum of Berlin show some understanding of the proportions of the human body." Great Bassam is called by Hecquard the "Fatherland of Smiths." The Mandingo in the northwest are remarkable workers in iron, silver, and gold, we are told by Mungo Park (1800), while there is a mass of testimony as to the work in the northwest of Africa in gold, tin, weaving, and dyeing. Caille found the Negroes in Bambana manufacturing gunpowder (1824–28), and the Hausa make soap; so, too, Negroes in Uganda and other parts have made guns after seeing European models.

So marked has been the work of Negro artisans and traders in the manufacture and exchange of iron implements that a growing number of archeologists are disposed to-day to consider the Negro as the originator of the art of smelting iron. Gabriel de Mortillet (1883) declared Negroes the only iron users among primitive people. Some would, therefore, argue that the Negro learned it from other folk, but Andree declares that the Negro developed his own "Iron Kingdom." Schweinfurth, Von Luschan, Boaz, and others incline to the belief that the Negroes invented the smelting of iron and passed it on to the Egyptians and to modern Europe.

Boaz says, "It seems likely that at a time when the European was still satisfied with rude stone tools, the African had invented or adopted the art of smelting iron. Consider for a moment what this invention has meant for the advance of the human race. As long as the hammer, knife, saw, drill, the spade, and the hoe had to be chipped out of stone, or had to be made of shell or hard wood, effective industrial work was not impossible, but difficult. A great progress was made when copper found in large nuggets was hammered out into tools and later on shaped by melting, and when bronze was introduced; but the true advancement of industrial life did not begin until the hard iron was discovered. It seems not unlikely that the people who made the marvelous discovery of reducing iron ores by smelting were the African Negroes. Neither ancient Europe, nor ancient western Asia, nor ancient China knew the iron, and everything points to its introduction from Africa. At the time of the great African discoveries toward the end of the past century, the trade of the blacksmith was found all over Africa, from north to south and from east to west. With his simple bellows and a charcoal fire he reduced the ore that is found in many parts of the continent and forged implements of great usefulness and beauty." [1]

Torday has argued recently, "I feel convinced by certain arguments that seem to prove to my satisfaction that we are indebted to the Negro for the very keystone of our modern civilization and that we owe him the discovery of iron. That iron could be discovered by accident in Africa seems beyond doubt: if this is so in other parts of the world, I am not competent to say. I will only remind you that Schweinfurth and Petherick record the fact that in the northern part of East Africa smelting furnaces are worked without artificial air current and, on the other hand, Stuhlmann and Kollmann found near Victoria Nyanza that the natives simply mixed powdered ore with charcoal and by introduction of air currents obtained the metal. These simple processes make it simple that iron should have been discovered in East or Central Africa. No bronze implements have ever been found in black Africa; had the Africans received iron from the Egyptians, bronze would have preceded this metal and all traces of it would not have disappeared. Black Africa was for a long time an exporter of iron, and even in the twelfth century exports to India and Java are recorded by Idrisi.

"It is difficult to imagine that Egypt should have obtained it from Europe where the oldest

[1] Atlanta University Leaflet, No. 19.

find (in Hallstadt) cannot be of an earlier period than 800 B.C., or from Asia, where iron is not known before 1000 B.C., and where, in the times of Ashur Nazir Pal, it was still used concurrently with bronze, while iron beads have been only recently discovered by Messrs. G. A. Wainwright and Bushe Fox in a predynastic grave, and where a piece of this metal, possibly a tool, was found in the masonry of the great pyramid." [1]

The Negro is a born trader. Lenz says, "our sharpest European merchants, even Jews and Armenians, can learn much of the cunning and trade of the Negroes." We know that the trade between Central Africa and Egypt was in the hands of Negroes for thousands of years, and in early days the cities of the Sudan and North Africa grew rich through Negro trade.

Leo Africanus, writing of Timbuktu in the sixteenth century, said, "It is a wonder to see what plentie of Merchandize is daily brought hither and how costly and sumptuous all things be. . . . Here are many shops of artificers and merchants and especially of such as weave linnen and cloth."

Long before cotton weaving was a British industry, West Africa and the Sudan were supplying a large part of the world with cotton cloth. Even to-day cities like Kuka on the west shore of Lake Chad and Sokota are manufacturing centers where cotton is spun and woven,

[1] *Journal of the Royal Anthropological Institute,* **XLIII,** 414, 415. Cf. also *The Crisis,* Vol. **IX,** p. 234.

skins tanned, implements and iron ornaments made.

"Travelers," says Bücher, "have often observed this tribal or local development of industrial technique. 'The native villages,' relates a Belgian observer of the Lower Congo, "'are often situated in groups. Their activities are based upon reciprocality, and they are to a certain extent the complements of one another. Each group has its more or less strongly defined specialty. One carries on fishing; another produces palm wine; a third devotes itself to trade and is broker for the others, supplying the community with all products from outside; another has reserved to itself work in iron and copper, making weapons for war and hunting, various utensils, etc. None may, however, pass beyond the sphere of its own specialty without exposing itself to the risk of being universally proscribed.'"

From the Loango Coast, Bastian tells of a great number of centers for special products of domestic industry. "Loango excels in mats and fishing baskets, while the carving of elephants' tusks is specially followed in Chilungo. The so-called Mafooka hats with raised patterns are drawn chiefly from the bordering country of Kakongo and Mayyume. In Bakunya are made potter's wares, which are in great demand; in Basanza, excellent swords; in Basundi, especially beautiful ornamented copper rings; on the Congo, clever wood and tablet carvings; in Loango, ornamented clothes and intricately designed mats; in Mayumbe, clothing of finely woven mat-work; in Kakongo, embroidered hats and also burnt clay pitchers; and among the Bayakas and Mantetjes, stuffs of woven grass." [1]

A native Negro student tells of the development of trade among the Ashanti. "It was a part of the state system of Ashanti to encourage trade. The king once in every forty days, at the Adai custom, distributed among a number of chiefs various sums of gold dust with a charge to turn the same to good account. These chiefs then sent down to the coast caravans of tradesmen, some of whom would be their slaves, sometimes some two or three hundred strong, to barter ivory for European goods, or buy such goods with gold dust, which the king obtained from the royal alluvial workings. Down to 1873 a constant stream of Ashanti traders might be seen daily wending their way to the merchants of the coast and back again, yielding more certain wealth and prosperity to the merchants of the Gold Coast and Great Britain than may be expected for some time yet to come from the mining industry and railway development put together. The trade chiefs would, in due time, render a faithful account to the king's stewards, being allowed to retain a fair portion of the profit. In the king's household, too, he would have special men who directly traded for him. Important chiefs carried on the same system

[1] Bücher: *Industrial Revolution* (tr. by Wickett), pp. 57–58.

of trading with the coast as did the king. Thus every member of the state, from the king downward, took an active interest in the promotion of trade and in the keeping open of trade routes into the interior." [1]

The trade thus encouraged and carried on in various parts of West Africa reached wide areas. From the Fish River to Kuka, and from Lagos to Zanzibar, the markets have become great centers of trade, the leading implement to civilization. Permanent markets are found in places like Ujiji and Nyangwe, where everything can be bought and sold from earthenware to wives; from the one to three thousand traders flocked here.

"How like is the market traffic, with all its uproar and sound of human voices, to one of our own markets! There is the same rivalry in praising the goods, the violent, brisk movements, the expressive gesture, the inquiring, searching glance, the changing looks of depreciation or triumph, of apprehension, delight, approbation. So says Stanley. Trade customs are not everywhere alike. If when negotiating with the Bangalas of Angola you do not quickly give them what they want, they go away and do not come back. Then perhaps they try to get possession of the coveted object by means of theft. It is otherwise with the Songos and Kiokos, who let you deal with them in the usual way. To buy even a small article you must go to the market; people avoid

[1] Hayford: *Native Institutions*, pp. 95–96.

trading anywhere else. If a man says to another;
'Sell me this hen' or 'that fruit,' the answer as
a rule will be, 'Come to the market place.' The
crowd gives confidence to individuals, and the
inviolability of the visitor to the market, and of
the market itself, looks like an idea of justice consecrated by long practice. Does not this remind
us of the old Germanic 'market place'?" [1]

Turning now to Negro family and social life
we find, as among all primitive peoples, polygamy and marriage by actual or simulated purchase. Out of the family develops the typical
African village organization, which is thus described in Ashanti by a native Gold Coast writer:
"The headman, as his name implies, is the head
of a village community, a ward in a township, or
of a family. His position is important, inasmuch
as he has directly to deal with the composite
elements of the general bulk of the people.

"It is the duty of the head of a family to bring
up the members thereof in the way they should
go; and by 'family' you must understand the
entire lineal descendants of a materfamilias, if
I may coin a convenient phrase. It is expected
of him by the state to bring up his charge in the
knowledge of matters political and traditional.
It is his work to train up his wards in the ways
of loyalty and obedience to the powers that be.
He is held responsible for the freaks of recalcitrant
members of his family, and he is looked to to
keep them within bounds and to insist upon

[1] Ratzel, II, 376.

conformity of their party with the customs, laws, and traditional observances of the community. In early times he could send off to exile by sale a troublesome relative who would not observe the laws of the community.

"It is a difficult task that he is set to, but in this matter he has all-powerful helpers in the female members of the family, who will be either the aunts, or the sisters, or the cousins, or the nieces of the headman; and as their interests are identical with his in every particular, the good women spontaneously train up their children to implicit obedience to the headman, whose rule in the family thus becomes a simple and an easy matter. 'The hand that rocks the cradle rules the world.' What a power for good in the native state system would the mothers of the Gold Coast and Ashanti become by judicious training upon native lines!

"The headman is par excellence the judge of his family or ward. Not only is he called upon to settle domestic squabbles, but frequently he sits judge over more serious matters arising between one member of the ward and another; and where he is a man of ability and influence, men from other wards bring him their disputes to settle. When he so settles disputes, he is entitled to a hearing fee, which, however, is not so much as would be payable in the regular court of the king or chief.

"The headman is naturally an important member of his company and often is a captain thereof. When he combines the two offices of headman and captain, he renders to the community a very important service. For in times of war, where the members of the ward would not serve cordially under a stranger, they would in all cases face any danger with their own kinsman as their leader. The headman is always succeeded by his uterine brother, cousin, or nephew — the line of succession, that is to say, following the customary law." [1]

We may contrast this picture with the more warlike Bantus of Southeast Africa. Each tribe lived by itself in a town with from five to fifteen thousand inhabitants, surrounded by gardens of millet, beans, and watermelon. Beyond these roamed their cattle, sheep, and goats. Their religion was ancestor worship with sacrifice to spirits and the dead, and some of the tribes made mummies of the corpses and clothed them for burial. They wove cloth of cotton and bark, they carved wood and built walls of unhewn stone. They had a standing military organization, and the tribes had their various totems, so that they were known as the Men of Iron, the Men of the Sun, the Men of the Serpents, Sons of the Corn Cleaners, and the like. Their system of common law was well conceived and there were organized tribunals of justice. In difficult cases precedents were sought and learned antiquaries consulted. At the age of fifteen or sixteen the boys were circumcised and formed into

[1] Hayford: *Native Institutions*, pp. 76 ff.

guilds. The land was owned by the tribe and apportioned to the chief by each family, and the main wealth of the tribe was in its cattle.

In general, among the African clans the idea of private property was but imperfectly developed and never included land. The main mass of visible wealth belonged to the family and clan rather than to the individual; only in the matter of weapons and ornaments was exclusive private ownership generally recognized.

The government, vested in fathers and chiefs, varied in different tribes from absolute despotisms to limited monarchies, almost republican. Viewing the Basuto National Assembly in South Africa, Lord Bryce recently wrote, "The resemblance to the primary assemblies of the early peoples of Europe is close enough to add another to the arguments which discredit the theory that there is any such thing as an Aryan type of institutions." [1]

While women are sold into marriage throughout Africa, nevertheless their status is far removed from slavery. In the first place the tracing of relationships through the female line, which is all but universal in Africa, gives the mother great influence. Parental affection is very strong, and throughout Negro Africa the mother is the most influential councilor, even in cases of tyrants like Chaka or Mutesa.

"No mother can love more tenderly or be more deeply beloved than the Negro mother. Robin

[1] *Impressions of South Africa*, 3d ed., p. 352.

tells of a slave in Martinique who, with his savings, freed his mother instead of himself. 'Everywhere in Africa,' writes Mungo Park, 'I have noticed that no greater affront can be offered a Negro than insulting his mother. 'Strike me,' cried a Mandingo to his enemy, 'but revile not my mother!' . . . The Herero swears 'By my mother's tears!' . . The Angola Negroes have a saying, 'As a mist lingers on the swamps, so lingers the love of father and mother.'" [1]

Black queens have often ruled African tribes. Among the Ba-Lolo, we are told, women take part in public assemblies where all-important questions are discussed. The system of educating children among such tribes as the Yoruba is worthy of emulation by many more civilized peoples.

Close knit with the family and social organization comes the religious life of the Negro. The religion of Africa is the universal animism or fetishism of primitive peoples, rising to polytheism and approaching monotheism chiefly, but not wholly, as a result of Christian and Islamic missions. Of fetishism there is much misapprehension. It is not mere senseless degradation. It is a philosophy of life. Among primitive Negroes there can be, as Miss Kingsley reminds us, no such divorce of religion from practical life as is common in civilized lands. Religion is life, and fetish an expression of the practical recog-

[1] William Schneider.

nition of dominant forces in which the Negro lives. To him all the world is spirit. Miss Kingsley says, "If you want, for example, to understand the position of man in nature according to fetish, there is, as far as I know, no clearer statement of it made than is made by Goethe in his superb 'Prometheus.'" [1] Fetish is a severely logical way of accounting for the world in terms of good and malignant spirits.

"It is this power of being able logically to account for everything that is, I believe, at the back of the tremendous permanency of fetish in Africa, and the cause of many of the relapses into it by Africans converted to other religions; it is also the explanation of the fact that white men who live in the districts where death and danger are everyday affairs, under a grim pall of boredom, are liable to believe in fetish, though ashamed of so doing. For the African, whose mind has been soaked in fetish during his early and most impressionable years, the voice of fetish is almost irresistible when affliction comes to him." [2]

Ellis tells us of the spirit belief of the Ewe people, who believe that men and all nature have the indwelling "Kra," which is immortal; that the man himself after death may exist as a ghost, which is often conceived of as departed from the "Kra," a shadowy continuing of the man. Bryce, speaking of the Kaffirs of South Africa,

[1] *West African Studies*, Chap. V.
[2] *Op. cit.*

says, "To the Kaffirs, as to the most savage races, the world was full of spirits — spirits of the rivers, the mountains, and the woods. Most important were the ghosts of the dead, who had power to injure or help the living, and who were, therefore, propitiated by offerings at stated periods, as well as on occasions when their aid was especially desired. This kind of worship, the worship once most generally diffused throughout the world, and which held its ground among the Greeks and Italians in the most flourishing period of ancient civilization, as it does in China and Japan to-day, was, and is, virtually the religion of the Kaffirs." [1]

African religion does not, however, stop with fetish, but, as in the case of other peoples, tends toward polytheism and monotheism. Among the Yoruba, for instance, Frobenius shows that religion and city-state go hand in hand.

"The first experienced glance will here detect the fact that this nation originally possessed a clear and definite organization so duly ordered and so logical that we but seldom meet with its like among all the peoples of the earth. And the basic idea of every clan's progeniture is a powerful God; the legitimate order in which the descendants of a particular clan unite in marriage to found new families, the essential origin of every new-born babe's descent in the founder of its race and its consideration as a part of the God in

[1] *Impressions of South Africa.*

Chief; the security with which the newly wedded wife not only may, but should, minister to her own God in an unfamiliar home." [1]

The Yoruba have a legend of a dying divinity. "This people . . . give evidence of a generalized system; a theocratic scheme, a well-conceived perceptible organization, reared in rhythmically proportioned manner."

Miss Kingsley says, "The African has a great Over God." [2] Nassau, the missionary, declares, "After more than forty years' residence among these tribes, fluently using their language, conversant with their customs, dwelling intimately in their huts, associating with them in the various relations of teacher, pastor, friend, master, fellow-traveler, and guest, and in my special office as missionary, searching after their religious thought (and therefore being allowed a deeper entrance into the arcana of their soul than would be accorded to a passing explorer), I am able unhesitatingly to say that among all the multitude of degraded ones with whom I have met, I have seen or heard of none whose religious thought was only a superstition.

"Standing in the village street, surrounded by a company whom their chief has courteously summoned at my request, when I say to him, 'I have come to speak to your people,' I do not need to begin by telling them that there is a God. Looking on that motley assemblage of villagers,

[1] Frobenius: *Voice of Africa*, Vol. I.
[2] *West African Studies*, p. 107.

— the bold, gaunt cannibal with his armament of gun, spear, and dagger; the artisan with rude adze in hand, or hands soiled at the antique bellows of the village smithy; women who have hasted from their kitchen fire with hands white with the manioc dough or still grasping the partly scaled fish; and children checked in their play with tiny bow and arrow or startled from their dusty street pursuit of dog or goat, — I have yet to be asked, 'Who is God?'" [1]

The basis of Egyptian religion was "of a purely Nigritian character," [2] and in its developed form Sudanese tribal gods were invoked and venerated by the priests. In Upper Egypt, near the confines of Ethiopia, paintings repeatedly represent black priests conferring on red Egyptian priests the instruments and symbols of priesthood. In the Sudan to-day Frobenius distinguishes four principal religions: first, earthly ancestor worship; next, the social cosmogony of the Atlantic races; third, the religion of the Bori, and fourth, Islam. The Bori religion spreads from Nubia as far as the Hausa, and from Lake Chad in the Niger as far as the Yoruba. It is the religion of possession and has been connected by some with Asiatic influences.

From without have come two great religious influences, Islam and Christianity. Islam came by conquest, trade, and proselytism. As a con-

[1] Nassau: *Fetishism in West Africa*, p. 36.
[2] *Encyclopædia Britannica*, 9th ed., XX, 362.

queror it reached Egypt in the seventh century and had by the end of the fourteenth century firm footing in the Egyptian Sudan. It overran the central Sudan by the close of the seventeenth century, and at the beginning of the nineteenth century had swept over Senegambia and the whole valley of the Niger down to the Gulf of Guinea. On the east Islam approached as a trader in the eighth century; it spread into Somaliland and overran Nubia in the fourteenth century. To-day Islam dominates Africa north of ten degrees north latitude and is strong between five and ten degrees north latitude. In the east it reaches below the Victoria Nyanza.

Christianity early entered Africa; indeed, as Mommsen says, "It was through Africa that Christianity became the religion of the world. Tertullian and Cyprian were from Carthage, Arnobius from Sicca Veneria, Lactantius, and probably in like manner Minucius Felix, in spite of their Latin names, were natives of Africa, and not less so Augustine. In Africa the Church found its most zealous confessors of the faith and its most gifted defenders." [1]

The Africa referred to here, however, was not Negroland, but Africa above the desert, where Negro blood was represented in the ancient Mediterranean race and by intercourse across the desert. On the other hand Christianity was early represented in the valley of the Nile under "the most holy pope and patriarch of the great city

[1] *The African Provinces*, II, 345.

of Alexandria and of all of the land of Egypt, of Jerusalem, the holy city, of Nubia, Abyssinia, and Pentapolis, and all the preaching of St. Mark." This patriarchate had a hundred bishoprics in the fourth century and included thousands of black Christians. Through it the Cross preceded the Crescent in some of the remotest parts of black Africa.

All these beginnings were gradually overthrown by Islam except among the Copts in Egypt, and in Abyssinia. The Portuguese in the sixteenth century began to replant the Christian religion and for a while had great success, both on the east and west coasts. Roman Catholic enterprise halted in the eighteenth century and the Protestants began. To-day the west coast is studded with English and German missions, South Africa is largely Christian through French and English influence, and the region about the Great Lakes is becoming christianized. The Roman Catholics have lately increased their activities, and above all the Negroes of America have entered with their own churches and with the curiously significant "Ethiopian" movement.

Coming now to other spiritual aspects of African culture, we can speak at present only in a fragmentary way. Roughly speaking, Africa can be divided into two language zones: north of the fifth degree of north latitude is the zone of diversity, with at least a hundred groups of widely divergent languages; south of the line

there is one minor language (Bushman-Hotten-
tot), spoken by less than fifty thousand people,
and elsewhere the predominant Bantu tongue
with its various dialects, spoken by at least
fifty million.   The Bantu tongue, which thus
rules all Central, West, and South Africa, is an
agglutinative tongue which makes especial use
of prefixes. The hundreds of Negro tongues or
dialects in the north represent most probably
the result of war and migration and the breaking
up of ancient centers of culture. In Abyssinia
and the great horn of East Africa the influence
of Semitic tongues is noted. Despite much effort
on the part of students, it has been impossible
to show any Asiatic origin for the Egyptian language. As Sergi maintains, "everything favors
an African origin." [1] The most brilliant suggestion of modern days links together the Egyptian
of North Africa and the Hottentot and Bushmen
tongues of South Africa.

Language was reduced to writing among the
Egyptians and Ethiopians and to some extent
elsewhere in Africa. Over 100 manuscripts of
Ethiopian and Ethiopic-Arabian literature are
extant, including a version of the Bible and historical chronicles. The Arabic was used as the
written tongue of the Sudan, and Negroland has
given us in this tongue many chronicles and
other works of black authors. The greatest of
these, the Epic of the Sudan (Tarikh-es-Soudan),
deserves to be placed among the classics of all

[1] *Mediterranean Race*, p. 10.

literature. In other parts of Africa there was no written language, but there was, on the other hand, an unusual perfection of oral tradition through bards, and extraordinary efficiency in telegraphy by drum and horn.

The folklore and proverbs of the African tribes are exceedingly rich. Some of these have been made familiar to English writers through the work of "Uncle Remus." Others have been collected by Johnston, Ellis, and Theal.

A black bard of our own day has described the onslaught of the Matabili in poetry of singular force and beauty:

> They saw the clouds ascend from the plains:
> It was the smoke of burning towns.
> The confusion of the whirlwind
> Was in the heart of the great chief of the blue-colored cattle.
> The shout was raised,
> "They are friends!"
> But they shouted again,
> "They are foes!"
> Till their near approach proclaimed them Matabili.
> The men seized their arms,
> And rushed out as if to chase the antelope.
> The onset was as the voice of lightning,
> And their javelins as the shaking of the forest in the autumn storm.[1]

There can be no doubt of the Negro's deep and delicate sense of beauty in form, color, and sound. Soyaux says of African industry, "Whoever denies to them independent invention and individual taste in their work either shuts his eyes intentionally before perfectly evident facts,

[1] Stowe: *Native Races*, etc., pp. 553–554.

or lack of knowledge renders him an incompetent judge." [1] M. Rutot had lately told us how the Negro race brought art and sculpture to pre-historic Europe. The bones of the European Negroids are almost without exception found in company with drawings and sculpture in high and low relief; some of their sculptures, like the Wellendorff "Venus," are unusually well finished for primitive man. So, too, the painting and carving of the Bushmen and their fore-runners in South Africa has drawn the admira-tion of students. The Negro has been prolific in the invention of musical instruments and has given a new and original music to the western world.

Schweinfurth, who has preserved for us much of the industrial art of the Negroes, speaks of their delight in the production of works of art for the embellishment and convenience of life. Frobenius expressed his astonishment at the originality of the African in the Yoruba temple which he visited. "The lofty veranda was divided from the passageway by fantastically carved and colored pillars. On the pillars were sculptured knights, men climbing trees, women, gods, and mythical beings. The dark chamber lying beyond showed a splendid red room with stone hatchets, wooden figures, cowry beads, and jars. The whole picture, the columns carved in colors in front of the colored altar, the old man sitting in the circle of those who reverenced him, the open scaffold-

[1] Quoted in Schneider.

ing of ninety rafters, made a magnificent impression." [1]

The Germans have found, in Kamarun, towns built, castellated, and fortified in a manner that reminds one of the prehistoric cities of Crete. The buildings and fortifications of Zymbabwe have already been described and something has been said of the art of Benin, with its brass and bronze and ivory. All the work of Benin in bronze and brass was executed by casting, and by methods so complicated that it would be no easy task for a modern European craftsman to imitate them.

Perhaps no race has shown in its earlier development a more magnificent art impulse than the Negro, and the student must not forget how far Negro genius entered into the art in the valley of the Nile from Meroe and Nepata down to the great temples of Egypt.

Frobenius has recently directed the world's attention to art in West Africa. Quartz and granite he found treated with great dexterity. But more magnificent than the stone monument is the proof that at some remote era glass was made and molded in Yorubaland and that the people here were brilliant in the production of terra-cotta images. The great mass of potsherds, lumps of glass, heaps of slag, etc., "proves, at all events, that the glass industry flourished in this locality in ages past. It is plain that the glass beads found to have been so very common

[1] Frobenius: *Voice of Africa*, Vol. I, Chap. XIV.

in Africa were not only not imported, but were actually manufactured in great quantities at home."

The terra-cotta pieces are "remains of another ancient and fine type of art" and were "eloquent of a symmetry, a vitality, a delicacy of form, and practically a reminiscence of the ancient Greeks." The antique bronze head Frobenius describes as "a head of marvelous beauty, wonderfully cast," and "almost equal in beauty and, at least, no less noble in form, and as ancient as the terra-cotta heads." [1]

In a park of monuments Frobenius saw the celebrated forge and hammer: a mighty mass of iron, like a falling drop in shape, and a block of quartz fashioned like a drum. Frobenius thinks these were relics dating from past ages of culture, when the manipulation of quartz and granite was thoroughly understood and when iron manipulation gave evidence of a skill not met with to-day.

Even when we contemplate such revolting survivals of savagery as cannibalism we cannot jump too quickly at conclusions. Cannibalism is spread over many parts of Negro Africa, yet the very tribes who practice cannibalism show often other traits of industry and power. "These cannibal Bassonga were, according to the types we met with, one of those rare nations of the African interior which can be classed with the most esthetic and skilled, most discreet and in-

[1] Frobenius: *Voice of Africa*, Vol. I.

telligent of all those generally known to us as the so-called natural races. Before the Arabic and European invasion they did not dwell in 'hamlets,' but in towns with twenty or thirty thousand inhabitants, in towns whose highways were shaded by avenues of splendid palms planted at regular intervals and laid out with the symmetry of colonnades. Their pottery would be fertile in suggestion to every art craftsman in Europe. Their weapons of iron were so perfectly fashioned that no industrial art from abroad could improve upon their workmanship. The iron blades were cunningly ornamented with damascened copper, and the hilts artistically inlaid with the same metal. Moreover, they were most industrious and capable husbandmen, whose careful tillage of the suburbs made them able competitors of any gardener in Europe. Their sexual and parental relations evidenced an amount of tact and delicacy of feelings unsurpassed among ourselves, either in the simplicity of the country or the refinements of the town. Originally their political and municipal system was organized on the lines of a representative republic. True, it is on record that these well-governed towns often waged an internecine warfare; but in spite of this it had been their invariable custom from time immemorial, even in times of strife, to keep the trade routes open and to allow their own and foreign merchants to go their ways unharmed. And the commerce of these nations ebbed and flowed along a road of unknown age, running from Itimbiri to Batubenge, about six hundred miles in length. This highway was destroyed by the 'missionaries of civilization' from Arabia only toward the close of the eighteenth century. But even in my own time there were still smiths who knew the names of places along that wonderful trade route driven through the heart of the 'impenetrable forests of the Congo.' For every scrap of imported iron was carried over it." [1]

In disposition the Negro is among the most lovable of men. Practically all the great travelers who have spent any considerable time in Africa testify to this and pay deep tribute to the kindness with which they were received. One has but to remember the classic story of Mungo Park, the strong expressions of Livingstone, the words of Stanley and hundreds of others to realize this.

Ceremony and courtesy mark Negro life. Livingstone again and again reminds us of "true African dignity." "When Ilifian men or women salute each other, be it with a plain and easy curtsey (which is here the simplest form adopted), or kneeling down, or throwing oneself upon the ground, or kissing the dust with one's forehead, no matter which, there is yet a deliberateness, a majesty, a dignity, a devoted earnestness in the manner of its doing, which brings to light with every gesture, with every fold of clothing, the deep significance and essential import of every single action. Everyone may, without too

[1] Frobenius: _Voice of Africa_, I, 14–15.

greatly straining his attention, notice the very striking precision and weight with which the upper and lower native classes observe these niceties of intercourse." [1]

All this does not mean that the African Negro is not human with the all-too-well-known foibles of humanity. Primitive life among them is, after all, as bare and cruel as among primitive Germans or Chinese, but it is not more so, and the more we study the Negro the more we realize that we are dealing with a normal human stock which under reasonable conditions has developed and will develop in the same lines as other men. Why is it, then, that so much of misinformation and contempt is widespread concerning Africa and its people, not simply among the unthinking mass, but among men of education and knowledge?

One reason lies undoubtedly in the connotation of the term "Negro." In North America a Negro may be seven-eighths white, since the term refers to any person of Negro descent. If we use the term in the same sense concerning the inhabitants of the rest of the world, we may say truthfully that Negroes have been among the leaders of civilization in every age of the world's history from ancient Babylon to modern America; that they have contributed wonderful gifts in art, industry, political organization, and religion, and that they are doing the same to-day in all parts of the world.

In sharp contrast to this usage the term "Negro"

[1] Frobenius: *Voice of Africa*, I, 272.

in Africa has been more and more restricted until some scientists, late in the last century, declared that the great mass of the black and brown people of Africa were not Negroes at all, and that the "real" Negro dwells in a small space between the Niger and the Senegal. Ratzel says, "If we ask what justifies so narrow a limitation, we find that the hideous Negro type, which the fancy of observers once saw all over Africa, but which, as Livingstone says, is really to be seen only as a sign in front of tobacco shops, has on closer inspection evaporated from all parts of Africa, to settle no one knows how in just this region. If we understand that an extreme case may have been taken for the genuine and pure form, even so we do not comprehend the ground of its geographical limitation and location; for wherever dark, woolly-haired men dwell, this ugly type also crops up. We are here in the presence of a refinement of science which to an unprejudiced eye will hardly hold water." [1]

In this restricted sense the Negro has no history, culture, or ability, for the simple fact that such human beings as have history and evidence culture and ability are not Negroes! Between these two extreme definitions, with unconscious adroitness, the most extraordinary and contradictory conclusions have been reached.

Let it therefore be said, once for all, that racial inferiority is not the cause of anti-Negro prejudice. Boaz, the anthropologist, says, "An unbiased

[1] Ratzel: *History of Mankind*, II, 313.

estimate of the anthropological evidence so far brought forward does not permit us to countenance the belief in a racial inferiority which would unfit an individual of the Negro race to take his part in modern civilization. We do not know of any demand made on the human body or mind in modern life that anatomical or ethnological evidence would prove to be beyond the powers of the Negro." [1]

"We have every reason to suppose that all races are capable, under proper guidance, of being fitted into the complex scheme of our modern civilization, and the policy of artificially excluding them from its benefits is as unjustifiable scientifically as it is ethically abhorrent." [2] What is, then, this so-called "instinctive" modern prejudice against black folk?

Lord Bryce says of the intermingling of blacks and whites in South America, "The ease with which the Spaniards have intermingled by marriage with the Indian tribes — and the Portuguese have done the like, not only with the Indians, but with the more physically dissimilar Negroes — shows that race repugnance is no such constant and permanent factor in human affairs as members of the Teutonic peoples are apt to assume. Instead of being, as we Teutons suppose, the rule in the matter, we are rather the exception, for in the ancient world there seems to have been little race repulsion."

[1] Atlanta University Publications, No. 11.
[2] Robert Lowie in the *New Review*, Sept., 1914.

In nearly every age and land men of Negro descent have distinguished themselves. In literature there is Terence in Rome, Nosseyeb and Antar in Arabia, Es-Sa'di in the Sudan, Pushkin in Russia, Dumas in France, Al Kanemi in Spain, Heredia in the West Indies, and Dunbar in the United States, not to mention the alleged Negro strain in Æsop and Robert Browning. As rulers and warriors we remember such Negroes as Queen Nefertari and Amenhotep III among many others in Egypt; Candace and Ergamenes in Ethiopia; Mansa Musa, Sonni Ali, and Mohammed Askia in the Sudan; Diaz in Brazil, Toussaint L'Ouverture in Hayti, Hannivalov in Russia, Sakanouye Tamuramaro in Japan, the elder Dumas in France, Calembe and Chaka among the Bantu, and Menelik, of Abyssinia; the numberless black leaders of India, and the mulatto strain of Alexander Hamilton. In music and art we recall Bridgewater, the friend of Beethoven, and the unexplained complexion of Beethoven's own father; Coleridge-Taylor in England, Tanner in America, Gomez in Spain; Ira Aldridge, the actor, and Johnson, Cook, and Burleigh, who are making the new American syncopated music. In the Church we know that Negro blood coursed in the veins of many of the Catholic African fathers, if not in certain of the popes; and there were in modern days Benoit of Palermo, St. Benedict, Bishop Crowther, the Mahdi who drove England from the Sudan, and Americans like Allen, Lot Carey, and Alexander Crummell.

In science, discovery, and invention the Negroes claim Lislet Geoffroy of the French Academy, Latino and Amo, well known in European university circles; and in America the explorers Dorantes and Henson; Banneker, the almanac maker; Wood, the telephone improver; McCoy, inventor of modern lubrication; Matseliger, who revolutionized shoemaking. Here are names representing all degrees of genius and talent from the mediocre to the highest, but they are strong human testimony to the ability of this race.

We must, then, look for the origin of modern color prejudice not to physical or cultural causes, but to historic facts. And we shall find the answer in modern Negro slavery and the slave trade.

CHAPTER IX

THE TRADE IN MEN

COLOR was never a badge of slavery in the ancient or medieval world, nor has it been in the modern world outside of Christian states. Homer sings of a black man, a "reverend herald"

> Of visage solemn, sad, but sable hue,
> Short, woolly curls, o'erfleeced his bending head, . . .
> Eurybiates, in whose large soul alone,
> Ulysses viewed an image of his own.

Greece and Rome had their chief supplies of slaves from Europe and Asia. Egypt enslaved races of all colors, and if there were more blacks than others among her slaves, there were also more blacks among her nobles and Pharaohs, and both facts are explained by her racial origin and geographical position. The fall of Rome led to a cessation of the slave trade, but after a long interval came the white slave trade of the Saracens and Moors, and finally the modern trade in Negroes.

Slavery as it exists universally among primitive people is a system whereby captives in war are put to tasks about the homes and in the fields, thus releasing the warriors for systematic fighting and the women for leisure. Such slavery has been common among all peoples and was widespread in Africa. The relative number of African slaves under these conditions was small and the labor not hard; they were members of the family and might and did often rise to high position in the tribe.

Remembering that in the fifteenth century there was no great disparity between the civilization of Negroland and that of Europe, what made the striking difference in subsequent development? European civilization, cut off by physical barriers from further incursions of barbaric races, settled more and more to systematic industry and to the domination of one religion; African culture and industries were threatened by powerful barbarians from the west and central regions of the continent and by the Moors in the north, and Islam had only partially converted the leading peoples.

When, therefore, a demand for workmen arose in America, European exportation was limited by religious ties and economic stability. African exportation was encouraged not simply by the Christian attitude toward heathen, but also by the Moslem enmity toward the unconverted Negroes. Two great modern religions, therefore, agreed at least in the policy of enslaving heathen blacks, while the overthrow of black Askias by the Moors at Tenkadibou brought that economic chaos among the advanced Negro peoples and movement among the more barbarous tribes which proved of prime advantage to the development of a systematic trade in men.

The modern slave trade began with the Mohammedan conquests in Africa, when heathen Negroes were seized to supply the harems, and as soldiers and servants. They were bought from the masters and seized in war, until the growing wealth and luxury of the conquerors demanded larger numbers. Then Negroes from the Egyptian Sudan, Abyssinia, and Zanzibar began to pass into Arabia, Persia, and India in increased numbers. As Negro kingdoms and tribes rose to power they found the slave trade lucrative and natural, since the raids in which slaves were captured were ordinary inter-tribal wars. It was not until the eighteenth and nineteenth centuries that the demand for slaves in Christian lands made slaves the object, and not the incident, of African wars.

In Mohammedan countries there were gleams of hope in slavery. In fiction and in truth the black slave had a chance. Once converted to Islam, he became a brother to the best, and the brotherhood of the faith was not the sort of idle lie that Christian slave masters made it. In Arabia black leaders arose like Antar; in India black slaves carved out principalities where their descendants still rule.

Some Negro slaves were brought to Europe by the Spaniards in the fourteenth century, and a small trade was continued by the Portuguese, who conquered territory from the "tawny"

Moors of North Africa in the early fifteenth
century. Later, after their severe repulse at Al-
Kasr-Al-Kabu, the Portuguese began to creep
down the west coast in quest of trade. They
reached the River of Gold in 1441, and their
story is that their leader seized certain free
Moors and the next year exchanged them for
ten black slaves, a target of hide, ostrich eggs,
and some gold dust. The trade was easily justified on the ground that the Moors were Mohammedans and refused to be converted to Christianity, while heathen Negroes would be better
subjects for conversion and stronger laborers.
In the next few years a small number of Negroes
continued to be imported into Spain and Portugal as servants. We find, for instance, in 1474,
that Negro slaves were common in Seville. There
is a letter from Ferdinand and Isabella in the
year 1474 to a celebrated Negro, Juan de Valla-
dolid, commonly called the "Negro Count"
(El Conde Negro), nominating him to the office
of "mayoral of the Negroes" in Seville. The
slaves were apparently treated kindly, allowed
to keep their own dances and festivals, and to
have their own chief, who represented them in the
courts, as against their own masters, and settled
their private quarrels.

Between 1455 and 1492 little mention is made
of slaves in the trade with Africa. Columbus is
said to have suggested Negroes for America, but
Ferdinand and Isabella refused. Nevertheless,
by 1501, we have the first incidental mention of

Negroes going to America in a declaration that Negro slaves "born in the power of Christians were to be allowed to pass to the Indies, and the officers of the royal revenue were to receive the money to be paid for their permits."

About 1501 Ovando, Governor of Spanish America, was objecting to Negro slaves and "solicited that no Negro slaves should be sent to Hispaniola, for they fled amongst the Indians and taught them bad customs, and never could be captured." Nevertheless a letter from the king to Ovando, dated Segovia, the fifteenth of September, 1505, says, "I will send more Negro slaves as you request; I think there may be a hundred. At each time a trustworthy person will go with them who may have some share in the gold they may collect and may promise them ease if they work well."[1] There is a record of a hundred slaves being sent out this very year, and Diego Columbus was notified of fifty to be sent from Seville for the mines in 1510.

After this time frequent notices show that Negroes were common in the new world.[2] When Pizarro, for instance, had been slain in Peru, his body was dragged to the cathedral by two Negroes. After the battle of Anaquito the head of the viceroy was cut off by a Negro, and during the great earthquake in Guatemala a most remarkable figure was a gigantic Negro seen in various parts of the city. Nunez had thirty Negroes with

---

[1] Cf. Helps: *Spanish Conquest*, IV, 401.
[2] Helps, *op. cit.*, I, 219–220.

him on the top of the Sierras, and there was rumor of an aboriginal tribe of Negroes in South America. One of the last acts of King Ferdinand was to urge that no more Negroes be sent to the West Indies, but under Charles V, Bishop Las Casas drew up a plan of assisted migration to America and asked in 1517 the right for immigrants to import twelve Negro slaves, in return for which the Indians were to be freed.

Las Casas, writing in his old age, owns his error: "This advice that license should be given to bring Negro slaves to these lands, the Clerigo Casas first gave, not considering the injustice with which the Portuguese take them and make them slaves; which advice, after he had apprehended the nature of the thing, he would not have given for all he had in the world. For he always held that they had been made slaves unjustly and tyrannically; for the same reason holds good of them as of the Indians." [1]

As soon as the plan was broached a Savoyard, Lorens de Gomenot, Governor of Bresa, obtained a monopoly of this proposed trade and shrewdly sold it to the Genoese for twenty-five thousand ducats. Other monopolies were granted in 1523, 1527, and 1528.[2] Thus the American trade became established and gradually grew, passing successively into the hands of the Portuguese, the Dutch, the French, and the English.

At first the trade was of the same kind and

[1] Helps, *op. cit.*, II, 18–19.
[2] Helps, *op. cit.*, III, 211–212.

volume as that already passing northward over the desert routes. Soon, however, the American trade developed. A strong, unchecked demand for brute labor in the West Indies and on the continent of America grew until it culminated in the eighteenth century, when Negro slaves were crossing the Atlantic at the rate of fifty to one hundred thousand a year. This called for slave raiding on a scale that drew upon every part of Africa — upon the west coast, the western and Egyptian Sudan, the valley of the Congo, Abyssinia, the lake regions, the east coast, and Madagascar. Not simply the degraded and weaker types of Negroes were seized, but the strong Bantu, the Mandingo and Songhay, the Nubian and Nile Negroes, the Fula, and even the Asiatic Malay, were represented in the raids.

There was thus begun in modern days a new slavery and slave trade. It was different from that of the past, because more and more it came in time to be founded on racial caste, and this caste was made the foundation of a new industrial system. For four hundred years, from 1450 to 1850, European civilization carried on a systematic trade in human beings of such tremendous proportions that the physical, economic, and moral effects are still plainly to be remarked throughout the world. To this must be added the large slave trade of Mussulman lands, which began with the seventh century and raged almost unchecked until the end of the nineteenth century.

These were not days of decadence, but a period that gave the world Shakespeare, Martin Luther, and Raphael, Haroun-al-Raschid and Abraham Lincoln. It was the day of the greatest expansion of two of the world's most pretentious religions and of the beginnings of the modern organization of industry. In the midst of this advance and uplift this slave trade and slavery spread more human misery, inculcated more disrespect for and neglect of humanity, a greater callousness to suffering, and more petty, cruel, human hatred than can well be calculated. We may excuse and palliate it, and write history so as to let men forget it; it remains the most inexcusable and despicable blot on modern human history.

The Portuguese built the first slave-trading fort at Elmina, on the Gold Coast, in 1482, and extended their trade down the west coast and up the east coast. Under them the abominable traffic grew larger and larger, until it became far the most important in money value of all the commerce of the Zambesi basin. There could be no extension of agriculture, no mining, no progress of any kind where it was so extensively carried on.[1]

It was the Dutch, however, who launched the oversea slave trade as a regular institution. They began their fight for freedom from Spain in 1579; in 1595, as a war measure against Spain, who at that time was dominating Portugal, they

[1] Theal: *History and Ethnography of South Africa before 1795*, I, 476.

made their first voyage to Guinea. By 1621 they had captured Portugal's various slave forts on the west coast and they proceeded to open sixteen forts along the coast of the Gulf of Guinea. Ships sailed from Holland to Africa, got slaves in exchange for their goods, carried the slaves to the West Indies or Brazil, and returned home laden with sugar. In 1621 the private companies trading in the west were all merged into the Dutch West India Company, which sent in four years fifteen thousand four hundred and thirty Negroes to Brazil, carried on war with Spain, supplied even the English plantations, and gradually became the great slave carrier of the day.

The commercial supremacy of the Dutch early excited the envy and emulation of the English. The Navigation Ordinance of 1651 was aimed at them, and two wars were necessary to wrest the slave trade from them and place it in the hands of the English. The final terms of peace, among other things, surrendered New Netherlands to England and opened the way for England to become henceforth the world's greatest slave trader.

The English trade began with Sir John Hawkins' voyages in 1562 and later, in which "the Jesus, our chiefe shippe" played a leading part. Desultory trade was kept up by the English until the middle of the seventeenth century, when English chartered slave-trading companies began to appear. In 1662 the "Royal Adventurers," including the king, the queen dowager, and the Duke of York, invested in the trade, and finally the Royal African Company, which became the world's chief slave trader, was formed in 1672 and carried on a growing trade for a quarter of a century. Jamaica had finally been captured and held by Oliver Cromwell in 1655 and formed a West Indian base for the trade in men.

The chief contract for trade in Negroes was the celebrated "Asiento" or agreement of the King of Spain to the importation of slaves into Spanish domains. The Pope's Bull or Demarkation, 1493, debarred Spain from African possessions, and compelled her to contract with other nations for slaves. This contract was in the hands of the Portuguese in 1600; in 1640 the Dutch received it, and in 1701 the French. The War of the Spanish Succession brought this monopoly to England.

This Asiento of 1713 was an agreement between England and Spain by which the latter granted the former a monopoly of the Spanish colonial slave trade for thirty years, and England engaged to supply the colonies within that time with at least one hundred and forty-four thousand slaves at the rate of forty-eight hundred per year. The English counted this prize as the greatest result of the Treaty of Utrecht (1713), which ended the mighty struggle against the power of Louis XIV. The English held the monopoly until the Treaty of Aix-la-Chapelle

(1748), although they had to go to war over it in 1739.

From this agreement the slave traders reaped a harvest. The trade centered at Liverpool, and that city's commercial greatness was built largely on this foundation. In 1709 it sent out one slaver of thirty tons' burden; encouraged by Parliamentary subsidies which amounted to nearly half a million dollars between 1729 and 1750, the trade amounted to fifty-three ships in 1751; eighty-six in 1765, and at the beginning of the nineteenth century one hundred and eighty-five, which carried forty-nine thousand two hundred and thirteen slaves in one year.

The slave trade thus begun by the Portuguese, enlarged by the Dutch, and carried to its culmination by the English centered on the west coast near the seat of perhaps the oldest and most interesting culture of Africa. It came at a critical time. The culture of Yoruba, Benin, Mossiland, and Nupe had exhausted itself in a desperate attempt to stem the on-coming flood of Mohammedan culture. It had succeeded in maintaining its small, loosely federated city-states suited to trade, industry, and art. It had developed strong resistance toward the Sudan state builders toward the north, as in the case of the fighting Mossi; but behind this warlike resistance lay the peaceful city life which gave industrial ideas to Byzantium and shared something of Ethiopian and Mediterranean culture.

The first advent of the slave traders increased

and encouraged native industry, as is evidenced by the bronze work of Benin; but soon this was pushed into the background, for it was not bronze metal but bronze flesh that Europe wanted. A new tyranny, bloodthirsty, cruel, and built on war, forced itself forward in the Niger delta. The powerful state of Dahomey arose early in the eighteenth century and became a devastating tyranny, reaching its highest power early in the nineteenth century. Ashanti, a similar kingdom, began its conquests in 1719 and grew with the slave trade. Thus state building in West Africa began to replace the city economy, but it was a state built on war and on war supported and encouraged largely for the sake of trade in human flesh. The native industries were changed and disorganized. Family ties and government were weakened. Far into the heart of Africa this devilish disintegration, coupled with Christian rum and Mohammedan raiding, penetrated. The face of Africa was turned south on these slave traders instead of northward toward the Mediterranean, where for two thousand years and more Europe and Africa had met in legitimate trade and mutual respect. The full significance of the battle of Tenkadibou, which overthrew the Askias, was now clear. Hereafter Africa for centuries was to appear before the world, not as the land of gold and ivory, of Mansa Musa and Meroe, but as a bound and captive slave, dumb and degraded.

The natural desire to avoid a painful subject

has led historians to gloss over the details of the slave trade and leave the impression that it was a local west-coast phenomenon and confined to a few years. It was, on the contrary, continent wide and centuries long and an economic, social, and political catastrophe probably unparalleled in human history.

The exact proportions of the slave trade can be estimated only approximately. From 1680 to 1688 we know that the English African Company alone sent 249 ships to Africa, shipped there 60,783 Negro slaves, and after losing 14,387 on the middle passage, delivered 46,396 in America.

It seems probable that 25,000 Negroes a year arrived in America between 1698 and 1707. After the Asiento of 1713 this number rose to 30,000 annually, and before the Revolutionary War it had reached at least 40,000 and perhaps 100,000 slaves a year.

The total number of slaves imported is not known. Dunbar estimates that nearly 900,000 came to America in the sixteenth century, 2,750,000 in the seventeenth, 7,000,000 in the eighteenth, and over 4,000,000 in the nineteenth, perhaps 15,000,000 in all. Certainly it seems that at least 10,000,000 Negroes were expatriated. Probably every slave imported represented on the average five corpses in Africa or on the high seas. The American slave trade, therefore, meant the elimination of at least 60,000,000 Negroes from their fatherland. The Mohammedan slave trade meant the expatriation or forcible migration in Africa of nearly as many more. It would be conservative, then, to say that the slave trade cost Negro Africa 100,000,000 souls. And yet people ask to-day the cause of the stagnation of culture in that land since 1600!

Such a large number of slaves could be supplied only by organized slave raiding in every corner of Africa. The African continent gradually became revolutionized. Whole regions were depopulated, whole tribes disappeared; villages were built in caves and on hills or in forest fastnesses; the character of peoples like those of Benin developed their worst excesses of cruelty instead of the already flourishing arts of peace. The dark, irresistible grasp of fetish took firmer hold on men's minds.

Further advances toward civilization became impossible. Not only was there the immense demand for slaves which had its outlet on the west coast, but the slave caravans were streaming up through the desert to the Mediterranean coast and down the valley of the Nile to the centers of Mohammedanism. It was a rape of a continent to an extent never paralleled in ancient or modern times.

In the American trade there was not only the horrors of the slave raid, which lined the winding paths of the African jungles with bleached bones, but there was also the horrors of what was called the "middle passage," that is, the voyage across the Atlantic. As Sir William Dolben said,

"The Negroes were chained to each other hand and foot, and stowed so close that they were not allowed above a foot and a half for each in breadth. Thus crammed together like herrings in a barrel, they contrácted putrid and fatal disorders; so that they who came to inspect them in a morning had occasionally to pick dead slaves out of their rows, and to unchain their carcases from the bodies of their wretched fellow-sufferers to whom they had been fastened." [1]

It was estimated that out of every one hundred lot shipped from Africa only about fifty lived to be effective laborers across the sea, and among the whites more seamen died in that trade in one year than in the whole remaining trade of England in two. The full realization of the horrors of the slave trade was slow in reaching the ears and conscience of the modern world, just as to-day the treatment of dark natives in European colonies is brought to publicity with the greatest difficulty. The first move against the slave trade in England came in Parliament in 1776, but it was not until thirty-one years later, in 1807, that the trade was banned through the arduous labors of Clarkson, Wilberforce, Sharpe, and others.

Denmark had already abolished the trade, and the United States attempted to do so the following year. Portugal and Spain were induced to abolish the trade between 1815 and 1830. Notwithstanding these laws, the contraband

[1] Ingram: *History of Slavery,* p. 152.

trade went on until the beginning of the Civil War in America. The reasons for this were the enormous profit of the trade and the continued demand of the American slave barons, who had no sympathy with the efforts to stop their source of cheap labor supply.

However, philanthropy was not working alone to overthrow Negro slavery and the slave trade. It was seen, first in England and later in other countries, that slavery as an industrial system could not be made to work satisfactorily in modern times. Its cost was too great, and one of the causes of this cost was the slave insurrections from the very beginning, when the slaves rose on the plantation of Diego Columbus down to the Civil War in America. Actual and potential slave insurrection in the West Indies, in North and South America, kept the slave owners in apprehension and turmoil, or called for a police system difficult to maintain. In North America revolt finally took the form of organized running away to the North, and this, with the growing scarcity of suitable land and the moral revolt, led to the Civil War and the disappearance of the American slave trade.

There was still, however, the Mohammedan slave trade to deal with, and this has been the work of the nineteenth and early twentieth centuries. In the last quarter of the nineteenth century ten thousand slaves annually were being distributed on the southern and eastern coast of the Mediterranean and at the great slave market in Bornu.

On the east coast of Africa in 1862 nineteen thousand slaves were passed into Zanzibar and thence into Arabia and Persia. As late as 1880, three thousand annually were being thus transplanted, but now the trade is about stopped. To-day the only centers of actual slave trading may be said to be the cocoa plantations of the Portuguese Islands on the west coast of Africa, and the Congo Free State.

Such is the story of the Rape of Ethiopia — a sordid, pitiful, cruel tale. Raphael painted, Luther preached, Corneille wrote, and Milton sung; and through it all, for four hundred years, the dark captives wound to the sea amid the bleaching bones of the dead; for four hundred years the sharks followed the scurrying ships; for four hundred years America was strewn with the living and dying millions of a transplanted race; for four hundred years Ethiopia stretched forth her hands unto God.

CHAPTER X

THAT was a wonderful century, the fifteenth, when men realized that beyond the scowling waste of western waters were dreams come true. Curious and yet crassly human it is that, with all this poetry and romance, arose at once the filthiest institution of the modern world and the costliest. For on Negro slavery in America was built, not simply the abortive cotton kingdom, but the foundations of that modern imperialism which is based on the despising of backward men.

According to some accounts Alonzo, "the Negro," piloted one of the ships of Columbus, and certainly there was Negro blood among his sailors. As early as 1528 there were nearly ten thousand Negroes in the new world. We hear of them in all parts. In Honduras, for instance, a Negro is sent to burn a native village; in 1555 the town council of Santiago de Chile voted to allow an enfranchised Negro possession of land in the town, and evidently treated him just as white applicants were treated. D'Allyon, who explored the coast of Virginia in the first quarter of the sixteenth century, used Negro slaves (who afterward revolted) to build his ships and help in exploration; Balboa had with him thirty Negroes, who, in 1513, helped to build the first ships on the Pacific coast; Cortez had three hundred Negro porters in 1522.

Before 1530 there were enough Negroes in Mexico to lead to an insurrection, where the Negroes fought desperately, but were overcome and their ringleaders executed.   Later the followers of another Negro insurgent, Bayano, were captured and sent back to Spain. Negroes founded the town of Santiago del Principe in 1570, and in 1540 a Negro slave of Hernandez de Alarcon was the only one of the party to carry a message across the country to the Zunis of New Mexico. A Negro, Stephen Dorantes, discovered New Mexico. This Stephen or "Estevanico" was sent ahead by certain Spanish friars to the "Seven Cities of Cibola." "As soon as Stephen had left said friars, he determined to earn all the reputation and honor for himself, and that the boldness and daring of having alone discovered those villages of high stories so much spoken of throughout that country should be attributed to him; and carrying along with him the people who followed him, he endeavored to cross the wilderness which is between Cibola and the country he had gone through, and he was so far ahead of the friars that when they arrived at Chichilticalli, which is on the edge of the wilderness, he was already at Cibola, which is eighty leagues of wilderness beyond." But the Indians of the new and strange country took alarm and concluded that Stephen "must be a spy or guide for some nations who intended to come and conquer them, because it seemed to them unreasonable for him to say that the people were white in the country from which he came, being black himself and being sent by them." [1]

Slaves imported under the Asiento treaties went to all parts of the Americas. Spanish America had by the close of the eighteenth century ten thousand in Santo Domingo, eighty-four thousand in Cuba, fifty thousand in Porto Rico, sixty thousand in Louisiana and Florida, and sixty thousand in Central and South America.

The history of the Negro in Spanish America centered in Cuba, Venezuela, and Central America. In the sixteenth century slaves began to arrive in Cuba and Negroes joined many of the exploring expeditions from there to various parts of America. The slave trade greatly increased in the latter part of the eighteenth century, and after the revolution in Hayti large numbers of French emigrants from that island settled in Cuba. This and Spanish greed increased the harshness of slavery and eventually led to revolt among the Negroes. In 1844 Governor O'Donnell began a cruel persecution of the blacks on account of a plot discovered among them. Finally in 1866 the Ten Years' War broke out in which Negro and white rebels joined. They demanded the abolition of slavery and equal political rights for natives

[1] H. O. Flipper's translation of Castaneda de Nafera's narrative.

and foreigners, whites and blacks. The war was cruel and bloody but ended in 1878 with the abolition of slavery, while a further uprising the following year secured civil rights for Negroes. Spanish economic oppression continued, however, and the leading chiefs of the Ten Years' War including such leaders as the mulatto, Antonio Maceo, with large numbers of Negro soldiers, took the field again in 1895. The result was the freeing of Cuba by the intervention of the United States. Negro regiments from the United States played here a leading role. A number of leaders in Cuba in political, industrial, and literary lines have been men of Negro descent.

Slavery was abolished by Guatemala in 1824 and by Mexico in 1829. Argentine, Peru, Bolivia, Chile, and Paraguay ceased to recognize it about 1825. Between 1840 and 1845 it came to an end in Colombia, Venezuela, and Ecquador. Bolivar, Paez, Sucre, and other South American leaders used Negro soldiers in fighting for freedom (1814–16), and Hayti twice at critical times rendered assistance and received Bolivar twice as a refugee.

Brazil was the center of Portuguese slavery, but slaves were not introduced in large numbers until about 1720, when diamonds were discovered in the territory above Rio Janeiro. Gradually the seaboard from Pernambuco to Rio Janeiro and beyond became filled with Negroes, and although the slave trade north of the equator was theoretically abolished by Portugal in 1815

and south of the equator in 1830, and by Brazil
in these regions in 1826 and 1830, nevertheless
between 1825 and 1850 over a million and a quarter of Negroes were introduced. Not until
Brazil abolished slavery in 1888 did the importation wholly cease. Brazilian slavery allowed
the slave to purchase his freedom, and the color
line was not strict. Even in the eighteenth century there were black clergy and bishops;
indeed the Negro clergy seem to have been on a
higher moral level than the whites.

Insurrection was often attempted, especially
among the Mohammedan Negroes around Bahia.
In 1695 a tribe of revolted slaves held out for a
long time. In 1719 a widespread conspiracy
failed, but many of the leaders fled to the forest.
In 1828 a thousand rose in revolt at Bahia, and
again in 1830. From 1831 to 1837 revolt was in
the air, and in 1835 came the great revolt of the
Mohammedans, who attempted to enthrone a
queen. The Negroes fought with furious bravery,
but were finally defeated.

By 1872 the number of free Negroes had very
greatly increased, so that emancipation did not
come as a shock. While Mohammedan Negroes
still gave trouble and were in some cases sent
back to Africa, yet on the whole emancipation
was peaceful, and whites, Negroes, and Indians
are to-day amalgamating into a new race. "At
the present moment there is scarcely a lowly or a
highly placed federal or provincial official at the
head of or within any of the great departments

of state that has not more or less Negro or Amer-Indian blood in his veins." [1]

Lord Bryce says, "It is hardly too much to say that along the coast from Rio to Bahia and Pernambuco, as well as in parts of the interior behind these two cities, the black population predominates. . . . The Brazilian lower class inter-marries freely with the black people; the Brazilian middle class intermarries with mulattoes and Quadroons. Brazil is the one country in the world, besides the Portuguese colonies on the east and west coasts of Africa, in which a fusion of the European and African races is proceeding unchecked by law or custom. The doctrines of human equality and human solidarity have here their perfect work. The result is so far satisfactory that there is little or no class friction. The white man does not lynch or maltreat the Negro; indeed I have never heard of a lynching anywhere in South America except occasionally as part of a political convulsion. The Negro is not accused of insolence and does not seem to develop any more criminality than naturally belongs to any ignorant population with loose notions of morality and property.

"What ultimate effect the intermixture of blood will have on the European element in Brazil I will not venture to predict. If one may judge from a few remarkable cases, it will not necessarily reduce the intellectual standard.

[1] Johnston: *Negro in the New World*, p. 109.

One of the ablest and most refined Brazilians I have known had some color; and other such cases have been mentioned to me. Assumptions and preconceptions must be eschewed, however plausible they may seem." [1]

A Brazilian writer said at the First Races Congress: "The coöperation of the *metis* [2] in the advance of Brazil is notorious and far from inconsiderable. They played the chief part during many years in Brazil in the campaign for the abolition of slavery. I could quote celebrated names of more than one of these *metis* who put themselves at the head of the literary movement. They fought with firmness and intrepidity in the press and on the platform. They faced with courage the gravest perils to which they were exposed in their struggle against the powerful slave owners, who had the protection of a conservative government. They gave evidence of sentiments of patriotism, self-denial, and appreciation during the long campaign in Paraguay, fighting heroically at the boarding of the ships in the naval battle of Riachuelo and in the attacks on the Brazilian army, on numerous occasions in the course of this long South American war. It was owing to their support that the republic was erected on the ruins of the empire." [3]

The Dutch brought the first slaves to the

[1] Bryce: *South America*, pp. 479–480.
[2] I.e., mulattoes.
[3] *Inter-Racial Problems*, p. 381.

North American continent. John Rolfe relates that the last of August, 1619, there came to Virginia "a Dutch man of warre that sold us twenty Negars." [1] This was probably one of the ships of the numerous private Dutch trading companies which early entered into the developed and the lucrative African slave trade. Although the Dutch thus commenced the continental slave trade they did not actually furnish a very large number of slaves to the English colonies outside the West Indies. A small trade had by 1698 brought a few thousand to New York and still fewer to New Jersey.

The Dutch found better scope for slaves in Guiana, which they settled in 1616. Sugar cane became the staple crop, but the Negroes early began to revolt and the Dutch brought in East Indian coolies. The slaves were badly treated and the runaways joined the revolted Bush Negroes in the interior. From 1715 to 1775 there was continuous fighting with the Bush Negroes or insurrections, until at last in 1749 a formal treaty between sixteen hundred Negroes and the Dutch was made. Immediately a new group revolted under a Mohammedan, Arabi, and they obtained land and liberty. In 1763 the coast Negroes revolted. They were checked, but made terms and settled in the interior. The Bush Negroes fought against both French and English to save Guiana to the Dutch, but Guiana was eventually divided between the three. The

[1] Smith: *General History of Virginia.*

Bush Negroes still maintain their independence and vigor.

The French encouraged settlements in the West Indies in the seventeenth century, but at last, finding that French immigrants would not come, they began about 1642 to import Negroes. Owing to wars with England, slaves were supplied by the Dutch and Portuguese, although the Royal Senegal Company held the coveted Asiento from 1701 to 1713.

It was in the island of Hayti, however, that French slavery centered. Pirates from many nations, but chiefly French, began to frequent the island, and in 1663 the French annexed the eastern part, thus dividing the island between France and Spain. By 1680 there were so many slaves and mulattoes that Louis XIV issued his celebrated Code Noir, which was notable in compelling bachelor masters, fathers of slave children, to marry their concubines. Children followed the condition of the mother as to slavery or freedom; they could have no property; harsh punishments were provided for, but families could not be separated by sale except in the case of grown children; emancipation with full civil rights was made possible for any slave twenty years of age or more. When Louisiana was settled and the Alabama coast, slaves were introduced there. Louisiana was transferred to Spain in 1762, against the resistance of both settlers and slaves, but Spain took possession in 1769 and introduced more Negroes.

Later, in Hayti, a more liberal policy encouraged trade; war was over and capital and slaves poured in. Sugar, coffee, chocolate, indigo, dyes, and spices were raised. There were large numbers of mulattoes, many of whom were educated in France, and many masters married Negro women who had inherited large properties, just as in the United States to-day white men are marrying eagerly the landed Indian women in the West. When white immigration increased in 1749, however, prejudice arose against these mulattoes and severe laws were passed depriving them of civil rights, entrance into the professions, and the right to hold office; severe edicts were enforced as to clothing, names, and social intercourse. Finally, after 1777, mulattoes were forbidden to come to France.

When the French Revolution broke out, the Haytians managed to send two delegates to Paris. Nevertheless the planters maintained the upper hand, and one of the colored delegates, Oge, on returning, started a small rebellion. He and his companions were killed with great brutality. This led the French government to grant full civil rights to free Negroes. Immediately planters and free Negroes flew to arms against each other and then, suddenly, August 22, 1791, the black slaves, of whom there were four hundred and fifty-two thousand, arose in revolt to help the free Negroes.

For many years runaway slaves had hidden in the mountains under their own chiefs. One of the earliest of these chiefs was Polydor, in 1724, who was succeeded by Macandal. The great chief of these runaways or "Maroons" at the time of the slave revolt was Jean François, who was soon succeeded by Biassou.

Pierre Dominic Toussaint, known as Toussaint L'Ouverture, joined these Maroon bands, where he was called "the doctor of the armies of the king," and soon became chief aid to Jean François and Biassou. Upon their deaths Toussaint rose to the chief command. He acquired complete control over the blacks, not only in military matters, but in politics and social organization; "the soldiers regarded him as a superior being, and the farmers prostrated themselves before him. All his generals trembled before him (Dessalines did not dare to look in his face), and all the world trembled before his generals." [1]

The revolt once started, blacks and mulattoes murdered whites without mercy and the whites retaliated. Commissioners were sent from France, who asked simply civil rights for freedmen, and not emancipation. Indeed that was all that Toussaint himself had as yet demanded. The planters intrigued with the British and this, together with the beheading of the king (an impious act in the eyes of Negroes), induced Toussaint to join the Spaniards. In 1793 British troops were landed and the French commissioners

---

[1] La Croix: *Mémoires sur la Révolution*, I, 253, 408.

in desperation declared the slaves emancipated. This at once won back Toussaint from the Spaniards. He became supreme in the north, while Rigaud, leader of the mulattoes, held the south and the west. By 1798 the British, having lost most of their forces by yellow fever, surrendered Mole St. Nicholas to Toussaint and departed. Rigaud finally left for France, and Toussaint in 1800 was master of Hayti. He promulgated a constitution under which Hayti was to be a self-governing colony; all men were equal before the law, and trade was practically free. Toussaint was to be president for life, with the power to name his successor.

Napoleon Bonaparte, master of France, had at this time dreams of a great American empire, and replied to Toussaint's new government by sending twenty-five thousand men under his brother-in-law to subdue the presumptuous Negroes, as a preliminary step to his occupation and development of the Mississippi valley. Fierce fighting and yellow fever decimated the French, but matters went hard with the Negroes too, and Toussaint finally offered to yield. He was courteously received with military honors and then, as soon as possible, treacherously seized, bound, and sent to France. He was imprisoned at Fort Joux and died, perhaps of poison, after studied humiliations, April 7, 1803.

Thus perished the greatest of American Negroes and one of the great men of all time, at the age of fifty-six. A French planter said, "God in his terrestrial globe did not commune with a purer spirit." [1]   Wendell Phillips said, "Some doubt the courage of the Negro. Go to Hayti and stand on those fifty thousand graves of the best soldiers France ever had and ask them what they think of the Negro's sword. I would call him Napoleon, but Napoleon made his way to empire over broken oaths and through a sea of blood. This man never broke his word. I would call him Cromwell, but Cromwell was only a soldier, and the state he founded went down with him into his grave. I would call him Washington, but the great Virginian held slaves. This man risked his empire rather than permit the slave trade in the humblest village of his dominions. You think me a fanatic, for you read history, not with your eyes, but with your prejudices. But fifty years hence, when Truth gets a hearing, the Muse of history will put Phocion for the Greek, Brutus for the Roman, Hampden for the English, La Fayette for France, choose Washington as the bright, consummate flower of our earlier civilization, then, dipping her pen in the sunlight, will write in the clear blue, above them all, the name of the soldier, the statesman, the martyr, Toussaint L'Ouverture."

The treacherous killing of Toussaint did not conquer Hayti. In 1802 and 1803 some forty thousand French soldiers died of war and fever. A new colored leader, Dessalines, arose and all

[1] Marquis d'Hermonas. Cf. Johnston: *Negro in the New World*, p. 158.

the eight thousand remaining French surrendered to the blockading British fleet.

The effect of all this was far-reaching. Napoleon gave up his dream of American empire and sold Louisiana for a song. "Thus, all of Indian Territory, all of Kansas and Nebraska and Iowa and Wyoming and Montana and the Dakotas, and most of Colorado and Minnesota, and all of Washington and Oregon states, came to us as the indirect work of a despised Negro. Praise, if you will, the work of a Robert Livingstone or a Jefferson, but to-day let us not forget our debt to Toussaint L'Ouverture, who was indirectly the means of America's expansion by the Louisiana Purchase of 1803." [1]

With the freedom of Hayti in 1801 came a century of struggle to fit the people for the freedom they had won. They were yet slaves, crushed by a cruel servitude, without education or religious instruction. The Haytian leaders united upon Dessalines to maintain the independence of the republic. Dessalines, like Toussaint and his lieutenant Christophe, was noted in slavery days for his severity toward his fellows and the discipline which he insisted on. He had other characteristics of African chieftains. "There were seasons when he broke through his natural sullenness and showed himself open, affable, and even generous. His vanity was excessive and manifested itself in singular per-

[1] DeWitt Talmage, in *Christian Herald*, November 28, 1906.

versities." [1] He was a man of great personal
bravery and succeeded in maintaining the independence of Hayti, which had already cost
the Frenchmen fifty thousand lives.

On January 1, 1804, at the place whence
Toussaint had been treacherously seized and
sent to France, the independence of Hayti was
declared by the military leaders. Dessalines was
made governor-general for life and afterward
proclaimed himself emperor. This was not an
act of grandiloquence and mimicry. "It is truer
to say that in it both Dessalines and later Christophe were actuated by a clear insight into the
social history and peculiarities of their people.
There was nothing in the constitution which did
not have its companion in Africa, where the organization of society was despotic, with elective-
hereditary chiefs, royal families, polygamic mar-
riages, councils, and regencies." [2]

The population was divided into soldiers and
laborers. The territory was parceled out to
chiefs, and the laborers were bound to the soil
and worked under rigorous inspection; part of
the products were reserved for their support,
and the rest went to the chiefs, the king, the
general government, and the army. The army
was under stern discipline and military service
was compulsory. Women did much of the agricultural labor. Under Toussaint the adminis-

[1] Aimes: *African Institutions in America* (reprinted from
Journal of American Folk Lore), p. 25.
[2] Brown: *History of San Domingo*, II, 158-159.

tration of this system was committed to Dessalines, who carried it out with rigor; it was afterward followed by Christophe. The latter even
imported four thousand Negroes from Africa,
from whom he formed a national guard for pa-
trolling the land. These regulations brought back
for a time a large part of the former prosperity
of the island.

The severity with which Dessalines enforced
the laws soon began to turn many against him.
The educated mulattoes especially objected to
submission to the savage African *mores*. Dessalines started to suppress their revolt, but was
killed in ambush in October, 1806.

Great Britain now began to intrigue for a protectorate over the island and the Spanish end of
the island threatened attack. These difficulties
were overcome, but at a cost of great internal
strain. After the death of Dessalines it seemed
that Hayti was about to dissolve into a number of
petty subdivisions. At one time Christophe was
ruling as king in the north, Petion as president
at Port au Prince, Rigaud in the south, and a
semi-brigand, Goman, in the extreme southwest.
Very soon, however, the rivalry narrowed down
to Petion and Christophe. Petion was a man of
considerable ability and did much, not simply for
Hayti, but for South America. Already as early
as 1779, before the revolution in Hayti, the
Haytian Negroes had helped the United States.
The British had captured Savannah in 1778.
The French fleet appeared on the coast of Georgia

late that year and was ordered to recruit men in Hayti. Eight hundred young freedmen, blacks and mulattoes, offered to take part in the expedition, and they fought valiantly in the siege and covered themselves with glory. It was this legion that made the charge on the British and saved the retreating American army. Among the men who fought there was Christophe.

When Simon Bolivar, Commodore Aury, and many Venezuelan families were driven from their country in 1815, they and their ships took temporary refuge in Hayti. Notwithstanding the embarrassed condition of the republic, Petion received them and gave them four thousand rifles with ammunition, provisions, and last and best a printing press. He also settled some international quarrels among members of the groups, and Bolivar expressed himself afterward as being "overwhelmed with magnanimous favors." [1]

Petion died in 1818 and was succeeded by his friend Boyer. Christophe committed suicide the following year and Boyer became not simply ruler of western Hayti, but also, by arrangement with the eastern end of the island, gained the mastery there, where they were afraid of Spanish aggression. Thus from 1822 to 1843 Boyer, a man of much ability, ruled the whole of the island and gained the recognition of Haytian independence from France and other nations.

France, under Charles X, demanded an indemnity of thirty million dollars to reimburse the

[1] See Leger: *Hayti*, Chap. XI.

planters for confiscated lands and property. This Hayti tried to pay, but the annual installment was a tremendous burden to the impoverished country. Further negotiations were entered into. Finally in 1838 France recognized the independence of the republic and the indemnity was reduced to twelve million dollars. Even this was a large burden for Hayti, and the payment of it for years crippled the island.

The United States and Great Britain in 1825–26 recognized the independence of Hayti. A concordat was arranged with the Pope for governing the church in Hayti, and finally in 1860 the church placed under the French hierarchy. Thus Boyer did unusually well; but his necessary concessions to France weakened his influence at home, and finally an earthquake, which destroyed several towns in 1842, raised the superstititious of the populace against him. He resigned in 1843, leaving the treasury well filled; but with his withdrawal the Spanish portion of the island was lost to Hayti.

The subsequent history of Hayti since 1843 has been the struggle of a small divided country to maintain political independence. The rich resources of the country called for foreign capital, but outside capital meant political influence from abroad, which the little nation rightly feared. Within, the old antagonism between the freedman and the slave settled into a color line between the mulatto and the black, which for a time meant the difference between educated liberalism and reactionary ignorance. This difference has largely disappeared, but some vestiges of the color line remain. The result has been reaction and savagery under Soulouque, Dominique, and Nord Alexis, and decided advance under presidents like Nissage-Saget, Solomon, Legitime, and Hyppolite.

In political life Hayti is still in the sixteenth century; but in economic life she has succeeded in placing on their own little farms the happiest and most contented peasantry in the world, after raising them from a veritable hell of slavery. If modern capitalistic greed can be restrained from interference until the best elements of Hayti secure permanent political leadership the triumph of the revolution will be complete.

In other parts of the French-American dominion the slaves achieved freedom also by insurrection. In Guadeloupe they helped the French drive out the British, and thus gained emancipation. In Martinique it took three revolts and a civil war to bring freedom.

The English slave empire in America centered in the Bermudas, Barbadoes, Jamaica and the lesser islands, and in the United States. Barbadoes developed a savage slave code, and the result was attempted slave insurrections in 1674, 1692, and 1702. These were not successful, but a rising in 1816 destroyed much property under the leadership of a mulatto, Washington Franklin, and the repeal of bad laws and eventual enfranchisement of the colored people followed. One

Barbadian mulatto, Sir Conrad Reeves, has held the position of chief justice in the island and was knighted. A Negro insurrection in Dominica under Farcel greatly exercised England in 1791 and 1794 and delayed slave trade abolition; in 1844 and 1847 further uprisings took place, and these continued from 1853 to 1893.

The chief island domain of English slavery was Jamaica. It was Oliver Cromwell who, in his zeal for God and the slave trade, sent an expedition to seize Hayti. His fleet, driven off there, took Jamaica in 1655. The English found the mountains already infested with runaway slaves known as "Maroons," and more Negroes joined them when the English arrived. In 1663 the freedom of the Maroons was acknowledged, land was given them, and their leader, Juan de Bolas, was made a colonel in the militia. He was killed, however, in the following year, and from 1664 to 1738 the three thousand or more black Maroons fought the British Empire in guerrilla warfare. Soldiers, Indians, and dogs were sent against them, and finally in 1738 Captain Cudjo and other chiefs made a formal treaty of peace with Governor   Trelawney.   They   were   granted twenty-five hundred acres and their freedom was recognized.

The peace lasted until 1795, when they rebelled again and gave the British a severe drubbing, besides murdering planters. Bloodhounds again were imported. The Maroons offered to surrender on the express condition that none of their number should be deported from the island, as the legislature wished. General Walpole hesitated, but could get peace on no other terms and gave his word. The Maroons surrendered their arms, and immediately the whites seized six hundred of the ringleaders and transported them to the snows of Nova Scotia! The legislature then voted a sword worth twenty-five hundred dollars to General Walpole, which he indignantly refused to accept. Eventually these exiled Maroons found their way to Sierra Leone, West Africa, in time to save that colony to the British crown.[1]

The pressing desire for peace with the Maroons on the part of the white planters arose from the new sugar culture introduced in 1673. A greatly increased demand for slaves followed, and between 1700 and 1786 six hundred and ten thousand slaves were imported; nevertheless, so severely were they driven, that there were only three hundred thousand Negroes in Jamaica in the latter year.

Despite the Moravian missions and other efforts late in the eighteenth century, unrest among the Jamaica slaves and freedmen grew and was increased by the anti-slavery agitation in England and the revolt in Hayti. There was an insurrection in 1796; and in 1831 again the Negroes of northwest Jamaica, impatient because of the slow progress of the emancipation, arose in revolt and destroyed nearly three and a half million dollars' worth of property, well-nigh ruin-

---

[1] Cf. Chapter V, p. 69.

ing the planters there. The next year two hundred and fifty-five thousand slaves were set free, for which the planters were paid nearly thirty million dollars. There ensued a discouraging condition of industry. The white officials sent out in these days were arbitrary and corrupt. Little was done for the mass of the people and there was outrageous over-taxation. Nevertheless the backwardness of the colony was attributed to the Negro. Governor Eyre complained in 1865 that the young and strong were good for nothing and were filling the jails; but a simultaneous report by a missionary told the truth concerning the officials. This aroused the colored people, and a mulatto, George William Gordon, called a meeting. Other meetings were afterward held, and finally the Negro peasantry began a riot in 1861, in which eighteen people were killed, only a few of whom were white.

The result was that Governor Eyre tried and executed by court-martial 354 persons, and in addition to this killed without trial 85, a total of 439. One thousand Negro homes were burned to the ground and thousands of Negroes flogged or mutilated. Children had their brains dashed out, pregnant women were murdered, and Gordon was tried by court-martial and hanged. In fact the punishment was, as the royal commissioners said, "reckless and positively barbarous." [1]

This high-handed act aroused England. Eyre was not punished, but the island was made a

[1] Johnston: *Negro in the New World.*

crown colony in 1866, and given representation in the legislature in 1886.

In the island of St. Vincent, Indians first sought to enslave the fugitive Negroes wrecked there, but the Negroes took the Carib women and then drove the Indian men away. These "black Caribs" fought with Indians, English, and others for three quarters of a century, until the Indians were exterminated. The British took possession in 1763. The black Caribs resisted, and after hard fighting signed a treaty in 1773, receiving one-third of the island as their property. They afterward helped the French against the British, and were finally deported to the island of Ruatan, off Honduras. In Trinidad and British Guiana there have been mutinies and rioting of slaves and a curious mingling of races.

Other parts of South America must be dismissed briefly, because of insufficient data. Colombia and Venezuela, with perhaps eight million people, have at least one-third of their population of Negro and Indian descent. Here Simon Bolivar with his Negro, mulatto, and Indian forces began the war that liberated South America. Central America has a smaller proportion of Negroids, perhaps one hundred thousand in all. Bolivia and Peru have small amounts of Negro blood, while Argentine and Uruguay have very little. The Negro population in these lands is everywhere in process of rapid amalgamation with whites and Indians.

CHAPTER XI

THERE were half a million slaves in the confines of the United States when the Declaration of Independence declared "that all men are created equal; that they are endowed by their Creator with certain unalienable rights; that among these are life, liberty, and the pursuit of happiness." The land that thus magniloquently heralded its advent into the family of nations had supported the institution of human slavery for one hundred and fifty-seven years and was destined to cling to it eighty-seven years longer.

The greatest experiment in Negro slavery as a modern industrial system was made on the mainland of North America and in the confines of the present United States. And this experiment was on such a scale and so long-continued that it is profitable for study and reflection. There were in the United States in its dependencies, in 1910, 9,828,294 persons of acknowledged Negro descent, not including the considerable infiltration of Negro blood which is not acknowledged and often not known. To-day the number of persons called Negroes is probably about ten and a quarter millions. These persons are almost entirely descendants of African slaves, brought to America in the sixteenth, seventeenth, eighteenth, and nineteenth centuries.

The importation of Negroes to the mainland of North America was small until the British got the coveted privilege of the Asiento in 1713. Before that Northern States like New York had received some slaves from the Dutch, and New England had early developed a trade by which she imported a number of house servants. Ships went out to the African coast with rum, sold the rum, and brought the slaves to the West Indies; there they exchanged the slaves for sugar and molasses and brought the molasses back to New England, to be made into rum for further exploits. After the Asiento treaty the Negro population increased in the eighteenth century from about 50,000 in 1710 to 220,000 in 1750 and to 462,000 in 1770. When the colonies became independent, the foreign slave trade was soon made illegal; but illicit trade, annexation of territory and natural increase enlarged the Negro population from a little over a million at the beginning of the nineteenth century to four and a half millions at the outbreak of the Civil War and to about ten and a quarter millions in 1914.

The present so-called Negro population of the United States is:

1. A mixture of the various African populations, Bantu, Sudanese, west-coast Negroes, some dwarfs, and some traces of Arab, Berber, and Semitic blood.

2. A mixture of these strains with the blood of white Americans through a system of concubinage of colored women in slavery days, together with some legal intermarriage.

The figures as to mulattoes [1] have been from time to time officially acknowledged to be understatements. Probably one-third of the Negroes of the United States have distinct traces of white blood. This blending of the races has led to interesting human types, but racial prejudice has hitherto prevented any scientific study of the matter. In general the Negro population in the United States is brown in color, darkening to almost black and shading off in the other direction to yellow and white, and is indistinguishable in some cases from the white population.

Much has been written of the black man in America, but most of this has been from the point of view of the whites, so that we know of the

[1] The figures given by the census are as follows:

1850, mulattoes formed 11.2 per cent of the total Negro population.

1860, mulattoes formed 13.2 per cent of the total Negro population.

1870, mulattoes formed 12 per cent of the total Negro population.

1890, mulattoes formed 15.2 per cent of the total Negro population.

1910, mulattoes formed 20.9 per cent of the total Negro population.

Or in actual numbers:

1850, 405,751 mulattoes.
1860, 588,352 mulattoes.
1870, 585,601 mulattoes.
1890, 1,132,060 mulattoes.
1910, 2,050,686 mulattoes.

effect of Negro slavery on the whites, the strife among the whites for and against abolition, and the consequent problem of the Negro so far as the white population is concerned.

This chapter, however, is dealing with the matter more from the point of view of the Negro group itself, and seeking to show what slavery meant to them, how they reacted against it, what they did to secure their freedom, and what they are doing with their partial freedom to-day.

The slaves landing from 1619 onward were received by the colonies at first as laborers, on the same plane as other laborers. For a long time there was in law no distinction between the indented white servant from England and the black servant from Africa, except in the term of their service. Even here the distinction was not always observed, some of the whites being kept beyond term of their service and Negroes now and then securing their freedom. Gradually the planters realized the advantage of laborers held for life, but they were met by certain moral difficulties. The opposition to slavery had from the first been largely stilled when it was stated that this was a method of converting the heathen to Christianity. The corollary was that when a slave was converted he became free. Up to 1660 or thereabouts it seemed accepted in most colonies and in the English West Indies that baptism into a Christian church would free a Negro slave. Masters, therefore, were reluctant in the seventeenth century to have their slaves receive Christian instruction. Massachusetts first apparently legislated on this matter by enacting in 1641 that slavery should be confined to captives in just wars "and such strangers as willingly sell themselves or are sold to us,"[1] meaning by "strangers" apparently heathen, but saying nothing as to the effect of conversion. Connecticut adopted similar legislation in 1650, and Virginia declared in 1661 that Negroes "are incapable of making satisfaction" for time lost in running away by lengthening their time of services, thus implying that they were slaves for life. Maryland declared in 1663 that Negro slaves should serve *durante vita*, but it was not until 1667 that Virginia finally plucked up courage to attack the issue squarely and declared by law: "Baptism doth not alter the condition of the person as to his bondage or freedom, in order that diverse masters freed from this doubt may more carefully endeavor the propagation of Christianity."[2]

The transplanting of the Negro from his African clan life to the West Indian plantation was a social revolution. Marriage became geographical and transient, while women and girls were without protection.

The private home as a self-protective, independent unit did not exist. That powerful institution, the polygamous African home, was al-

[1] Cf. "The Spanish Jurist Solorzaris," quoted in Helps: *Spanish Conquest,* IV, 381.
[2] Hurd: *Law of Freedom and Bondage.*

most completely destroyed, and in its place in America arose sexual promiscuity, a weak community life, with common dwelling, meals, and child nurseries. The internal slave trade tended further to weaken natural ties. A small number of favored house servants and artisans were raised above this — had their private homes, came in contact with the culture of the master class, and assimilated much of American civilization. This was, however, exceptional; broadly speaking, the greatest social effect of American slavery was to substitute for the polygamous Negro home a new polygamy less guarded, less effective, and less civilized.

At first sight it would seem that slavery completely destroyed every vestige of spontaneous movement among the Negroes. This is not strictly true. The vast power of the priest in the African state is well known; his realm alone — the province of religion and medicine — remained largely unaffected by the plantation system. The Negro priest, therefore, early became an important figure on the plantation and found his function as the interpreter of the supernatural, the comforter of the sorrowing, and as the one who expressed, rudely but picturesquely, the longing and disappointment and resentment of a stolen people. From such beginnings arose and spread with marvelous rapidity the Negro church, the first distinctively Negro American social institution. It was not at first by any means a Christian church, but a mere adaptation of those rites of fetish which in America is termed obe worship, or "voodooism."[1]   Association and missionary effort soon gave these rites a veneer of Christianity and gradually, after two centuries, the church became Christian, with a simple Calvinistic creed, but with many of the old customs still clinging to the services.   It is this historic fact, that the Negro church of to-day bases itself upon the sole surviving social institution of the African fatherland, that accounts for its extraordinary growth and vitality.

The slave codes at first were really labor codes based on an attempt to reëstablish in America the waning feudalism of Europe.   The laborers were mainly black and were held for life.   Above them came the artisans, free whites with a few blacks, and above them the master class.   The feudalism called for the plantation system, and the plantation system as developed in America, and particularly in Virginia, was at first a feudal domain.   On these plantations the master was practically supreme.   The slave codes in early days were but moderately harsh, allowing punishment by the master, but restraining him in ex-

---

[1] "Obi (Obeah, Obiah, or Obia) is the adjective; Obe or Obi, the noun. It is of African origin, probably connected with Egyptian Ob, Aub, or Obron, meaning 'serpent.' Moses forbids Israelites ever to consult the demon Ob, i.e., 'Charmer, Wizard.' The Witch of Endor is called Oub or Ob. Oubaois is the name of the Baselisk or Royal Serpent, emblem of the Sun, and, according to Horus Appollo, 'the Ancient Deity of Africa.'" — Edwards: *West Indies*, ed. 1819, II, 106–119. Cf. Johnston: *Negro in the New World*, pp. 65–66; *also Atlanta University Publications*, No. 8, pp. 5–6.

treme cases and providing for care of the slaves and of the aged. With the power, however, solely in the hands of the master class, and with the master supreme on his own plantation, his power over the slave was practically what he wished it to be. In some cases the cruelty was as great as on the worst West Indian plantations. In other cases the rule was mild and paternal.

Up through this American feudalism the Negro began to rise. He learned in the eighteenth century the English language, he began to be identified with the Christian church, he mingled his blood to a considerable extent with the master class. The house servants particularly were favored, in some cases receiving education, and the number of free Negroes gradually increased.

Present-day students are often puzzled at the apparent contradictions of Southern slavery. One hears, on the one hand, of the staid and gentle patriarchy, the wide and sleepy plantations with lord and retainers, ease and happiness; on the other hand one hears of barbarous cruelty and unbridled power and wide oppression of men. Which is the true picture? The answer is simple: both are true. They are not opposite sides of the same shield; they are different shields. They are pictures, on the one hand, of house service in the great country seats and in the towns, and on the other hand of the field laborers who raised the great tobacco, rice, and cotton crops. We have thus not only carelessly mixed pictures of what were really different kinds of slavery, but of that which represented different degrees in the development of the economic system. House service was the older feudal idea of personal retainership, developed in Virginia and Carolina in the seventeenth and eighteenth centuries. It had all the advantages and disadvantages of such a system; the advantage of the strong personal tie and the disadvantage of unyielding caste distinctions, with the resultant immoralities. At its worst, however, it was a matter primarily of human relationships.

Out of this older type of slavery in the northern South there developed, during the eighteenth and nineteenth centuries, in the southern South the type of slavery which corresponds to the modern factory system in its worst conceivable form. It represented production of a staple product on a large scale; between the owner and laborer were interposed the overseer and the drivers. The slaves were whipped and driven to a mechanical task system. Wide territory was needed, so that at last absentee landlordship was common. It was this latter type of slavery that marked the cotton kingdom, and the extension of the area of this system southward and westward marked the aggressive world-conquering visions of the slave barons. On the other hand it was the milder and far different Virginia house service and the personal retainership of town life in which most white children grew up; it was this that impressed their imaginations and which they have so vividly portrayed. The Negroes, however, knew the other side, for it was under the harsher, heartless driving of the fields that fully nine-tenths of them lived.

There early began to be some internal development and growth of self-consciousness among the Negroes: for instance, in New England towns Negro "governors" were elected. This was partly an African custom transplanted and partly an endeavor to put the regulation of the slaves into their own hands. Negroes voted in those days: for instance, in North Carolina until 1835 the Constitution extended the franchise to every freeman, and when Negroes were disfranchised in 1835, several hundred colored men were deprived of the vote. In fact, as Albert Bushnell Hart says, "In the colonies freed Negroes, like freed indentured white servants, acquired property, founded families, and came into the political community if they had the energy, thrift, and fortune to get the necessary property." [1]

The humanitarian movement of the eighteenth century was active toward Negroes, because of the part which they played in the Revolutionary War. Negro regiments and companies were raised in Connecticut and Rhode Island, and a large number of Negroes were members of the continental armies elsewhere. Individual Negroes distinguished themselves. It is estimated that five thousand Negroes fought in the American armies.

The mass of the Americans considered at the

[1] *Boston Transcript*, March 24, 1906.

time of the adoption of the Constitution that Negro slavery was doomed. There soon came a series of laws emancipating slaves in the North: Vermont began in 1779, followed by judicial decision in Massachusetts in 1780 and gradual emancipation in Pennsylvania beginning the same year; emancipation was accomplished in New Hampshire in 1783, and in Connecticut and Rhode Island in 1784. The momentous exclusion of slavery in the Northwest Territory took place in 1787, and gradual emancipation began in New York and New Jersey in 1799 and 1804.

Beneficial and insurance societies began to appear among colored people. Nearly every town of any size in Virginia in the early eighteenth century had Negro organizations for caring for the sick and burying the dead. As the number of free Negroes increased, particularly in the North, these financial societies began to be openly formed. One of the earliest was the Free African Society of Philadelphia. This eventually became the present African Methodist Church, which has to-day half a million members and over eleven million dollars' worth of property.

Negroes began to be received into the white church bodies in separate congregations, and before 1807 there is the record of the formation of eight such Negro churches. This brought forth leaders who were usually preachers in these churches. Richard Allen, the founder of the African Methodist Church, was one; Lot Carey, one of the founders of Liberia, was another. In the South there was John Chavis, who passed through a regular course of studies at what is now Washington and Lee University. He started a school for young white men in North Carolina and had among his pupils a United States senator, sons of a chief justice of North Carolina, a governor of the state, and many others. He was a full-blooded Negro, but a Southern writer says that "all accounts agree that John Chavis was a gentleman. He was received socially among the best whites and asked to table." [1]

In the war of 1812 thirty-three hundred Negroes helped Jackson win the battle of New Orleans, and numbers fought in New York State and in the navy under Perry, Channing, and others. Phyllis Wheatley, a Negro girl, wrote poetry, and the mulatto, Benjamin Banneker, published one of the first American series of almanacs.

In fine, it seemed in the early years of the nineteenth century that slavery in the United States would gradually disappear and that the Negro would have, in time, a man's chance. A change came, however, between 1820 and 1830, and it is directly traceable to the industrial revolution of the nineteenth century.

Between 1738 and 1830 there had come a remarkable series of inventions which revolutionized the methods of making cloth. This series included the invention of the fly shuttle, the carding machine, the steam engine, and the power

[1] Bassett: *North Carolina*, pp. 73–76.

loom. The world began to look about for a cheaper and larger supply of fiber for weaving. It was found in the cotton plant, and the southern United States was especially adapted to its culture. The invention of the cotton gin removed the last difficulties. The South now had a crop which could be attended to by unskilled labor and for which there was practically unlimited demand. There was land, and rich land, in plenty. The result was that the cotton crop in the United States increased from 8,000 bales in 1790 to 650,000 bales in 1820, to 2,500,000 bales in 1850, and to 4,000,000 bales in 1860.

In this growth one sees the economic foundation of the new slavery in the United States, which rose in the second decade of the nineteenth century. Manifestly the fatal procrastination in dealing with slavery in the eighteenth century received in the nineteenth century its terrible reward. The change in the attitude toward slavery was manifest in various ways. The South no longer excused slavery, but began to defend it as an economic system. The enforcement of the slave trade laws became notoriously lax and there was a tendency to make slave codes harsher.

This led to retaliation on the part of the Negroes. There had not been in the United States before this many attempts at insurrection. The slaves were distributed over a wide territory, and before they became intelligent enough to coöperate the chance of emancipation was held before them. Several small insurrections are alluded to in South Carolina early in the eighteenth century, and one by Cato at Stono in 1740 caused widespread alarm. The Negro plot in New York in 1712 put the city into hysterics. There was no further plotting on any scale until the Haytian revolt, when Gabriel in Virginia made an abortive attempt. In 1822 a free Negro, Denmark Vesey, in South Carolina, failed in a well-laid plot, and ten years after that, in 1831, Nat Turner led his insurrection in Virginia and killed fifty-one persons. The result of this insurrection was to crystallize tendencies toward harshness which the economic revolution was making advisable.

A wave of legislation passed over the South, prohibiting the slaves from learning to read and write, forbidding Negroes to preach, and interfering with Negro religious meetings. Virginia declared in 1831 that neither slaves nor free Negroes might preach, nor could they attend religious service at night without permission. In North Carolina slaves and free Negroes were forbidden to preach, exhort, or teach "in any prayer meeting or other association for worship where slaves of different families are collected together" on penalty of not more than thirty-nine lashes. Maryland and Georgia and other states had similar laws.

The real effective revolt of the Negro against slavery was not, however, by fighting, but by running away, usually to the North, which had been recently freed from slavery. From the beginning of the nineteenth century slaves began to escape in considerable numbers. Four geographical paths were chiefly followed: one, leading southward, was the line of swamps along the coast from Norfolk, Virginia, to the northern border of Florida. This gave rise to the Negro element among the Indians in Florida and led to the two Seminole wars of 1817 and 1835. These wars were really slave raids to make the Indians give up the Negro and half-breed slaves domiciled among them. The wars cost the United States ten million dollars and two thousand lives.

The great Appalachian range, with its abutting mountains, was the safest path northward. Through Tennessee and Kentucky and the heart of the Cumberland Mountains, using the limestone caverns, was the third route, and the valley of the Mississippi was the western tunnel.

These runaways and the freedmen of the North soon began to form a group of people who sought to consider the problem of slavery and the destiny of the Negro in America. They passed through many psychological changes of attitude in the years from 1700 to 1850. At first, in the early part of the eighteenth century, there was but one thought: revolt and revenge. The development of the latter half of the century brought an attitude of hope and adjustment and emphasized the differences between the slave and the free Negro. The first part of the nineteenth century brought two movements: among the free Negroes an effort at self-development and protection through organization; among slaves and recent fugitives a distinct reversion to the older idea of revolt.

As the new industrial slavery, following the rise of the cotton kingdom, began to press harder, a period of storm and stress ensued in the black world, and in 1829 came the first full-voiced, almost hysterical protest of a Negro against slavery and the color line in David Walker's Appeal, which aroused Southern legislatures to action.

The decade 1830–40 was a severe period of trial. Not only were the chains of slavery tighter in the South, but in the North the free Negro was beginning to feel the ostracism and competition of white workingmen, native and foreign. In Philadelphia, between 1829 and 1849, six mobs of hoodlums and foreigners murdered and maltreated Negroes. In the Middle West harsh black laws which had been enacted in earlier days were hauled from their hiding places and put into effect. No Negro was allowed to settle in Ohio unless he gave bond within twenty days to the amount of five thousand dollars to guarantee his good behavior and support. Harboring or concealing fugitives was heavily fined, and no Negro could give evidence in any case where a white man was party. These laws began to be enforced in 1829 and for three days riots went on in Cincinnati and Negroes were shot and killed. Aroused, the Negroes sent a deputation to Canada where they were offered asylum. Fully two thousand migrated from Ohio. Later large numbers from other parts of the United States joined them.

In 1830–31 the first Negro conventions were called in Philadelphia to consider the desperate condition of the Negro population, and in 1833 the convention met again and local societies were formed. The first Negro paper was issued in New York in 1827, while later emancipation in the British West Indies brought some cheer in the darkness.

A system of separate Negro schools was established and the little band of abolitionists led by Garrison and others appeared. In spite of all the untoward circumstances, therefore, the internal development of the free Negro in the North went on. The Negro population increased twenty-three per cent between 1830 and 1840; Philadelphia had, in 1838, one hundred small beneficial societies, while Ohio Negroes had ten thousand acres of land. The slave mutiny on the *Creole*, the establishment of the Negro Odd Fellows, and the growth of the Negro churches all indicated advancement.

Between 1830 and 1850 the concerted coöperation to assist fugitives came to be known as the Underground Railroad. It was an organization not simply of white philanthropists, but the coöperation of Negroes in the most difficult part of the work made it possible. Hundreds of Negroes visited the slave states to entice the slaves away, and the list of Underground Railroad operators given by Siebert contains one hundred and twenty-eight names of Negroes. In Canada and in the northern United States there was a secret society, known as the League of Freedom, which especially worked to help slaves run away. Harriet Tubman was one of the most energetic of these slave conductors and brought away several thousand slaves. William Lambert, a colored man, was reputed between 1829 and 1862 to have aided in the escape of thirty thousand.

The decade 1840–50 was a period of hope and uplift for the Negro group, with clear evidences of distinct self-assertion and advance. A few well-trained lawyers and physicians appeared, and colored men took their place among the abolition orators. The catering business in Philadelphia and other cities fell largely into their hands, and some small merchants arose here and there. Above all, Frederick Douglass made his first speech in 1841 and thereafter became one of the most prominent figures in the abolition crusade. A new series of national conventions began to assemble late in the forties, and the delegates were drawn from the artisans and higher servants, showing a great increase of efficiency in the rank and file of the free Negroes.

By 1850 the Negroes had increased to three and a half million. Those in Canada were being organized in settlements and were accumulating

property. The escape of fugitive slaves was
systematized and some of the most representative conventions met. One particularly, in 1854,
grappled frankly with the problem of emigration.
It looked as though it was going to be impossible
for Negroes to remain in the United States and
be free. As early as 1788 a Negro union of New-
port, Rhode Island, had proposed a general
exodus to Africa. John and Paul Cuffe, after
petitioning for the right to vote in 1780, started
in 1815 for Africa, organizing an expedition at
their own expense which cost four thousand
dollars. Lot Carey organized the African Mission Society in 1813, and the first Negro college
graduate went to Liberia in 1829 and became
superintendent of public schools. The Colonization Society encouraged this migration, and the
Negroes themselves had organized the Canadian
exodus.

The Rochester Negro convention in 1853 pro-
nounced against migration, but nevertheless
emissaries were sent in various directions to
see what inducements could be offered. One
went to the Niger valley, one to Central America,
and one to Hayti. The Haytian trip was successful and about two thousand black emigrants
eventually settled in Hayti.

Delaney, who went to Africa, concluded a
treaty with eight kings offering inducements to
Negroes, but nothing came of it. In 1853 Negroes
like Purvis and Barbadoes helped in the formation of the American Anti-slavery society, and

for a while colored men coöperated with John Brown and probably would have given him considerable help if they had thoroughly known his plans. As it was, six or seven of his twenty-two followers were Negroes.

Meantime the slave power was impelled by the high price of slaves and the exhaustion of cotton land to make increased demands. Slavery was forced north of Mason and Dixon's line in 1820; a new slave empire with thousands of slaves was annexed in 1850, and a fugitive slave law was passed which endangered the liberty of every free Negro; finally a determined attempt was made to force slavery into the Northwest in competition with free white labor, and less effective but powerful movements arose to annex more slave territory to the south and to reopen the African slave trade.

It looked like a triumphal march for the slave barons, but each step cost more than the last. Missouri gave rise to the early abolitionist movement. Mexico and the fugitive slave law aroused deep opposition in the North, and Kansas developed an attack upon the free labor system, not simply of the North, but of the civilized world. The result was war; but the war was not against slavery. It was fought to protect free white laborers against the competition of slaves, and it was thought possible to do this by segregating slavery.

The first thing that vexed the Northern armies on Southern soil during the war was the question of the disposition of the fugitive slaves, who immediately began to arrive in increasing numbers. Butler confiscated them, Fremont freed them, and Halleck caught and returned them; but their numbers swelled to such large proportions that the mere economic problem of their presence overshadowed everything else, especially after the Emancipation Proclamation. Lincoln was glad to have them come after once he realized their strength to the Confederacy.

The Emancipation Proclamation was forced, not simply by the necessity of paralyzing industry in the South, but also by the necessity of employing Negro soldiers. During the first two years of the war no one wanted Negro soldiers. It was declared to be a "white man's war." General Hunter tried to raise a regiment in South Carolina, but the War Department disavowed the act. In Louisiana the Negroes were anxious to enlist, but were held off. In the meantime the war did not go as well as the North had hoped, and on the twenty-sixth of January, 1863, the Secretary of War authorized the Governor of Massachusetts to raise two regiments of Negro troops. Frederick Douglass and others began the work with enthusiasm, and in the end one hundred and eighty-seven thousand Negroes enlisted in the Northern armies, of whom seventy thousand were killed and wounded. The conduct of these troops was exemplary. They were indispensable in camp duties and brave on the field, where they fought in two hundred and thirteen battles. General Banks wrote, "Their conduct was heroic. No troops could be more determined or more daring." [1]

The assault on Fort Wagner, led by a thousand black soldiers under the white Colonel Shaw, is one of the greatest deeds of desperate bravery on record. On the other hand the treatment of Negro soldiers when captured by the Confederates was barbarous. At Fort Pillow, after the surrender of the federal troops, the colored regiment was indiscriminately butchered and some of them were buried alive.

Abraham Lincoln said, "The slightest knowledge of arithmetic will prove to any man that the rebel armies cannot be destroyed with Democratic strategy. It would sacrifice all the white men of the North to do it. There are now in the service of the United States near two hundred thousand able-bodied colored men, most of them under arms, defending and acquiring Union territory. . . . Abandon all the posts now garrisoned by black men; take two hundred thousand men from our side and put them in the battlefield or cornfield against us, and we would be compelled to abandon the war in three weeks." [2] Emancipation thus came as a war measure to break the power of the Confederacy, preserve the Union, and gain the sympathy of the civilized world.

However, two hundred and forty-four years

[1] Cf. Wilson: *The Black Phalanx.*
[2] Wilson: *The Black Phalanx*, p. 108.

of slavery could not be stopped by edict. There were legal difficulties, the whole slow problem of economic readjustment, and the subtle and far-reaching questions of future race relations.

The peculiar circumstances of emancipation forced the legal and political difficulties to the front, and these were so striking that they have since obscured the others in the eyes of students. Quite unexpectedly and without forethought the nation had emancipated four million slaves. Once the deed was done, the majority of the nation was glad and recognized that this was, after all, the only result of a fearful four years' war which in any degree justified it. But how was the result to be secured for all time? There were three possibilities: (1) to declare the slave free and leave him at the mercy of his former masters; (2) to establish a careful government guardianship designed to guide the slave from legal to real economic freedom; (3) to give the Negro the political power to guard himself as well as he could during this development. It is very easy to forget that the United States government tried each one of these in succession and was literally forced to adopt the third, because the first had utterly failed and the second was thought too "paternal" and especially too costly. To leave the Negroes helpless after a paper edict of emancipation was manifestly impossible. It would have meant that the war had been fought in vain.

Carl Schurz, who traversed the South just

after the war, said, "A veritable reign of terror prevailed in many parts of the South. The Negro found scant justice in the local courts against the white man. He could look for protection only to the military forces of the United States still garrisoning the states lately in rebellion and to the Freedmen's Bureau." [1]   This Freedmen's Bureau was proposed by Charles Sumner. If it had been presented to-day instead of fifty years ago, it would have been regarded as a proposal far less revolutionary than the state insurance of England and Germany. A half century ago, however, and in a country which gave the *laisser faire* economics their extremest trial, the Freedmen's Bureau struck the whole nation as unthinkable, save as a very temporary expedient and to relieve the more pointed forms of distress following war. Yet the proposals of the Bureau were both simple and sensible:

1. To oversee the making and enforcement of wage contracts for freedmen.

2. To appear in the courts as the freedmen's best friend.

3. To furnish the freedmen with a minimum of land and of capital.

4. To establish schools.

5. To furnish such institutions of relief as hospitals, outdoor relief stations, etc.

How a sensible people could expect really to conduct a slave into freedom with less than this it is hard to see. Even with such tutelage ex-

[1] *American Historical Review*, Vol. XV.

tending over a period of two or three decades, the ultimate end had to be enfranchisement and political and social freedom for those freedmen who attained a certain set standard. Otherwise the whole training had neither object nor guarantee. Precisely on this account the former masters opposed the Freedmen's Bureau with all their influence. They did not want the Negro trained or really freed, and they criticized mercilessly the many mistakes of the new Bureau.

The North at first thought to pay for the main cost of the Freedmen's Bureau by confiscating the property of former slave owners; but finding this not in accordance with law, they realized that they were embarking on an enterprise which bade fair to add many millions to the already staggering cost of the war. When, therefore, they saw that the abolition of slavery could not be left to the white South and could not be done by the North without time and money, they determined to put the responsibility on the Negro himself. This was without a doubt a tremendous experiment, but with all its manifest mistakes it succeeded to an astonishing degree. It made the immediate reëstablishment of the old slavery impossible, and it was probably the only quick method of doing this. It gave the freedmen's sons a chance to begin their education. It diverted the energy of the white South slavery to the recovery of political power, and in this interval, small as it was, the Negro took his first steps toward economic freedom.

The difficulties that stared reconstruction politicians in the face were these: (1) They must act quickly. (2) Emancipation had increased the political power of the South by one-sixth. Could this increased political power be put in the hands of those who, in defense of slavery, had disrupted the Union? (3) How was the abolition of slavery to be made effective? (4) What was to be the political position of the freedmen?

The Freedmen's Bureau in its short life accomplished a great task. Carl Schurz, in 1865, felt warranted in saying that "not half of the labor that has been done in the South this year, or will be done there next year, would have been or would be done but for the exertions of the Freedmen's Bureau. . . . No other agency except one placed there by the national government could have wielded that moral power whose interposition was so necessary to prevent Southern society from falling at once into the chaos of a general collision between its different elements." [1] Notwithstanding this the Bureau was temporary, was regarded as a makeshift, and soon abandoned.

Meantime partial Negro suffrage seemed not only just, but almost inevitable. Lincoln, in 1864, "cautiously" suggested to Louisiana's private consideration "whether some of the colored people may not be let in as, for instance, the very intelligent, and especially those who

[1] Report to President Johnson.

fought gallantly in our ranks. They would probably help in some trying time to come, to keep
the jewel of liberty in the family of freedom."
Indeed, the "family of freedom" in Louisiana
being somewhat small just then, who else was
to be intrusted with the "jewel"? Later and
for different reasons Johnson, in 1865, wrote to
Mississippi, "If you could extend the elective
franchise to all persons of color who can read the
Constitution of the United States in English and
write their name, and to all persons of color who
own real estate valued at not less than two hundred and fifty dollars, and pay taxes thereon,
you would completely disarm the adversary and
set an example the other states will follow. This
you can do with perfect safety, and you thus
place the Southern States, in reference to free
persons of color, upon the same basis with the
free states. I hope and trust your convention
will do this."

The Negroes themselves began to ask for
the suffrage. The Georgia convention in
Augusta (1866) advocated "a proposition to
give those who could write and read well and
possessed a certain property qualification the
right of suffrage." The reply of the South to
these suggestions was decisive. In Tennessee
alone was any action attempted that even suggested possible Negro suffrage in the future, and
that failed. In all other states the "Black
Codes" adopted were certainly not reassuring
to the friends of freedom. To be sure, it was not

a time to look for calm, cool, thoughtful action on the part of the white South. Their economic condition was pitiable, their fear of Negro freedom genuine. Yet it was reasonable to expect from them something less than repression and utter reaction toward slavery. To some extent this expectation was fulfilled. The abolition of slavery was recognized on the statute book, and the civil rights of owning property and appearing as a witness in cases in which he was a party were generally granted the Negro; yet with these in many cases went harsh and unbearable regulations which largely neutralized the concessions and certainly gave ground for an assumption that, once free, the South would virtually reenslave the Negro. The colored people themselves naturally feared this, protesting, as in Mississippi, "against the reactionary policy prevailing and expressing the fear that the legislature will pass such proscriptive laws as will drive the freedmen from the state, or practically reënslave them."

The codes spoke for themselves. As Burgess says, "Almost every act, word, or gesture of the Negro, not consonant with good taste and good manners as well as good morals, was made a crime or misdemeanor for which he could first be fined by the magistrates and then be consigned to a condition of almost slavery for an indefinite time, if he could not pay the bill." [1]

All things considered, it seems probable that,

[1] *Reconstruction and the Constitution.*

if the South had been permitted to have its way in 1865, the harshness of Negro slavery would have been mitigated so as to make slave trading difficult, and so as to make it possible for a Negro to hold property and appear in some cases in court; but that in most other respects the blacks would have remained in slavery.

What could prevent this? A Freedmen's Bureau established for ten, twenty, or forty years, with a careful distribution of land and capital and a system of education for the children, might have prevented such an extension of slavery. But the country would not listen to such a comprehensive plan. A restricted grant of the suffrage voluntarily made by the states would have been a reassuring proof of a desire to treat the freedmen fairly and would have balanced in part, at least, the increased political power of the South. There was no such disposition evident.

In Louisiana, for instance, under the proposed reconstruction "not one Negro was allowed to vote, though at that very time the wealthy intelligent free colored people of the state paid taxes on property assessed at fifteen million dollars and many of them were well known for their patriotic zeal and love for the Union." [1]

Thus the arguments for universal Negro suffrage from the start were strong and are still strong, and no one would question their strength were it not for the assumption that the experi-

[1] Brewster: *Sketches*, etc.

ment failed. Frederick Douglass said to President Johnson, "Your noble and humane predecessor placed in our hands 'the sword to assist in saving the nation, and we do hope that you, his able successor, will favorably regard the placing in our hands the ballot with which to save ourselves." [1]

Carl Schurz wrote, "It is idle to say that it will be time to speak of Negro suffrage when the whole colored race will be educated, for the ballot may be necessary to him to secure his education." [2]

The granting of full Negro suffrage meant one of two alternatives to the South: (1) The uplift of the Negro for sheer self-preservation. This is what Schurz and the saner North expected. As one Southern school superintendent said, "The elevation of this class is a matter of prime importance, since a ballot in the hands of a black citizen is quite as potent as in the hands of a white one." Or (2) Negro suffrage meant a determined concentration of Southern effort by actual force to deprive the Negro of the ballot or nullify its use. This last is what really happened. But even in this case, so much energy was taken in keeping the Negro from voting that the plan for keeping him in virtual slavery and denying him education partially failed. It took ten years to nullify Negro suffrage in part and twenty years to escape the fear of federal intervention. In these

[1] McPherson: *Reconstruction*, p. 52.
[2] Report to the President, 1865.

twenty years a vast number of Negroes had arisen so far as to escape slavery forever. Debt peonage could be fastened on part of the rural South and was; but even here the new Negro landholder appeared. Thus despite everything the Fifteenth Amendment, and that alone, struck the death knell of slavery.

The steps toward the Fifteenth Amendment were taken slowly. First Negroes were allowed to take part in reconstructing the state governments. This was inevitable if loyal governments were to be obtained. Next the restored state governments were directed to enfranchise all citizens, black or white, or have their representation in Congress cut down proportionately. Finally the United States said the last word of simple justice: the states may regulate the suffrage, but no state may deprive a person of the right to vote simply because he is a Negro or has been a slave.

For such reasons the Negro was enfranchised. What was the result? No language has been spared to describe these results as the worst imaginable. This is not true. There were bad results, and bad results arising from Negro suffrage; but those results were not so bad as usually painted, nor was Negro suffrage the prime cause of many of them. Let us not forget that the white South believed it to be of vital interest to its welfare that the experiment of Negro suffrage should fail ignominiously and that almost to a man the whites were willing to insure this failure either by active force or passive acquiescence; that besides this there were, as might be expected, men, black and white, Northern and Southern, only too eager to take advantage of such a situation for feathering their own nests. Much evil must result in such case; but to charge the evil to Negro suffrage is unfair. It may be charged to anger, poverty, venality, and ignorance, but the anger and poverty were the almost inevitable aftermath of war; the venality was much greater among whites than Negroes both North and South, and while ignorance was the curse of Negroes, the fault was not theirs and they took the initiative to correct it.

The chief charges against the Negro governments are extravagance, theft, and incompetency of officials. There is no serious charge that these governments threatened civilization or the foundations of social order. The charge is that they threatened property and that they were inefficient. These charges are in part undoubtedly true, but they are often exaggerated. The South had been terribly impoverished and saddled with new social burdens. In other words, states with smaller resources were asked not only to do a work of restoration, but a larger social work. The property holders were aghast. They not only demurred, but, predicting ruin and revolution, they appealed to secret societies, to intimidation, force, and murder. They refused to believe that these novices in government and their friends were aught but scamps and fools. Under the circumstances occurring directly after the war, the wisest statesman would have been compelled to resort to increased taxation and would have, in turn, been execrated as extravagant, dishonest, and incompetent. It is easy, therefore, to see what flaming and incredible stories of Reconstruction governments could gain wide currency and belief. In fact the extravagance, although great, was not universal, and much of it was due to the extravagant spirit pervading the whole country in a day of inflated currency and speculation.

That the Negroes, led by the astute thieves, became at first tools and received some small share of the spoils is true. But two considerations must be added: much of the legislation which resulted in fraud was represented to the Negroes as good legislation, and thus their votes were secured by deliberate misrepresentation. Take, for instance, the land frauds of South Carolina. A wise Negro leader of that state, advocating the state purchase of farm lands, said, "One of the greatest of slavery bulwarks was the infernal plantation system, one man owning his thousand, another his twenty, another fifty thousand acres of land. This is the only way by which we will break up that system, and I maintain that our freedom will be of no effect if we allow it to continue. What is the main cause of the prosperity of the North? It is because every man has his own farm and is free and independent. Let the lands of the South be similarly divided." [1]

[1] *American Historical Review*, Vol. XV, No. 4.

From such arguments the Negroes were induced to aid a scheme to buy land and distribute it. Yet a large part of eight hundred thousand dollars appropriated was wasted and went to the white landholders' pockets.

The most inexcusable cheating of the Negroes took place through the Freedmen's Bank. This bank was incorporated by Congress in 1865 and had in its list of incorporators some of the greatest names in America including Peter Cooper, William Cullen Bryan and John Jay. Yet the bank was allowed to fail in 1874 owing the freedmen their first savings of over three millions of dollars. They have never been reimbursed.

Many Negroes were undoubtedly venal, but more were ignorant and deceived. The question is: Did they show any signs of a disposition to learn to better things? The theory of democratic government is not that the will of the people is always right, but rather that normal human beings of average intelligence will, if given a chance, learn the right and best course by bitter experience. This is precisely what the Negro voters showed indubitable signs of doing. First they strove for schools to abolish ignorance, and second, a large and growing number of them revolted against the extravagance and stealing that marred the beginning of Reconstruction, and joined with the best elements to institute reform. The greatest stigma on the white South is not that it opposed Negro suffrage and resented theft and incompetence, but that, when it saw the reform movements growing and even in some cases triumphing, and a larger and larger number of black voters learning to vote for honesty and ability, it still preferred a Reign of Terror to a campaign of education and disfranchised Negroes instead of punishing rascals.

No one has expressed this more convincingly than a Negro who was himself a member of the Reconstruction legislature of South Carolina, and who spoke at the convention which disfranchised him against one of the onslaughts of Tillman. "We were eight years in power. We had built school houses, established charitable institutions, built and maintained the penitentiary system, provided for the education of the deaf and dumb, rebuilt the jails and court houses, rebuilt the bridges, and reëstablished the ferries. In short, we had reconstructed the state and placed it upon the road to prosperity, and at the same time, by our acts of financial reform, transmitted to the Hampton government an indebtedness not greater by more than two and a half million dollars than was the bonded debt of the state in 1868, before the Republican Negroes and their white allies came into power." [1]

So, too, in Louisiana in 1872, and in Mississippi later, the better element of the Republicans triumphed at the polls and, joining with the Democrats, instituted reforms, repudiated the worst extravagance, and started toward better things. Unfortunately there was one thing

[1] *Occasional Papers*, American Negro Academy, No. 6.

that the white South feared more than Negro
dishonesty, ignorance, and incompetency, and
that was Negro honesty, knowledge, and efficiency.

In the midst of all these difficulties the Negro
governments in the South accomplished much of
positive good. We may recognize three things
which Negro rule gave to the South: (1) democratic government, (2) free public schools, (3) new
social legislation.

In general, the words of Judge Albion W.
Tourgee, a white "carpet bagger," are true when
he says of the Negro governments, "They obeyed
the Constitution of the United States and annulled
the bonds of states, counties, and cities which
had been issued to carry on the War of Rebellion
and maintain armies in the field against the
Union. They instituted a public school system
in a realm where public schools had been unknown.
They opened the ballot box and the jury box to
thousands of white men who had been debarred
from them by a lack of earthly possessions.
They introduced home rule into the South.
They abolished the whipping post, the branding
iron, the stocks, and other barbarous forms of
punishment which had up to that time prevailed. They reduced capital felonies from
about twenty to two or three. In an age of extravagance they were extravagant in the sums
appropriated for public works. In all of that
time no man's rights of persons were invaded
under the forms of law. Every Democrat's

life, home, fireside, and business were safe. No man obstructed any white man's way to the ballot box, interfered with his freedom of speech, or boycotted him on account of his political faith." [1]

A thorough study of the legislation accompanying these constitutions and its changes since shows the comparatively small amount of change in law and government which the overthrow of Negro rule brought about. There were sharp and often hurtful economies introduced, marking the return of property to power; there was a sweeping change of officials, but the main body of Reconstruction legislation stood. The Reconstruction democracy brought forth new leaders and definitely overthrew the old Southern aristocracy. Among these new men were Negroes of worth and ability. John R. Lynch, when Speaker of the Mississippi House of Representatives, was given a public testimonial by Republicans and Democrats, and the leading white paper said, "His bearing in office had been so proper, and his rulings in such marked contrast to the partisan conduct of the ignoble whites of his party who have aspired to be leaders of the blacks, that the conservatives cheerfully joined in the testimonial." [2]

Of the colored treasurer of South Carolina the white Governor Chamberlain said, "I have never heard one word or seen one act of Mr.

[1] *Occasional Papers*, American Negro Academy, No. 6.
[2] *Jackson (Miss.) Clarion*, April 24, 1873.

Cardoza's which did not confirm my confidence in his personal integrity and his political honor and zeal for the honest administration of the state government. On every occasion, and under all circumstances, he has been against fraud and robbery and in favor of good measures and good men."[1]

Jonathan C. Gibbs, a colored man and the first state superintendent of instruction in Florida, was a graduate of Dartmouth. He established the system and brought it to success, dying in harness in 1874. Such men — and there were others — ought not to be forgotten or confounded with other types of colored and white Reconstruction leaders.

There is no doubt that the thirst of the black man for knowledge, a thirst which has been too persistent and durable to be mere curiosity or whim, gave birth to the public school system of the South. It was the question upon which black voters and legislators insisted more than anything else, and while it is possible to find some vestiges of free schools in some of the Southern States before the war, yet a universal, well-established system dates from the day that the black man got political power.

Finally, in legislation covering property, the wider functions of the state, the punishment of crime and the like, it is sufficient to say that the laws on these points established by Reconstruction legislatures were not only different from and

[1] Allen: *Governor Chamberlain's Administration*, p. 82.

even revolutionary to the laws in the older South, but they were so wise and so well suited to the needs of the new South that, in spite of a retrogressive movement following the overthrow of the Negro governments, the mass of this legislation, with elaborations and development, still stands on the statute books of the South.[1]

The triumph of reaction in the South inaugurated a new era in which we may distinguish three phases: the renewed attempt to reduce the Negroes to serfdom, the rise of the Negro metayer, and the economic disfranchisement of the Southern working class.

The attempt to replace individual slavery had been frustrated by the Freedmen's Bureau and the Fifteenth Amendment. The disfranchisement of 1876 was followed by the widespread rise of "crime" peonage. Stringent laws on vagrancy, guardianship, and labor contracts were enacted and large discretion given judge and jury in cases of petty crime. As a result Negroes were systematically arrested on the slightest pretext and the labor of convicts leased to private parties. This "convict lease system" was almost universal in the South until about 1890, when its outrageous abuses and cruelties aroused the whole country. It still survives over wide areas, and is not only responsible for the impression that the Negro is a natural

[1] Reconstruction Constitutions, practically unaltered, were kept in Florida, 1868–85, seventeen years; Virginia, 1870–1902, thirty-two years; South Carolina, 1868–95, twenty-seven years; Mississippi, 1868–90, twenty-two years.

criminal, but also for the inability of the Southern
courts to perform their normal functions after
so long a prostitution to ends far removed from
justice.

In more normal economic lines the employers
began with the labor contract system. Before
the war they owned labor, land, and subsistence.
After the war they still held the land and subsistence. The laborer was hired and the subsistence "advanced" to him while the crop was
growing. The fall of the Freedmen's Bureau
hindered the transmutation of this system into
a modern wage system, and allowed the laborers
to be cheated by high interest charges on the
subsistence advanced and actual cheating often
in book accounts.

The black laborers became deeply dissatisfied
under this system and began to migrate from
the country to the cities, where there was an
increasing demand for labor. The employing
farmers complained bitterly of the scarcity of
labor and of Negro "laziness," and secured
the enactment of harsher vagrancy and labor
contract laws, and statutes against the "entice-
ment" of laborers. So severe were these laws
that it was often impossible for a laborer to stop
work without committing a felony. Nevertheless
competition compelled the landholders to offer
more inducements to the farm hand. The result
was the rise of the black share tenant: the
laborer securing better wages saved a little
capital and began to hire land in parcels of forty

to eighty acres, furnishing his own tools and seed and practically raising his own subsistence. In this way the whole face of the labor contract in the South was, in the decade 1880–90, in process of change from a nominal wage contract to a system of tenantry. The great plantations were apparently broken up into forty and eighty acre farms with black farmers. To many it seemed that emancipation was accomplished, and the black folk were especially filled with joy and hope.

It soon was evident, however, that the change was only partial. The landlord still held the land in large parcels. He rented this in small farms to tenants, but retained direct control. In theory the laborer was furnishing capital, but in the majority of cases he was borrowing at least a part of this capital from some merchant.

The retail merchant in this way entered on the scene as middle man between landlord and laborer. He guaranteed the landowner his rent and relieved him of details by taking over the furnishing of supplies to the laborer. He tempted the laborer by a larger stock of more attractive goods, made a direct contract with him, and took a mortgage on the growing crop. Thus he soon became the middle man to whom the profit of the transaction largely flowed, and he began to get rich.

If the new system benefited the merchant and the landlord, it also brought some benefits to the black laborers. Numbers of these were still held in peonage, and the mass were laborers working for scant board and clothes; but above these began to rise a large number of independent tenants and farm owners.

In 1890, therefore, the South was faced by this question: Are we willing to allow the Negro to advance as a free worker, peasant farmer, metayer, and small capitalist, with only such handicaps as naturally impede the poor and ignorant, or is it necessary to erect further artificial barriers to restrain the advance of the Negroes? The answer was clear and unmistakable. The advance of the freedmen had been too rapid and the South feared it; every effort must be made to "keep the Negro in his place" as a servile caste.

To this end the South strove to make the disfranchisement of the Negroes effective and final. Up to this time disfranchisement was illegal and based on intimidation. The new laws passed between 1890 and 1910 sought on their face to base the right to vote on property and education in such a way as to exclude poor and illiterate Negroes and admit all whites. In fact they could be administered so as to exclude nearly all Negroes. To this was added a series of laws designed publicly to humiliate and stigmatize Negro blood: as, for example, separate railway cars; separate seats in street cars, and the like; these things were added to the separation in schools and churches, and the denial of redress to seduced colored women, which had long been the custom in the South. All these new enactments meant not simply separation, but subordination, caste, humiliation, and flagrant injustice.

To all this was added a series of labor laws making the exploitation of Negro labor more secure. All this legislation had to be accomplished in the face of the labor movement throughout the world, and particularly in the South, where it was beginning to enter among the white workers. This was accomplished easily, however, by an appeal to race prejudice. No method of inflaming the darkest passions of men was unused. The lynching mob was given its glut of blood and egged on by purposely exaggerated and often wholly invented tales of crime on the part of perhaps the most peaceful and sweet-tempered race the world has ever known. Under the flame of this outward noise went the more subtle and dangerous work. The election laws passed in the states where three-fourths of the Negroes live, were so ingeniously framed that a black university graduate could be prevented from voting and the most ignorant white hoodlum could be admitted to the polls. Labor laws were so arranged that imprisonment for debt was possible and leaving an employer could be made a penitentiary offense. Negro schools were cut off with small appropriations or wholly neglected, and a determined effort was made with wide success to see that no Negro had any voice either in the making or the administration of local, state, or national law.

The acquiescence of the white labor vote of

the South was further insured by throwing white and black laborers, so far as possible, into rival competing groups and making each feel that the one was the cause of the other's troubles. The neutrality of the white people of the North was secured through their fear for the safety of large investments in the South, and through the fatalistic attitude common both in America and Europe toward the possibility of real advance on the part of the darker nations.

The reaction of the Negro Americans upon this wholesale and open attempt to reduce them to serfdom has been interesting. Naturally they began to organize and protest and in some cases to appeal to the courts. Then, to their astonishment, there arose a colored leader, Mr. Booker T. Washington, who advised them to yield to disfranchisement and caste and wait for greater economic strength and general efficiency before demanding full rights as American citizens. The white South naturally agreed with Mr. Washington, and the white North thought they saw here a chance for peace in the racial conflict and safety for their Southern investments.

For a time the colored people hesitated. They respected Mr. Washington for shrewdness and recognized the wisdom of his homely insistence on thrift and hard work; but gradually they came to see more and more clearly that, stripped of political power and emasculated by caste, they could never gain sufficient economic strength to take their place as modern men. They also realized that any lull in their protests would be taken advantage of by Negro haters to push their caste program. They began, therefore, with renewed persistence to fight for their fundamental rights as American citizens. The struggle tended at first to bitter personal dissension within the group. But wiser counsels and the advice of white friends eventually prevailed and raised it to the broad level of a fight for the fundamental principles of democracy. The launching of the "Niagara Movement" by twenty-nine daring colored men in 1905, followed by the formation of the National Association for the Advancement of Colored People in 1910, marked an epoch in the advance of the Negro. This latter organization, with its monthly organ, *The Crisis*, is now waging a nation-wide fight for justice to Negroes. Other organizations, and a number of strong Negro weekly papers are aiding in this fight. What has been the net result of this struggle of half a century?

In 1863 there were about five million persons of Negro descent in the United States. Of these, four million and more were just being released from slavery. These slaves could be bought and sold, could move from place to place only with permission, were forbidden to learn to read or write, and legally could never hold property or marry. Ninety per cent were totally illiterate, and only one adult in six was a nominal Christian.

Fifty years later, in 1913, there were in the

United States ten and a quarter million persons of Negro descent, an increase of one hundred and five per cent. Legal slavery has been abolished leaving, however, vestiges in debt slavery, peonage, and the convict lease system. The mass of the freedmen and their sons have

1. Earned a living as free and partially free laborers.

2. Shared the responsibilities of government.

3. Developed the internal organization of their race.

4. Aspired to spiritual self-expression.

The Negro was freed as a penniless, landless, naked, ignorant laborer. There were a few free Negroes who owned property in the South, and a larger number who owned property in the North; but ninety-nine per cent of the race in the South were penniless field hands and servants.

To-day there are two and a half million laborers, the majority of whom are efficient wage earners. Above these are more than a million servants and tenant farmers; skilled and semi-skilled workers make another million and at the top of the economic column are 600,000 owners and managers of farms and businesses, cash tenants, officials, and professional men. This makes a total of 5,192,535 colored breadwinners in 1910.

More specifically these breadwinners include 218,972 farm owners and 319,346 cash farm tenants and managers. There were in all 62,755 miners, 288,141 in the building and hand trades;

28,515 workers in clay, glass, and stone; 41,739 iron and steel workers; 134,102 employees on railways; 62,822 draymen, cab drivers, and liverymen; 133,245 in wholesale and retail trade; 32,170 in the public service; and 69,471 in professional service, including 29,750 teachers, 17,495 clergymen, and 4,546 physicians, dentists, trained nurses, etc. Finally, we must not forget 2,175,000 Negro homes, with their housewives, and 1,620,000 children in school.

Fifty years ago the overwhelming mass of these people were not only penniless, but were themselves assessed as real estate. By 1875 the Negroes probably had gotten hold of something between 2,000,000 and 4,000,000 acres of land through their bounties as soldiers and the low price of land after the war. By 1880 this was increased to about 6,000,000 acres; in 1890 to about 8,000,000 acres; in 1900 to over 12,000,000 acres. In 1910 this land had increased to nearly 20,000,000 acres, a realm as large as Ireland.

The 120,738 farms owned by Negroes in 1890 increased to 218,972 in 1910, or eighty-one per cent. The value of these farms increased from $179,796,639 in 1900 to $440,992,439 in 1910; Negroes owned in 1910 about 500,000 homes out of a total of 2,175,000. Their total property in 1900 was estimated at $300,000,000 by the American Economic Association. On the same basis of calculation it would be worth to-day not less than $800,000,000.

Despite the disfranchisement of three-fourths

of his voting population, the Negro to-day is a recognized part of the American government. He holds 7,500 offices in the executive service of the nation, besides furnishing four regiments in the army and a large number of sailors. In the state and municipal service he holds nearly 20,000 other offices, and he furnishes 500,000 of the votes which rule the Union.

In these same years the Negro has relearned the lost art of organization. Slavery was the almost absolute denial of initiative and responsibility. To-day Negroes have nearly 40,000 churches, with edifices worth at least $75,000,000 and controlling nearly 4,000,000 members. They raise themselves $7,500,000 a year for these churches.

There are 200 private schools and colleges managed and almost entirely supported by Negroes, and these and other public and private Negro schools have received in 40 years $45,000,000 of Negro money in taxes and donations. Five millions a year are raised by Negro secret and beneficial societies which hold at least $6,000,000 in real estate. Negroes support wholly or in part over 100 old folks' homes and orphanages, 30 hospitals, and 500 cemeteries. Their organized commercial life is extending rapidly and includes over 22,000 small retail businesses and 40 banks.

Above and beyond this material growth has gone the spiritual uplift of a great human race. From contempt and amusement they have passed to the pity, perplexity, and fear on the part of their neighbors, while within their own souls they have arisen from apathy and timid complaint to open protest and more and more manly self-assertion. Where nine-tenths of them could not read or write in 1860, to-day over two-thirds can; they have 300 papers and periodicals, and their voice and expression are compelling attention.

Already in poetry, literature, music, and painting the work of Americans of Negro descent has gained notable recognition. Instead of being led and defended by others, as in the past, American Negroes are gaining their own leaders, their own voices, their own ideals. Self-realization is thus coming slowly but surely to another of the world's great races, and they are to-day girding themselves to fight in the van of progress, not simply for their own rights as men, but for the ideals of the greater world in which they live: the emancipation of women, universal peace, democratic government, the socialization of wealth, and human brotherhood.

CHAPTER XII

THE NEGRO PROBLEMS

It is impossible to separate the population of the world accurately by race, since that is no scientific criterion by which to divide races. If we divide the world, however, roughly into African Negroes and Negroids, European whites, and Asiatic and American brown and yellow peoples, we have approximately 150,000,000 Negroes, 500,000,000 whites, and 900,000,000 yellow and brown peoples. Of the 150,000,000 Negroes, 121,000,000 live in Africa, 27,000,000[1] in the new world, and 2,000,000 in Asia.

What is to be the future relation of the Negro race to the rest of the world? The visitor from Altruria might see here no peculiar problem. He would expect the Negro race to develop along the lines of other human races. In Africa his economic and political development would restore and eventually outrun the ancient glories of Egypt, Ethiopia, and Yoruba; overseas the West Indies would become a new and nobler Africa, built in the very pathway of the new

[1] Sir Harry Johnston estimates 135,000,000 Negroes, of whom 24,591,000 live in America. See *Inter-Racial Problems*, p. 335.

highway of commerce between East and West — the real sea route to India; while in the United States a large part of its citizenship (showing for perhaps centuries their dark descent, but nevertheless equal sharers of and contributors to the civilization of the West) would be the descendants of the wretched victims of the seventeenth, eighteenth, and nineteenth century slave trade.

This natural assumption of a stranger finds, however, lodging in the minds of few present-day thinkers. On the contrary, such an outcome is usually dismissed summarily. Most persons have accepted that tacit but clear modern philosophy which assigns to the white race alone the hegemony of the world and assumes that other races, and particularly the Negro race, will either be content to serve the interests of the whites or die out before their all-conquering march. This philosophy is the child of the African slave trade and of the expansion of Europe during the nineteenth century.

The Negro slave trade was the first step in modern world commerce, followed by the modern theory of colonial expansion. Slaves as an article of commerce were shipped as long as the traffic paid. When the Americas had enough black laborers for their immediate demand, the moral action of the eighteenth century had a chance to make its faint voice heard.

The moral repugnance was powerfully reënforced by the revolt of the slaves in the West Indies and South America, and by the fact that North America early began to regard itself as the seat of advanced ideas in politics, religion, and humanity.

Finally European capital began to find better investments than slave shipping and flew to them. These better investments were the fruit of the new industrial revolution of the nineteenth century, with its factory system; they were also in part the result of the cheapened price of gold and silver, brought about by slavery and the slave trade to the new world. Commodities other than gold, and commodities capable of manufacture and exploitation in Europe out of materials furnishable by America, became enhanced in value; the bottom fell out of the commercial slave trade and its suppression became possible.

The middle of the nineteenth century saw the beginning of the rise of the modern working class. By means of political power the laborers slowly but surely began to demand a larger share in the profiting industry. In the United States their demand bade fair to be halted by the competition of slave labor. The labor vote, therefore, first confined slavery to limits in which it could not live, and when the slave power sought to exceed these territorial limits, it was suddenly and unintentionally abolished.

As the emancipation of millions of dark workers took place in the West Indies, North and South America, and parts of Africa at this time, it was natural to assume that the uplift of this working class lay along the same paths with that of European and American whites. This was the *first* suggested solution of the Negro problem. Consequently these Negroes received partial enfranchisement, the beginnings of education, and some of the elementary rights of wage earners and property holders, while the independence of Liberia and Hayti was recognized. However, long before they were strong enough to assert the rights thus granted or to gather intelligence enough for proper group leadership, the new colonialism of the later nineteenth and twentieth centuries began to dawn. The new colonial theory transferred the reign of commercial privilege and extraordinary profit from the exploitation of the European working class to the exploitation of backward races under the political domination of Europe. For the purpose of carrying out this idea the European and white American working class was practically invited to share in this new exploitation, and particularly were flattered by popular appeals to their inherent superiority to "Dagoes," "Chinks," "Japs," and "Niggers."

This tendency was strengthened by the fact that the new colonial expansion centered in Africa. Thus in 1875 something less than one-tenth of Africa was under nominal European control, but the Franco-Prussian War and the exploration of the Congo led to new and fateful things. Germany desired economic expansion and, being shut out from America by the Monroe

Doctrine, turned to Africa. France, humiliated in war, dreamed of an African empire from the Atlantic to the Red Sea. Italy became ambitious for Tripoli and Abyssinia. Great Britain began to take new interest in her African realm, but found herself largely checkmated by the jealousy of all Europe. Portugal sought to make good her ancient claim to the larger part of the whole southern peninsula. It was Leopold of Belgium who started to make the exploration and civilization of Africa an international movement. This project failed, and the Congo Free State became in time simply a Belgian colony. While the project was under discussion, the international scramble for Africa began. As a result the Berlin Conference and subsequent wars and treaties gave Great Britain control of 2,101,411 square miles of African territory, in addition to Egypt and the Egyptian Sudan with 1,600,000 square miles. This includes South Africa, Bechuanaland and Rhodesia, East Africa, Uganda and Zanzibar, Nigeria, and British West Africa. The French hold 4,106,950 square miles, including nearly all North Africa (except Tripoli) west of the Niger valley and Libyan Desert, and touching the Atlantic at four points. To this is added the Island of Madagascar. The Germans have 910,150 square miles, principally in Southeast and Southwest Africa and the Kamerun. The Portuguese retain 787,500 square miles in Southeast and Southwest Africa. The Belgians have 900,000 square miles, while Liberia (43,000 square miles) and Abyssinia (350,000 square miles) are independent. The Italians have about 600,000 square miles and the Spanish less than 100,000 square miles.

This partition of Africa brought revision of the ideas of Negro uplift. Why was it necessary, the European investors argued, to push a continent of black workers along the paths of social uplift by education, trades-unionism, property holding, and the electoral franchise when the workers desired no change, and the rate of European profit would suffer?

There quickly arose then the *second* suggestion for settling the Negro problem. It called for the virtual enslavement of natives in certain industries, as rubber and ivory collecting in the Belgian Congo, cocoa raising in Portuguese Angola, and diamond mining in South Africa. This new slavery or "forced" labor was stoutly defended as a necessary foundation for implanting modern industry in a barbarous land; but its likeness to slavery was too clear and it has been modified, but not wholly abolished.

The *third* attempted solution of the Negro sought the result of the *second* by less direct methods. Negroes in Africa, the West Indies, and America were to be forced to work by land monopoly, taxation, and little or no education. In this way a docile industrial class working for low wages, and not intelligent enough to unite in labor unions, was to be developed. The peonage systems in parts of the United States and the labor systems of many of the African colonies of Great Britain and Germany illustrate this phase of solution.[1] It is also illustrated in many of the West Indian islands where we have a predominant Negro population, and this population freed from slavery and partially enfranchised. Land and capital, however, have for the most part been so managed amd monopolized that the black peasantry have been reduced to straits to earn a living in one of the richest parts of the world. The problem is now going to be intensified when the world's commerce begins to sweep through the Panama Canal.

All these solutions and methods, however, run directly counter to modern philanthropy, and have to be carried on with a certain concealment and half-hypocrisy which is not only distasteful in itself, but always liable to be discovered and exposed by some liberal or religious movement of the masses of men and suddenly overthrown. These solutions are, therefore, gradually merging into a *fourth* solution, which is to-day very popular. This solution says: Negroes differ from whites in their inherent genius and stage of development. Their development must not, therefore, be sought along European lines,

[1] The South African natives, in an appeal to the English Parliament, show in an astonishing way the confiscation of their land by the English. They say that in the Union of South Africa 1,250,000 whites own 264,000,000 acres of land, while the 4,500,000 natives have only 21,000,000 acres. On top of this the Union Parliament has passed a law making even the future purchase of land by Negroes illegal save in restricted areas!

but along their own native lines. Consequently
the effort is made to-day in British Nigeria, in
the French Congo and Sudan, in Uganda and
Rhodesia to leave so far as possible the outward
structure of native life intact; the king or chief
reigns, the popular assemblies meet and act,
the native courts adjudicate, and native social
and family life and religion prevail. All this,
however, is subject to the veto and command of
a European magistracy supported by a native
army with European officers. The advantage of
this method is that on its face it carries no clue
to its real working. Indeed it can always point
to certain undoubted advantages: the abolition
of the slave trade, the suppression of war and
feud, the encouragement of peaceful industry.
On the other hand, back of practically all these
experiments stands the economic motive — the
determination to use the organization, the land,
and the people, not for their own benefit, but for
the benefit of white Europe. For this reason
education is seldom encouraged, modern religious
ideas are carefully limited, sound political development is sternly frowned upon, and industry
is degraded and changed to the demands of
European markets. The most ruthless class of
white mercantile exploiters is allowed large liberty,
if not a free hand, and protected by a concerted
attempt to deify white men as such in the eyes
of the native and in their own imagination.[1]

[1] The traveler Glave writes in the *Century Magazine*
(LIII, 913): "Formerly [in the Congo Free State] an ordinary

White missionary societies are spending perhaps as much as five million dollars a year in Africa and accomplishing much good, but at the same time white merchants are sending at least twenty million dollars' worth of European liquor into Africa each year, and the debauchery of the almost unrestricted rum traffic goes far to neutralize missionary effort.

Under this last mentioned solution of the Negro problems we may put the attempts at the segregation of Negroes and mulattoes in the United States and to some extent in the West Indies. Ostensibly this is "separation" of the races in society, civil rights, etc. In practice it is the subordination of colored people of all grades under white tutelage, and their separation as far as possible from contact with civilization in dwelling place, in education, and in public life.

On the other hand the economic significance of the Negro to-day is tremendous. Black Africa to-day exports annually nearly two hundred million dollars' worth of goods, and its economic development has scarcely begun. The black West Indies export nearly one hundred million dollars' worth of goods; to this must be added the labor value of Negroes in South Africa, Egypt, the West Indies, North, Central, and South America, where the result is blended in the common output of many races. The economic foun-

white man was merely called 'bwana' or 'Mzunga'; now the merest insect of a pale face earns the title of 'bwana Mkubwa' [big master]."

dation of the Negro problem can easily be seen
to be a matter of many hundreds of millions
to-day, and ready to rise to the billions to-
morrow.

Such figures and facts give some slight idea of
the economic meaning of the Negro to-day as a
worker and industrial factor. "Tropical Africa
and its peoples are being brought more irrevo-
cably every year into the vortex of the economic
influences that sway the western world." [1]

What do Negroes themselves think of these
their problems and the attitude of the world
toward them? First and most significant, they
are thinking. There is as yet no great single
centralizing of thought or unification of opinion,
but there are centers which are growing larger
and larger and touching edges. The most
significant centers of this new thinking are, perhaps naturally, outside Africa and in America:
in the United States and in the West Indies;
this is followed by South Africa and West Africa
and then, more vaguely, by South America, with
faint beginnings in East Central Africa, Nigeria,
and the Sudan.

The Pan-African movement when it comes will
not, however, be merely a narrow racial propaganda. Already the more far-seeing Negroes
sense the coming unities: a unity of the working
classes everywhere, a unity of the colored races,
a new unity of men. The proposed economic
solution of the Negro problem in Africa and

[1] E. D. Morel, in the *Nineteenth Century*.

America has turned the thoughts of Negroes toward a realization of the fact that the modern white laborer of Europe and America has the key to the serfdom of black folk, in his support of militarism and colonial expansion. He is beginning to say to these workingmen that, so long as black laborers are slaves, white laborers cannot be free. Already there are signs in South Africa and the United States of the beginning of understanding between the two classes.

In a conscious sense of unity among colored races there is to-day only a growing interest. There is slowly arising not only a curiously strong brotherhood of Negro blood throughout the world, but the common cause of the darker races against the intolerable assumptions and insults of Europeans has already found expression. Most men in this world are colored. A belief in humanity means a belief in colored men. The future world will, in all reasonable probability, be what colored men make it. In order for this colored world to come into its heritage, must the earth again be drenched in the blood of fighting, snarling human beasts, or will Reason and Good Will prevail? That such may be true, the character of the Negro race is the best and greatest hope; for in its normal condition it is at once the strongest and gentlest of the races of men: "Semper novi quid ex Africa!"

DISTRIBUTION OF NEGRO BLOOD, ANCIENT AND MODERN

AFTERWORD

Robert Gregg

It is a curious commentary on modern prejudice that most of this splendid history of civilization and uplift is unknown to-day, and men confidently assert that Negroes have no history.
                                        —*W.E.B. Du Bois*, The Negro

For some people, when you say "Timbuktu" it is like the end of the world, but that is not true. I am from Timbuktu, and I can tell you we are right at the heart of the world.
                                        —*Ali Farka Toure, "Talking Timbuktu"*

With the publication of *The Negro* in 1915, W.E.B. Du Bois lifted a veil from African history, one that had enabled Europeans to deny that Africans had a meaningful history comparable to their own and had justified (to their own satisfaction) their exploitation of African resources from the beginning of the Atlantic slave trade to the establishment of colonial regimes. Synthesizing the recent historical and anthropological scholarship in the most thorough and accessible account of Africa and the African diaspora till then written, Du Bois accomplished a feat that made it no longer possible for Europeans idly to repeat

245

Hegel's "ancient lie of 1833," that "alone of all the continents, the African has no history."

Unfortunately, few people at the present time are acquainted with Du Bois's formidable contribution in *The Negro*. While the significance of Du Bois's text was readily apparent when it was first published, especially among African and African American intellectuals, and remained so through the 1970s, when newly-independent African states had not yet begun to falter and Du Bois's writings were still fresh in the minds of many scholars, the book is remembered less well today.[1] Now scholars and students are more likely to be familiar with other writings by Du Bois, such as *The Philadelphia Negro* (which is considered a foundational text in sociology), *The Souls of Black Folk* (which cemented Du Bois's reputation in opposition to Booker T. Washington and provided a way of reevaluating black culture), and to a les-

1. George Shepperson, Introduction to *The Negro* (New York: Oxford University Press, 1970), vii–xxv, and Herbert Aptheker, Introduction to *Black Folk Then and Now* (Millwood, N.Y.: Kraus-Thomson, 1973 [1939]), 5–23, discussed the contemporary reaction to this work. See especially the influence of *The Negro* on the pioneering Africanist and Howard University professor William Hansberry in Shepperson, xxi. Their introductions and the influence they attributed to *The Negro* highlight the work's enduring appeal.

ser extent, *Black Reconstruction in America* (which has inspired leading historians of American Reconstruction).[2]

Even David Levering Lewis, in his monumental biography of Du Bois, downplays *The Negro*'s significance, devoting only a couple of paragraphs to an examination of the text. He describes *The Negro* as a "pioneering synthesis of the latest scholarship brilliantly beamed through a revisionist lens," but feels that the work seems to

2. For the influence of *The Philadelphia Negro* (Philadelphia: University of Pennsylvania Press, 1997 [1899]), see Michael B. Katz and Thomas J. Sugrue, eds., *W.E.B. DuBois, Race, and the City: The Philadelphia Negro and Its Legacy* (Philadelphia: University of Pennsylvania Press, 1998). *The Souls of Black Folk* (New York: Bantam, 1989 [1903]), with its concept of the double consciousness, is perhaps the most cited of Du Bois's works. See Adolph L. Reed, Jr., *W.E.B. Du Bois and American Political Thought: Fabianism and the Color Line* (New York: Oxford University Press, 1997) for a discussion of this concept and its pervasiveness in African American political discourse. The influence of *Black Reconstruction in America* (New York: Atheneum, 1979 [1935]) is most evident in the work of Eric Foner; see *Nothing But Freedom: Emancipation and Its Legacy* (Baton Rouge: Louisiana State University Press, 1983), 5–6. For further discussion of these, see Robert Gregg, "Giant Steps: W.E.B. DuBois and the Historical Enterprise," in Katz and Sugrue, *W.E.B. DuBois, Race, and the City*, 77–99.

show Du Bois's conformity to some of the racial and elitist assumptions of the period. He writes:

> In what was the first general history yet written in English on the subject, Du Bois casually informed readers that "in disposition the Negro is among the most lovable of men," that there could be "no doubt of the Negro's deep and delicate sense of beauty in form, color, and sound," or that Haiti's peasantry is "the happiest and most contented peasantry in the world."[3]

For Lewis, Du Bois was here clearly endorsing racial stereotypes and romanticizing the condition of peasants in Haiti, although I will argue later that this is not a fair reading of the text.[4] Nevertheless, even in his brief account Lewis ges-

3. David Levering Lewis, *WE.B. Du Bois—Biography of a Race, 1868–1919* (New York: Henry Holt, 1993), 461. The comment from DuBois about Haiti is found on p. 178.

4. Given Du Bois's extensive study of the conditions of the peasants of the American South, it is hard to imagine that he really intended to suggest that Haitian peasants were living in any kind of paradise. Instead, he was perhaps proclaiming his solidarity with Haitian peasants, which would be restated later in 1915 when Woodrow Wilson invaded the island. This occurred in spite of the fact that, to Du Bois's eye at least, conditions for Haitian peasants were better than those suffered by African Americans in the South. Haiti, Du Bois noted, "is more civilized than Texas"; "Hayti," *The Crisis* 10 (October 1915): 291.

tures to the work's major revisionist contribution, writing how "the pages of *The Negro* were littered with fallacious concepts exploded by Du Bois."[5] One of the book's most important contributions, according to Lewis, is to be found in the subsequent flourishing of Afrocentric scholarship: "*The Negro* was a large building block in an Afrocentric historiography," which "achieved its credibility through the writings of scholars such as Basil Davidson, Martin Bernal, and Cheikh Anta Diop."[6] Lewis refers here to the kind of scholarship that highlighted African development and preceded the emergence of European hegemony,

5. Lewis, *W.E.B. Du Bois*, 462.

6. Lewis, *W.E.B. Du Bois*, 462. The works cited by Lewis include Basil Davidson, *Black Mother, Africa: The Years of Trial* (London: Victor Gollancz, 1961); Martin Bernal, *Black Athena: The Afroasiatic Roots of Classical Civilization*, 2 vols. (New Brunswick, N.J.: Rutgers University Press, 1987, 1991); Cheikh Anta Diop, *Civilization and Barbarism: An Authentic Anthropology* (New York: Lawrence Hill Books, 1991). Shepperson fleshes out this influence on Afrocentric scholarship in his intriguing discussion of the connections between Du Bois and Melville J. Herskovits. The latter seems to have gained his ideas in *The Myth of the Negro Past* (New York and London: Harper, 1941) from Du Bois's works other than *The Negro*, however, so the influence of this book on that scholarship is indirect. Du Bois's later works, which Herskovits used liberally, were all built around the ideas first fully developed in *The Negro*. See Shepperson, "Introduction," xix.

and which in many instances laid the foundation for European cultural and economic development. We need to be careful, however, not to misinterpret this connection with Afrocentric scholarship. Labeling the work Afrocentric may leave the impression that it uncritically enshrined a transhistorical category of race, or conformed to a perspective that Kwame Anthony Appiah has rejected as "Egyptianist" (attributing everything to African origins), when the impetus of the book was actually in the opposite direction.[7] George Shepperson in his introduction to *The Negro* adds that this work shows the development of Du Bois's attitudes toward Pan-Africanism at a time when many persons believe that he had lost interest in the idea, a significant biographical point.[8] It is fortuitous, therefore, that the University of Pennsylvania Press has reissued *The Negro*. It is time, once again, to take a closer look at this path-breaking study.

On the surface, *The Negro* does appear to conform to many of the suppositions of the period, and its radical core is not at first evident. *The*

7. Kwame Anthony Appiah, *In My Father's House: Africa in the Philosophy of Culture* (New York: Oxford University Press, 1992). The kind of work to which Appiah refers is found in, for example, Molefi Kete Asante, *Afrocentricity*, rev. ed. (Trenton, N.J.: Africa World Press, 1988).

8. Shepperson, "Introduction," xxii.

Negro was published at a turning point in African history, when change seemed to be dawning throughout Africa, so the work's influence was likely to be determined in large measure by Du Bois's ability to predict the direction those changes would take. By 1915 the Scramble for Africa had contributed both to the outbreak of a World War and to the emergence of an increasingly vocal opposition to European colonial regimes. Reforms following revelations about the barbarity of the colonial regime in the Congo seemed to suggest that widespread abhorrence to injustice and cruelty might lead to change, not just in Leopold's Congo but also in colonies where rulers did not want to be tainted by association with the atrocities inflicted on the Congolese peoples.[9] But, while Du Bois's text was shaped by considerable optimism about the future for Africa, and he seemed to be predicting that changes would occur throughout the continent (especially given that the colonial rulers had extended themselves too far in the World War and were becoming increasingly dependent on assistance from their colonial

9. As Adam Hochschild has made clear, such events also provide the backdrop to events in Mobutu's Zaire (to which we can add more recent events such as the corruption of Laurent-Désiré Kabila and his subsequent assassination); Hochschild, *King Leopold's Ghost: A Story of Greed, Terror, and Heroism in Colonial Africa* (New York: Houghton Mifflin, 1999), 302–4.

subjects)[10] his optimism was not yet of an anti-colonial nature. In short, he did not predict the rise of nationalist movements in this book.[11] And since Africa ultimately moved in the direction of nationalism rather than toward the overarching Pan-Africanism to which Du Bois gestured in *The Negro*, the work could appear superficially to be dated.

In addition, Du Bois's own sensibility, that of a scholar living in the United States who had not yet visited Africa (he would do so in 1923), and who conformed in many ways to ideas shared by those who labeled themselves Progressives, further contributed to the feeling that the work was not especially innovative.[12] Du Bois was convinced of the benefits of western civilization, and he wrote at a time when a widespread belief in progress still prevailed. While proclaiming the importance of remembering the "tragedy" alongside the "romance" of Africa (as in the opening

10. Du Bois made this argument on several occasions in the pages of *The Crisis*.

11. His writing would become more anticolonial later, as in *Black Folk: Then and Now*.

12. The assertion that the book was not innovative was made erroneously by Francis L. Broderick, *W.E.B. Du Bois, Negro Leader in a Time of Crisis* (Stanford, Calif.: Stanford University Press, 1959), 228; see Aptheker, "Introduction," 15.

lines of *The Negro*), he seemed to feel that the ongoing engagement between Europe and Africa would ultimately elevate Africa to a status alongside other civilizations.[13] For Du Bois, the horrors of globalization (the slave trade and imperialism) still scarred Africa, but some progress for "the Negro" had occurred nonetheless and a process of uplift was likely to follow. Readers for much of the latter part of the twentieth century may have found such optimism hard to swallow, as neocolonialism seamlessly replaced colonialism, apartheid became entrenched in South Africa, and the continent witnessed ongoing problems of famine, disease, and war.

Added to this, Du Bois retained an academic distance throughout *The Negro*, endeavoring to reinterpret the archive of materials already assembled on the subject to represent African history anew. Dealing with and emerging out of an academic and political culture that valued highly the notion of objectivity and believed in paying homage to the recognized authorities, he felt that

13. In this assessment, Du Bois's text resembles that of Henry Louis Gates, Jr.'s recent *Wonders of the African World* (New York: Knopf, 1999). Gates, echoing Du Bois, writes: "With the restoration of the particularity of Africa's grand past, perhaps a century hence other writers will note that the future, the next millennium, belongs to Africa and to the Africans," 256.

he needed to challenge mainstream beliefs using an archive that was already firmly in place.[14] Though Du Bois had previously shown (in *The Souls of Black Folk*) the value of speaking as a representative of a people, highlighting the problem of the color line through his own personal experience, in *The Negro* he eschewed any such approach (while clearly identifying emotionally with the project). Here he seemed to suggest that this study could have been written by anyone acquainted with the evidence and aspiring to objectivity—in other words, anyone not blinded by color prejudice.

But the text's seeming conformity and narrow sensibility should be a first impression only. Indeed, while *The Negro* was intended to lay the foundation for an *Encyclopedia Africana* (thereby extending to Africa a long-standing Enlightenment and Eurocentric tradition),[15] it was also

14. See, for example, Peter Novick, *That Noble Dream: The "Objectivity Question" and the American Historical Profession* (New York: Cambridge University Press, 1988).

15. Du Bois's work on the *Encyclopedia Africana* would span the period from his work on *The Negro* to his death on the eve of the March on Washington in 1963. See W.E.B. Du Bois and Guy B. Johnson, *Encyclopedia of the Negro* (preparatory volume) (New York: Phelps-Stokes Fund, 1945). Arguably, the enterprise was completed by Kwame Anthony Appiah and Henry Louis Gates, Jr. in *Africana: The Encyclopedia of the African and African American Experience* (New York: Basic Civitas Books, 1999).

very much an opening salvo against the American academy for its neglect of Africa and African Americans, one that would be followed by other assaults on the ivory tower.[16] For, while Du Bois reached the pinnacle of academic achievement, he would mostly work outside the academy. He would hold only a temporary position at the University of Pennsylvania, when he was hired to undertake the research that would result in the publication of *The Philadelphia Negro*. He would be offered a long-term one only at Atlanta University, which enabled him to produce the widely respected Atlanta University sociological studies between 1897 and 1912. But none of the major American universities would offer Du Bois a position commensurate with his Harvard Ph.D. and graduate training in Berlin.[17] He remained an outsider, forced to launch his assault on the academy from his position as editor of the NAACP journal, *The Crisis*. Thus *The Negro* can be seen as a foundation stone for later works on both Africa and the United States, works that would lead him

16. At the time that he was publishing *The Negro* he was also in the process of writing "The African Roots of the War" at *Atlantic Monthly*, which as its title suggests attributed the causes of World War I to European imperialism; Lewis, *W.E.B. Du Bois*, 504. Although Lewis does not address this, *The Negro* must be read in the larger context of DuBois's response to this war.

17. Lewis, *W.E.B. Du Bois*, 145.

down the road toward a Marxian analysis of what he called the "propaganda of history," and that would culminate in his own exile to Ghana at the end of his life.[18]

Moreover, Du Bois's distanced location and manner led him to an expansive perspective of Africa, seen through diasporas, trade, and imperialism. Paradoxically, therefore, the American reader of *The Negro* could not remain as removed from the topic as the work's author seemed to be. Du Bois pulled his reader into the vortex of world history that is Africa writ large. Today our inclination might be to shrink Africa down to a place that "we" can appreciate more fully so that it may be better integrated into "our" global economy. But Du Bois would have us remember that this new economy is an extension of slavery and the slave trade (and the earlier Africa-centered global economy that preceded it). While we may feel obliged to remember the human tragedies or holocausts lest we become overly absorbed in the scramble once again for African commodities, Du Bois wanted his readers to go further than

18. "The Propaganda of History" was the concluding chapter of *Black Reconstruction in America*, 713–26; see Gregg, "Giant Steps," 80.

this. He was less concerned with memory than with interpretation. While we may now fear that history may be *forgotten*, Du Bois's hope was that this history might yet be *understood*.

Arising out of this particular sensibility, then, we see Du Bois in *The Negro* attempt to fashion a vision of an alternative world out of his study of Africa.[19] In *The Negro* Du Bois combines the romanticism that had been evident in *The Souls of Black Folk* with a rejuvenated faith in science gained from his attendance at the Universal Races Congress held in London in 1911. He had suggested in *Souls* that Africans had something to bring to the conversation of cultures—alongside Shakespeare there would be the Sorrow Song. Added to this, Du Bois derived a great deal of optimism from reading the work of the very people that he cited liberally throughout *The Negro*, attendees at the Congress like Franz Boas and Gustav Spiller, along with Friedrich Ratzel, who had died a few years earlier.[20] Although Du Bois's

19. Shepperson refers to theologian, historian, and activist Vincent Harding's reading of *The Negro*, which highlighted the book's messianic quality; "Introduction," xxi.

20. See the collected papers of the Congress in Gustav Spiller, *Papers on Inter-Racial Problems, Communicated to the first Universal Races Congress* (London: P.S. King and Son, 1911); also Friedrich Ratzel, *The History of Mankind* (London: Macmillan, 1896–98).

feelings toward the scientific method found in sociology had soured considerably, his feelings about history and anthropology, both of which would be the pillars of his work on the encyclopedia, remained positive. And with the fact that the civilization of Shakespeare and Goethe had now erupted in a "European civil war," he could hope that the special "gift of black folk" might receive a fairer hearing. It is in this context that Du Bois's comments that "in disposition the Negro is among the most lovable of men" and that there could be "no doubt of the Negro's deep and delicate sense of beauty in form, color, and sound" need to be read. As the war among Europeans was hardening into a bloodbath in Flanders, Du Bois's "casual declarations" of this sort may have seemed self-evident.

Hence, for Du Bois, the world might be redeemed in a different world order, as he proclaimed in *The Negro*'s final passage, which ends with, "Semper novi quid ex Africa." This Latin phrase (literally "Always something new from Africa") is in direct contrast to the contemporary beliefs that Africa was a stagnating dark continent; it is Africa, the land of migration and newness, that provides Du Bois with his beacon of light for the future. Such a hope for "unity among colored peoples" would animate his endeavors at the Pan-African Conference in Paris in 1919 and was very much evident in his later writings, such as *Dark Princess* and *Black Reconstruction in America*.[21]

One of the most radical aspects of *The Negro* derived from Du Bois's attempt to shift the focus of African history away from empires and geographical landmarks to (as the work's title suggests) those who peopled the continent. Earlier accounts of Africa had tended to be static, converting places of struggle and sites of contestation, into exotic wonders and cultural artifacts, "semper antiqui quid."[22] Getting from such a past to the present, reigniting the sense of relevance of this history for the American (as Du Bois hoped to do), was made more difficult by this approach.

Where such works were sympathetic to Africans, they tended to reduce the history of

21. Du Bois, *Dark Princess, a Romance* (Millwood, N.Y.: Kraus-Thomson, 1974 [1928]). He wrote in *Black Reconstruction*, for example: "in Africa, a black back runs red with the blood of the lash; in India, a brown girl is raped; in China, a coolie starves; in Alabama, seven darkies are more than lynched; while in London, the white limbs of a prostitute are hung with jewels and silk. Flames of jealous murder sweep the earth, while brains of little children smear the hills," 728.

22. Here, Mary Louise Pratt's discussion of travel writing tending to erase people from the landscape is relevant; *Imperial Eyes: Travel Writing and Transculturation* (New York: Routledge, 1992), 51–52, 59–60.

Africa either to the significance of the Middle Passage or to a celebration of the glorious civilizations of the past. In either case, the process of silencing (as Michel-Rolph Trouillot would describe it) large chunks of African history went uncontested.[23] The standard European historical trope about Africa, that it was merely the victim of world historical forces animated by Europe, continually "provincialized" the continent.[24] In addition, the very absence of these "lost" civilizations severely tested their power to pass muster against more recent ones.[25]

In contrast to such accounts, *The Negro* resembles the kind of work written later in the twentieth century by social historians. Du Bois cast his gaze firmly on people in Africa and its diaspora. He certainly noted all the empires that waxed and waned, but he was most interested in the

23. Michel-Rolph Trouillot, *Silencing the Past: Power and the Production of History* (Boston: Beacon Press, 1995).

24. Dipesh Chakrabarty uses the term provincializing to interrogate the lens through which South Asian history has been observed. Chakrabarty, *Provincializing Europe: Postcolonial Thought and Historical Difference* (Princeton, N.J.: Princeton University Press, 1999).

25. In our own day, we have seen the Soviet empire disappear, so we might understand with Gibbon that empires rise and fall. But for many Americans the collapse of that other empire only seems to have validated their own.

people as they moved around the continent, migrants all.[26] Indeed, though commentators have generally overlooked this, migration is of prime importance to this volume, defining the different peoples in all the various sections of Africa. We learn of the wandering herdsmen on the Senegal River in early times who then "changed to a Negro or dark mulatto people and lived scattered in small communities between the Atlantic and Darfur." We find out that in coastal West Africa "Movement and migration is evident along this coast in ancient and modern times." Also we learn that "the first clearly defined movement of modern times," the migration of the Bantu from central to southern Africa, began "at least a thousand years before Christ." And it is not just people who move. Trade routes circulate ideas, customs, and commodities around the continent and beyond its boundaries. It is this focus on migration (a major preoccupation of recent ethnic studies programs) that gives Du Bois's book its current feel, and which also enables it to speak to so many areas of historical scholarship about Africa and the world that have developed

26. Du Bois's interest in migration echoed some of the participants at the Universal Races Congress. See, for example, Felix von Luschan, "Anthropological View of Race," in Spiller, *Inter-Racial Problems*, 21.

since. The current rage to internationalize American history, for example, clearly has long roots, and one could hardly do better than take *The Negro* as a guide for such an enterprise.[27]

This migration perspective has important implications. First, it helps explain Du Bois's belief that "the character of the Negro race is the best and greatest hope" and his sense that the race has an important role to play in the emergence of a world order based on humanitarian principles. Africa has been connected to such transformations in the past, in the shaping of Egyptian and Greek civilizations, as a font of world religions, and providing the labor that would make possible the emergence of industrial capitalism. Its people had spread across the globe, and in all sections of it still felt the sting arising from racial prejudice, the kind of alienation that Marx saw as the basis of a revolutionary consciousness.[28]

Second, notions of race to which Du Bois had

27. See the 1999 special issues of the *Journal of American History* devoted to "Internationalizing American History."

28. A close parallel to Du Bois's "Negro" as migrant is Randolph S. Bourne's notion of a "Trans-National America"; see *War and the Intellectuals: Collected Essays, 1915–1919* (New York: Harper and Row, 1964). Also writing during World War I, Bourne saw the possibility for a humanitarian and peaceful society lying in the fulfillment of the United States as a multi-cultural and multi-ethnic society.

subscribed earlier in his career were clearly brought into question by his discussion of migration. If people are migrating they are also becoming "amalgamated," and we have to question a classificatory system that defines them as if they were immobile. In his earlier writings on race, like "The Conservation of Races," Du Bois had tended to romanticize the category of race.[29] According to Appiah, Du Bois attempted to assail racism by developing an alternative category of race in which racial characteristics were seen not as being related to biological or intrinsic moral differences but as socio-historical in nature—in other words, they were socially constructed. Yet, having taken form they developed histories and cultures and these gave races meaning. Thus, Du Bois had written, "the history of the world is the history, not of individuals, but of groups, not of nations, but of races."[30] In this history, according to Appiah "races have a 'message' for humanity," and each one differed. One was not better than another it was merely different. In short, Du Bois had

29. Du Bois, "The Conservation of Races," *American Negro Academy Occasional Papers* 2 (1897).

30. Appiah, *In My Father's House*, 28. See Robert Gregg, *Inside Out, Outside In: Essays in Comparative History* (London: Macmillan, 2000), 88–95.

wanted to take a concept of race that was constructed along a vertical, hierarchical axis (one
race is better than another) and give it a horizon-
tal reading.[31]

In *The Negro*, however, Du Bois seemed to rely
more heavily on the idea of race as a social construction, and, through his attention to migration, he came pretty close to throwing out a racial
classification system altogether. For example, he
quotes Friedrich Ratzel: "There is only one
species of man. The variations are numerous, but
do not go deep." He then goes on to explain:

> All this does not mean that the African Negro is
> not human with the all too well-known foibles
> of humanity. Primitive life among them is,
> after all, as bare and cruel as among primitive
> Germans or Chinese, but it is not more so, and
> the more we study the Negro the more we real-
> ize that we are dealing with a normal human
> stock that under reasonable conditions has
> developed and will develop in the same lines as
> other men.

31. So, Appiah notes, while the attempt to highlight certain "race abilities" might lead to a more equitable estimation
of the different contributions of the races, "it might just as
easily" he says, "lead to chauvinism or total incomprehen-
sion"; *In My Father's House*, 94.

Such cultural relativism obviously reflects the views then gaining currency in the work of Spiller and Boas, among others. But it also is not far removed from Appiah's own view that race cannot stand up to philosophical scrutiny, and that of a scholar like Paul Gilroy, who founds hopes for a new humanism, global and cosmopolitan, on the renunciation of race.[32]

But Du Bois's analysis takes a different turn in the ensuing passages. He asks why it is, if the African Negro shares this common humanity with others, that "misinformation and contempt is widespread concerning Africa and its people." One reason for this, he says, lies in the connotation of the term "Negro" and its changing definition in different contexts. There is the North American definition, with which Du Bois is all too familiar, that "a Negro may be seven-eighths white, since the term refers to any person of Negro descent." While this has led to widespread discrimination, it has, according to Du Bois, at least allowed for "the Negroes" to be recognized for being "among the leaders of civilization in every age of the world's history." "In

32. Appiah, *In My Father's House*, 45; Paul Gilroy, *Against Race: Imagining Political Culture Beyond the Color Line* (Cambridge, Mass: Belknap Press of Harvard University Press, 2000).

sharp contrast to this usage," Du Bois continues, "the term 'Negro' in Africa has been more and more restricted until some scientists, late in the last century, declared that the great mass of the black and brown people of Africa were not Negroes at all, and that the 'real' Negro dwells in a small space between the Niger and Senegal." In this way the achievements of people who in America would be classified "Negro" are attributed to other people. And then Du Bois comments wryly, in a fashion that might bring a gleam into the eye of the contemporary cultural critic: "In this restricted sense the Negro has no history, culture or ability, for the simple fact that such human beings as have history and evidence culture and ability are not Negroes!"

Many things can be said about this comment beyond the simplistic and erroneous reading that frequently accompanies it—that Du Bois here conforms to a belief that Africans contribute nothing unless they have received some infusion from without. Bearing in mind all the migration Du Bois describes in this volume, we can assume that he believes the American definition is the one that ought to be used for Africa. In the process African Americans are tied more closely to their African heritage, not because they can be traced through direct lineage to a particular people or area in Africa, but because they, like Africans, are products of different peoples coming together through historical processes. The narrow definition is inappropriate, not just because scholars motivated by prejudice have deployed it, but also because it is simply ahistorical. As such, there is an air of the "subaltern" to Du Bois's Negro: The category of Negro becomes quite unstable (in both positive and negative ways), taking on a dual function of representing both the contributor to great civilizations and one who has no history.[33] And here Du Bois realized once again the need for political activism to accompany his work as scholar. For it is not enough to highlight the contributions that a people have made to history, when those can be denied or silenced merely by altering the system of classification.[34]

With the category of race problematized and Africa, the continent of migration, established as the font of newness (and so also modernity),

---

33. Gyan Prakash, "Subaltern Studies as Postcolonial Criticism," *American Historical Review* (December 1994): 1475–90; see also Homi K. Bhabha, *The Location of Culture* (London: Routledge, 1994), 254–56.

34. It is not clear, however, to what degree Du Bois here appreciated that some of his own concepts, like "the talented tenth," might have contributed in the past to the process of excluding those who did not fit within his system, thereby attributing to them the narrow definition of "Negro," or people without history. See Trouillot, *Silencing the Past*.

Du Bois was in a position to develop other theories that either would be picked up and developed by later scholars or would lie dormant waiting to be unearthed and seen anew.[35] Take, for example, Du Bois's comment that in order to locate the origin of modern color prejudice it is necessary to look not to "physical or cultural causes, but to historic facts," which are "modern Negro slavery and the slave trade." Such a comment presaged Eric Williams's profound contribution to slavery scholarship in *Capitalism and Slavery*, as well as that of Edmund Morgan in *American Slavery, American Freedom*.[36] Echoes of *The Negro* are found elsewhere in historical writing. Du Bois's view of slavery, described in his chapter entitled "The American Negro," prefigured both the paternalist perspective of Eugene Genovese and, paradoxically, the materialist view that the system was part of the capitalist mode of produc-

35. Aptheker, "Introduction," 17, highlights a number of Du Bois's theories relating to American slavery that he himself would develop, along with those of Eric Williams, in *Capitalism and Slavery* (London: Andre Deutsch, 1964 [1944]). Shepperson's introduction is more expansive in this regard.

36. Williams, *Capitalism and Slavery*; Edmund S. Morgan, *American Slavery, American Freedom: The Ordeal of Colonial Virginia* (New York: Norton, 1975).

tion.[37] His discussion of Reconstruction preempted much later historiography, including his own *Black Reconstruction in America*, while his identification of segregation as an issue of class rather than race was almost forty years ahead of C. Vann Woodward's similar thesis.[38] However, historians have been reluctant to accept his outline of black contributions to the Civil War and to the process of emancipation.

But perhaps still most noteworthy is the underdevelopment thesis, later associated with Walter Rodney.[39] Du Bois sees the intervention of the

37. A long historiographical debate over whether slavery was capitalist has continued. Some examples of the debate can be found in Eugene Genovese, *The Political Economy of Slavery: Studies in the Economy & Society of the Slave South* (New York: Vintage, 1967); Robert William Fogel and Stanley L. Engerman, *Time on the Cross* (Boston: Little, Brown, 1974); and Gavin Wright, *The Political Economy of the Cotton South: Households, Markets, and Wealth in the Nineteenth Century* (New York: Norton, 1978). See also Drew Gilpin Faust, *James Henry Hammond and the Old South: A Design for Mastery* (Baton Rouge: Louisiana State University Press, 1982).

38. C. Vann Woodward, *Origins of the New South, 1817–1913* (Baton Rouge: Louisiana State University Press, 1951) and *The Strange Career of Jim Crow* (New York: Oxford University Press 1955).

39. Walter Rodney, *How Europe Underdeveloped Africa* (Washington, D.C.: Howard University Press, 1974).

slave trade completely undermining the continent
of Africa's ability to generate its own newness. As
such, Du Bois describes a continent that is moving from developed to underdeveloped, not vice
versa. "It was the slave trade," he writes, "that
turned the balance and set these lands back-
wards. . . . And, from the middle of the fifteenth
century until it was terminated in the last half of
the nineteenth, the American slave trade centered
in Guinea and devastated the coast morally,
socially, and physically." While it would be rash
not to attribute this idea directly to Du Bois's
own contemplation, it is interesting to speculate
whether he was influenced in this direction by his
interaction with scholars of India and the British
Empire at the Universal Races Congress, who
were very much conversant in the ideas associated
with drain theory, the idea that the coming of the
British Empire, and especially the growth of the
Manchester cotton industry (built on the products of African slave labor), had led to the dein-
dustrialization of the Indian subcontinent.[40]

The Negro, then, is compelling on so many levels—as history, anthropology, social commentary,

40. See Gokhale's address at the Congress, which while not
directly mentioning the drain theory is influenced by it; "East
and West in India," in Spiller, *Inter-Racial Problems*, 157–67.

as elegy on the condition of migrancy. But maybe it is Du Bois's appreciation of the process of globalization that will make people look again at this text and see it as if for the first time. Intellectually and historically prescient, Du Bois assumed globalization as a matter of course, so that his definition of the color line in *The Negro* linked all colonized peoples, not just people of African descent. The Pan-African movement, DuBois wrote, would "not be merely a narrow racial propaganda." With the resolution of the Cold War and the ascendancy of the global market, bringing new and old color lines into sharp relief, Du Bois's sweeping vision of Africans and the diaspora seems more relevant now than at any time in the past hundred years.

And perhaps, too, we can once again appreciate Du Bois's sense of optimism. Although one aspect of recent transformations in Africa has been the political instability arising from changing regimes, it has also been a time of possibility and opportunity all across Africa, beginning with Nelson Mandela's triumph in South Africa, through the recent attempts to end corruption in countries like Nigeria, and continuing in efforts by the Organization of African Unity to persuade African states to ratify the constitutive act of the African Union (a rebirth, perhaps, of Du Bois's Pan-Africanism). Such possibilities are accompanied also by the political and moral imperatives to engage with African nations to combat the scourge of AIDS and to ensure that the kinds of horrors witnessed in Somalia and Rwanda, which often have their roots in poverty, do not occur again. For Du Bois's discovery in *The Negro* was that Africa lay at the heart of the world. So, more even than remembering the litany of horrors inflicted by Europeans upon Africans, we need to learn from Du Bois that when change occurs for Africa and its peoples everyone feels the reverberations. "Semper novi quid ex Africa!"

SUGGESTIONS FOR FURTHER READING

THERE is no general history of the Negro race. Perhaps Sir Harry H. Johnston, in his various works on Africa, has come as near covering the subject as any one writer, but his valuable books have puzzling inconsistencies and inaccuracies. Keane's *Africa* is a helpful compendium, despite the fact that whenever Keane discovers intelligence in an African he immediately discovers that its possessor is no "Negro." The articles in the latest edition of the *Encylopædia Britannica* are of some value, except the ridiculous article on the "Negro" by T. A. Joyce. Frobenius' newly published *Voice of Africa* is broad-minded and informing, and Brown's *Story of Africa and its Explorers* brings together much material in readable form. The compendiums by Keltie and White, and Johnston's *Opening up of Africa* are the best among the shorter treatises.

None of these authors write from the point of view of the Negro as a man, or with anything but incidental acknowledgment of the existence or value of his history. We may, however, set down certain books under the various subjects which the chapters have treated. These books will consist of (1) standard works for wider reading and (2) special works on which the author has relied for his statements or which amplify his point of view. *The latter are starred.*

THE PHYSIOGRAPHY OF AFRICA

A. S. WHITE: *The Development of Africa*, 2d ed., 1892.
STANFORD'S COMPENDIUM OF GEOGRAPHY: *Africa*, by A. H. KEANE, 2d ed., 1904-7.
E. RECLUS: *Universal Geography*, Vols. X-XIII.

RACIAL DIFFERENCES AND THE ORIGIN AND CHARACTERISTICS
OF NEGROES

J. Deniker: *The Races of Man*, etc., New York, 1904.

*J. Finot: *Race Prejudice* (tr. by Wade-Evans), New York, 1907.

*W. Z. Ripley: *The Races of Europe*, etc., New York, 1899.

*Jacques Loeb: in *The Crisis*, Vol. VIII, p. 84, Vol. IX, p. 92.

Papers on Inter-Racial Problems Communicated to the First Universal Races Congress, etc. (ed. by G. Spiller), 1911.

*G. Sergi: *The Mediterranean Race*, etc., London, 1901.

*Franz Boas: *The Mind of Primitive Man*, New York, 1911.

C. B. Davenport: *Heredity of Skin Color in Negro-White Crosses*, 1913.

EARLY MOVEMENTS OF THE NEGRO RACE

*Sir Harry H. Johnston: *The Opening up of Africa* (Home University Library).

—— *A History of the Colonization of Africa by Alien Races*, Cambridge, 1905.

*G. W. Stowe: *The Native Races of South Africa* (ed. by G. M. Theal), London, 1910.

(Consult also Johnston's other works on Africa, and his article in Vol. XLIII of the *Journal of the Royal Anthropological Institute of Great Britain and Ireland*; also *Inter-Racial Problems*, and Deniker, noted above.)

NEGRO IN ETHIOPIA AND EGYPT

(The works of Breasted and Petrie, Maspero, Budge and Newberry and Garstang are the standard books on Egypt. They mention the Negro, but incidentally and often slightingly.)

*A. F. Chamberlain: "The Contribution of the Negro to Human Civilization" (*Journal of Race Development*, Vol. I, April, 1911).

T. E. S. Scholes: *Glimpses of the Ages*, etc., London, 1905.
W. H. Ferris: *The African Abroad*, etc., 2 vols., New Haven, 1913.
E. A. W. Budge: *The Egyptian Sudan*, 2 vols., 1907.
Archeological Survey of Nubia.
*A. Thompson and D. Randal McIver: *The Ancient Races of the Thebaid*, 1905.

ABYSSINIA

Job Ludolphus: *A New History of Ethiopia* (tr. by Gent), London, 1682.
W. S. Harris: *Highlands of Æthiopia*, 3 vols., London, 1844.
R. S. Whiteway: *The Portuguese Expedition to Abyssinia . . . as narrated by Castanhosa*, etc., 1902.

THE NIGER RIVER AND ISLAM

*F. L. Shaw (Lady Lugard): *A Tropical Dependency*, etc., London, 1906.
(The reader may dismiss as worthless Lady Lugard's definition of "Negro." Otherwise her book is excellent.)
*Es-Sa'di, Abderrahman Ben Abdallah, etc., translated into French by O. Houdas, Paris, 1900.
*F. DuBois: *Timbuktu the Mysterious* (tr. by White), 1896.
*W. D. Cooley: *The Negroland of the Arabs*, etc., 1841.
*H. Barth: *Travels and Discoveries in North and Central Africa*, etc., 5 vols., 1857–58.
*Ibn Batuta: *Travels*, etc. (tr. by Lee), 1829.
*Leo Africanus: *The History and Description of Africa*, etc. (tr. by Pory, ed. by R. Brown), 3 vols., 1896.
*E. W. Blyden: *Christianity, Islam, and the Negro Race*.
*Leo Frobenius: *The Voice of Africa* (tr. by Blind), 2 vols., 1913.
Mungo Park: *Travels in the Interior Districts of Africa*, 1799.

THE NEGRO ON THE GUINEA COAST

*Leo Frobenius (as above).
Sir Harry H. Johnston: *Liberia*, 2 vols., New York, 1906.
H. H. Foote: *Africa and the American Flag*, New York, 1859.

T. H. T. McPHERSON: *A History of Liberia*, Baltimore, Johns Hopkins Studies.

T. J. ALLDRIDGE: *A Transformed Colony* (Sierra Leone), London, 1910.

E. D. MOREL: *Affairs of West Africa*, 1902.

H. L. ROTH: *Great Benin and Its Customs*, 1903.

*F. STARR: *Liberia*, 1913.

W. JAY: *An Inquiry*, etc., 1835.

*A. B. ELLIS: *The Tshi-speaking Peoples of the Gold Coast*, 1887.

—— *The Ewe-speaking Peoples of the Slave Coast*, 1890.

—— *The Yoruba-speaking Peoples of the Slave Coast*, 1894.

C. H. READ and O. M. DALTON: *Antiquities from the City of Benin*, etc., 1899.

*M. H. KINGSLEY: *West African Studies*, 2d ed., 1904.

*G. W. ELLIS: *Negro Culture in West Africa* (Vai-speaking peoples), 1914.

THE CONGO VALLEY

*G. SCHWEINFURTH: *The Heart of Africa*, Vol. II, 1873.

*H. M. STANLEY: *Through the Dark Continent*, 2 vols., 1878.

—— *In Darkest Africa*, 2 vols., 1890.

—— *The Congo*, etc., 2 vols., London, 1885.

H. VON WISSMAN: *My Second Journey through Equatorial Africa*, 1891.

*H. R. FOX-BOURNE: *Civilization in Congoland*, 1903.

SIR HARRY H. JOHNSTON: *George Grenfell and the Congo*, 2 vols., London, 1908.

*E. D. MOREL: *Red Rubber*, London, 1906.

THE NEGRO IN THE REGION OF THE GREAT LAKES

*SIR HARRY H. JOHNSTON: *The Uganda Protectorate*, 2d ed., 2 vols., 1904.

—— *British Central Africa*, 1897.

—— *The Nile Quest*, 1903.

*D. RANDAL McIVER: *Mediæval Rhodesia*, 1906.

The Last Journals of David Livingstone in Central Africa (ed. by H. Waller), 1874.

J. Dos Santos: *Ethiopia Oriental* (Theal's *Records of South Africa*, Vol. VII).
C. Peters: "Ophir and Punt in South Africa" (*African Society Journal*, Vol. I).
De Barros: *De Asia.*
R. Burton: *Lake Regions of Central Africa*, 1860.
R. P. Ashe: *Chronicles of Uganda*, 1894.
  (See also Stanley's works, as above.)

THE NEGRO IN SOUTH AFRICA

*G. M. Theal: *History and Ethnography of South Africa of the Zambesi to 1795*, 3 vols., 1907–10.
—— *History of South Africa since September, 1795*, 5 vols., 1908.
—— *Records of South Eastern Africa*, 9 vols., 1898–1903.
*J. Bryce: *Impressions of South Africa*, 1897.
D. Livingstone: *Missionary Travels in South Africa*, 1857.
*South African Native Affairs Commission, 1903–5, *Reports*, etc., 5 vols., Cape Town, 1904–5.
G. Lagden: *The Basutos*, London, 1909.
J. Stewart: *Lovedale*, 1884.
  (See also Stowe, as above.)

ON NEGRO CIVILIZATION

J. Dowd: *The Negro Races*, 1907, 1914.
*H. Gregoire: *An Inquiry concerning the Intellectual and Moral Faculties and Literature of Negroes*, etc. (tr. by Warden), Brooklyn, 1810.
C. Bücher: *Industrial Evolution* (tr. by Wickett), New York, 1904.
*Franz Boas: "The Real Race Problem" (*The Crisis*, December, 1910).
—— *Commencement Address* (Atlanta University Leaflet, No. 19).
*F. Ratzel: *The History of Mankind* (tr. by Butler), 3 vols., 1904.
C. Hayford: *Gold Coast Institutions*, 1903.
A. B. Camphor: *Missionary Sketches and Folk Lore from Africa*, 1909.
R. H. Nassau: *Fetishism in West Africa*, 1907.

*WILLIAM SCHNEIDER: *Die Culturfähigkeit des Negers*, Frankfort, 1885.

*G. SCHWEINFURTH: *Artes Africanae*, etc., 1875.

DUKE OF MECKLENBURG: *From the Congo to the Niger and the Nile* (English tr.), Philadelphia, 1914.

D. CRAWFORD: *Thinking Black.*

R. N. CUST: *Sketch of Modern Languages of Africa*, 2 vols., 1883.

H. CHATELAIN: *The Folk Lore of Angola.*

D. KIDD: *The Essential Kaffir*, 1904.

—— *Savage Childhood*, 1906.

—— *Kaffir Socialism and the Dawn of Individualism*, 1908.

M. H. TONGUE: *Bushman Paintings*, Oxford, 1909.

   (See also the works of A. B. Ellis, Miss Kingsley, Sir Harry H. Johnston, Frobenius, Stowe, Theal, and Ibn Batuta; and particularly Chamberlain's article in the *Journal of Race Development*.)

THE SLAVE TRADE

T. K. INGRAM: *History of Slavery and Serfdom*, London, 1895. (Same article revised in *Encyclopædia Britannica*, 11th edition.)

JOHN R. SPEARS: *The American Slave Trade*, 1900.

*T. F. BUXTON: *The African Slave Trade and Its Remedy*, etc., 1896.

T. CLARKSON: *History . . . of the Abolition of the African Slave Trade*, etc., 2 vols., 1808.

R. DRAKE: *Revelations of a Slave Smuggler*, New York, 1860.

Report of the Lords of the Committee of Council, etc., London, 1789.

*B. MAYER: *Captain Canot or Twenty Years of an African Slaver*, etc., 1854.

W. E. B. DUBOIS: *The suppression of the African Slave-Trade to the U. S. A.*, 1896.

   (See also Bryan Edwards' *West Indies*.)

THE WEST INDIES AND SOUTH AMERICA

FLETCHER and KIDDER: *Brazil and the Brazilians*, 1879.

*BRYAN EDWARDS: *History . . . of the British West Indies*, 5 editions, Vols. II–V, 1793–1819.

*SIR HARRY H. JOHNSTON: *The Negro in the New World*, 1910.
T. G. STEWARD: *The Haitian Revolution, 1791–1804*, 1914.
J. N. LEGER: *Haiti*, etc., 1907.
J. BRYCE: *South America*, etc., 1912.
*J. B. DE LACERDA: "The Metis or Half-Breeds of Brazil" (*Inter-Racial Problems*, etc.).
A. K. FISKE: *History of the West Indies*, 1899.

THE NEGRO IN THE UNITED STATES

Walker's Appeal, 1829.
*G. W. WILLIAMS: *History of the Negro Race in America, 1619–1880*, 1882.
B. G. BRAWLEY: *A Short History of the American Negro*, 1913.
B. T. WASHINGTON: *Up from Slavery*, 1901.
—— *The Story of the Negro*, 2 vols., 1909.
The Autobiography of an Ex-Colored Man, 1912.
*G. E. STROUD: *Sketch of the Laws relating to Slavery*, etc., 1827.
The Human Way: Addresses on Race Problems at the Southern Sociological Congress, Atlanta, 1913 (ed. by J. E. McCulloch).
W. J. SIMMONS: *Men of Mark*, 1887.
*J. R. GIDDINGS: *The Exiles of Florida*, 1858.
W. E. NELL: *The Colored Patriots of the American Revolution*, etc., 1855.
C. W. CHESNUTT: *The Marrow of Tradition*, 1901.
P. L. DUNBAR: *Lyrics of Lowly Life*, 1896.
Life and Times of Frederick Douglass, revised edition, 1892.
*H. E. KREIHBEL: *Afro-American Folk Songs*, etc., 1914.
T. P. FENNER and others: *Cabin and Plantation Songs*, 3d ed., 1901.
W. F. ALLEN and others: *Slave Songs of the United States*, 1867.
W. E. B. DuBois: "The Negro Race in the United States of America" (*Inter-Racial Problems*, etc.).
—— "The Economics of Negro Emancipation" (*Sociological Review*, October, 1911).
—— *John Brown*.
—— *The Philadelphia Negro*, 1899.

W. E. B. DuBois: "Reconstruction and its Benefits" (*American Historical Review*, Vol. XV, No. 4).

—— editor, *The Crisis: A Record of the Darker Races*, monthly, 1910.

—— editor, *The Atlanta University Studies:*

No. 1. *Mortality Among Negroes in Cities*, 1896.

No. 2. *Social and Physical Conditions of Negroes in Cities*, 1897.

No. 3. *Some Efforts of Negroes for Social Betterment*, 1898.

No. 4. *The Negro in Business*, 1899.

No. 5. *The College Bred Negro*, 1900.

No. 6. *The Negro Common School*, 1901.

No. 7. *The Negro Artisan*, 1902.

No. 8. *The Negro Church*, 1903.

No. 9. *Notes on Negro Crime*, 1904.

No. 10. *A Select Bibliography of the Negro American*, 1905.

No. 11. *Health and Physique of the Negro American*, 1906.

No. 12. *Economic Co-operation among Negro Americans*, 1907.

No. 13. *The Negro American Family*, 1908.

No. 14. *Efforts for Social Betterment among Negro Americans*, 1909.

No. 15. *The College Bred Negro American*, 1910.

No. 16. *The Common School and the Negro American*, 1911.

No. 17. *The Negro American Artisan*, 1912.

No. 18. *Morals and Manners among Negro Americans*, 1913.

*G. W. Cable: *The Silent South*, etc., 1885.

*J. R. Lynch: *The Facts of Reconstruction*, 1913.

*J. T. Wilson: *The Black Phalanx*, 1897.

William Goodell: *Slavery and Anti-Slavery*, 1852.

G. S. Merriam: *The Negro and the Nation*, 1906.

A. B. Hart: *The Southern South*, 1910.

*G. Livermore: *An Historical Research respecting the Opinions of the Founders of the Republic on Negroes*, etc., 1862.

HARTSHORN and PENNIMAN: *An Era of Progress and Promise*, 1910 (profusely illustrated).

*JAMES BREWSTER: *Sketches of Southern Mystery, Treason, and Murder*.

WILLCOX and DuBOIS: *Negroes in the United States* (United States Census of 1900, Bulletin No. 8).

THE FUTURE OF THE NEGRO RACE

*J. S. KELTIE: *The Partition of Africa*, 2d ed., 1895.

B. T. WASHINGTON: *The Future of the Negro*.

W. E. B. DuBOIS: "The Future of the Negro Race in America" (*East and West*, Vol. II, No. 5).

—— *Souls of Black Folk*, 1913.

—— *Quest of the Silver Fleece*.

ALEXANDER CRUMMELL: *The Future of Africa*, 2d ed., 1862.

*CASELY HAYFORD: *Ethiopia Unbound*, 1911.

KELLY MILLER: *Out of the House of Bondage*, 1914.

—— *Race Adjustment*, 1908.

* J. ROYCE: *Race Questions*, etc., 1908.

*R. S. BAKER: *Following the Color Line*, 1908.

N. S. SHALER: *The Neighbor*.

E. D. MOREL: "Free Labor in Tropical Africa" (*Nineteenth Century and After*, 1914).

(See also FINOT, BOAS, *Inter-Racial Problems*, and WHITE'S *Development of Africa*.)

INDEX

12/11/01

races of mankind a transition stage from beast to man." [1]

Much has been made of the supposed smaller brain of the Negro race; but this is as yet an unproved assumption, based on the uncritical measurement of less than a thousand Negro brains as compared with eleven thousand or more European brains. Even if future measurement prove the average Negro brain lighter, the vast majority of Negro brain weights fall within the same limits as the whites; and finally, "neither size nor weight of the brain seems to be of importance" as an index of mental capacity. We may, therefore, say with Ratzel, "There is only one species of man. The variations are numerous, but do not go deep." [2]

To this we may add the word of the Secretary of the First Races Congress: "We are, then, under the necessity of concluding that an impartial investigator would be inclined to look upon the various important peoples of the world as to all intents and purposes essentially equal in intellect, enterprise, morality, and physique." [3]

If these conclusions are true, we should expect to see in Africa the human drama play itself out much as in other lands, and such has actually been the fact. At the same time we must expect peculiarities arising from the physiography of

---

[1] G. Finot: *Race Prejudice.* F. Herz: *Moderne Rassentheorien.*

[2] Ratzel: quoted in Spiller: *Inter-Racial Problems,* p. 31.

[3] Spiller: *Inter-Racial Problems,* p. 35.

the land — its climate, its rainfall, its deserts, and the peculiar inaccessibility of the coast.

Three principal zones of habitation appear: first, the steppes and deserts around the Sahara in the north and the Kalahari desert in the south; secondly, the grassy highlands bordering the Great Lakes and connecting these two regions; thirdly, the forests and rivers of Central and West Africa. In the deserts are the nomads, and the Pygmies are in the forest fastnesses. Herdsmen and their cattle cover the steppes and highlands, save where the tsetse fly prevents. In the open forests and grassy highlands are the agriculturists.

Among the forest farmers the village is the center of life, while in the open steppes political life tends to spread into larger political units. Political integration is, however, hindered by an ease of internal communication almost as great as the difficulty of reaching outer worlds beyond the continent. The narrow Nile valley alone presented physical barriers formidable enough to keep back the invading barbarians of the south, and even then with difficulty. Elsewhere communication was all too easy. For a while the Congo forests fended away the restless, but this only temporarily.

On the whole Africa from the Sahara to the Cape offered no great physical barrier to the invader, and we continually have whirlwinds of invading hosts rushing now southward, now northward, from the interior to the coast and from the coast inland, and hurling their force against states, kingdoms, and cities. Some resisted for generations, some for centuries, some but a few years. It is, then, this sudden change and the fear of it that marks African culture, particularly in its political aspects, and which makes it so difficult to trace this changing past. Nevertheless beneath all change rests the strong substructure of custom, religion, industry, and art well worth the attention of students.

Starting with agriculture, we learn that "among all the great groups of the 'natural' races, the Negroes are the best and keenest tillers of the ground. A minority despise agriculture and breed cattle; many combine both occupations. Among the genuine tillers the whole life of the family is taken up in agriculture, and hence the months are by preference called after the operations which they demand. Constant clearings change forests to fields, and the ground is manured with the ashes of the burnt thicket. In the middle of the fields rise the light watch-towers, from which a watchman scares grain-eating birds and other thieves. An African cultivated landscape is incomplete without barns. The rapidity with which, when newly imported, the most various forms of cultivation spread in Africa says much for the attention which is devoted to this branch of economy. Industries, again, which may be called agricultural, like the preparation of meal from millet and other crops, also from cassava, the fabrication of fermented drinks from grain, or the manufacture of cotton, are widely known and sedulously fostered." [1]

Bücher reminds us of the deep impression made upon travelers when they sight suddenly the well-attended fields of the natives on emerging from the primeval forests. "In the more thickly populated parts of Africa these fields often stretch for many a mile, and the assiduous care of the Negro women shines in all the brighter light when we consider the insecurity of life, the constant feuds and pillages, in which no one knows whether he will in the end be able to harvest what he has sown. Livingstone gives somewhere a graphic description of the devastations wrought by slave hunts; the people were lying about slain, the dwellings were demolished; in the fields, however, the grain was ripening and there was none to harvest it." [2]

Sheep, goat, and chickens are domestic animals all over Africa, and Von Franzius considers Africa the home of the house cattle and the Negro as the original tamer. Northeastern Africa especially is noted for agriculture, cattle raising, and fruit culture. In the eastern Sudan, and among the great Bantu tribes extending from the Sudan down toward the south, cattle are evidences of wealth; one tribe, for instance, having so many oxen that each village had ten or twelve thousand head. Lenz (1884), Bouet-Williaumez (1848), Hecquard (1854), Bosman (1805), and

---

[1] Ratzel: *History of Mankind*, II, 380 ff.
[2] *Industrial Evolution*, p. 47.

To my parents and brothers,
Gerhard and Martin

CONTENTS

PREFACE

This new edition seeks to update, expand, and revise the arguments of the previous two editions of *Globalism* in light of recent political and social developments. But the basic premise of the book has remained the same: globalization contains important discursive aspects in the form of ideologically charged narratives that put before the public a particular agenda of topics for discussion, questions to ask, and claims to make. The existence of these narratives suggests that globalization is not merely a set of material processes anchored in economics and technology. It is also reflected in conflicting systems of ideas and claims circulating in the global public realm as more or less coherent stories that define, describe, and evaluate the process of globalization.

In this new edition, however, I no longer refer to "globalism" in the singular to connote the most influential of these globalization stories—a market ideology that endows the concept of globalization with neoliberal norms, values, and meanings. I now speak of "globalisms" in the plural, for it has become abundantly clear that the dominant discourse of market globalism has been challenged by coherent globalisms on the political Left and Right. Articulating the rising global imaginary into concrete political programs and agendas, these ideologies deserve their own appellations: justice globalism and jihadist globalism. Market globalism has responded to these challengers by toughening up its ideological structure. I call this modified version "imperial globalism"—a political belief system that marries the market language of the 1990s with the security concerns of our post-9/11 world. In short, the neoliberal program of economic deregulation, privatization, free trade, unfettered capital movements, low taxation, and fiscal austerity has been merged with neoconservative attempts to shape the entire globe in the American image. But this aggressive projection of American power should not be mistaken for a revival of old-style nationalism. American Empire is as much part of globalization as the jihadist-globalist effort to galvanize the global *umma* (Muslim community of believers) into radical action or the justice-globalist attempt to build "another world." Wildly different in their values, beliefs, and political agendas, the three globalisms of our time nonetheless share a common conceptual framework and field of application: the global (though usually mediated through the local). Given that these different ways of articulating the global imaginary contribute to the development of concrete manifestations of globalization, it is only logical to conclude that market globalism, justice globalism, and jihadist globalism demand critical analyses in their own right.

What, exactly, are the core claims amd conceptual features of these globalisms? How does the imperial globalism of the 2000s differ from the market globalism of the 1990s? How has justice globalism managed to mature into a coherent ideology? What are the core concepts and main ideological claims of jihadist globalism? Where do national populists like Pat Buchanan or Hugo Chavez fit in? What are the most likely future trajectories of the great ideological struggle of the twenty-first century? These are the central questions I seek to answer in this new edition. The overarching intent of this study is not to denounce globalization but to contribute to a critical theory of globalization that encourages the reader to recognize the internal contradictions and biases of the various globalist discourses and thus provides people with a better understanding of how beliefs about globalization fashion their realities and how these ideas can be changed. Derived from the Greek verb *krinein* (to discern, to reflect, to judge) and the Greek noun *theoria* (contemplation), "critical theory" signifies the noble human impulse to contemplate the validity and desirability of social institutions. Guided by the regulative ideal of an equitable and peaceful global order, critical theories of globalization weaken the authoritarian tendency to silence dissent and eliminate freedom of opinion. Thus, ethically and historically informed criticisms represent the lifeblood of all democratic politics—past, present, and future.

ACKNOWLEDGMENTS

It is a pleasant duty to record my debts of gratitude. First and foremost, I want to thank my colleagues at the Royal Melbourne Institute of Technology's Globalism Research Centre and Global Cities Institute for their generous support and critical feedback. My thanks also go out to my colleagues at the University of Hawai'i at Manoa, particularly those connected to the Globalization Research Center and the Department of Political Science. Furthermore, I appreciate the opportunity to hone the ideas presented in this book at many invited lectures, academic colloquia, and research seminars in Australia and New Zealand, North America, Europe, and Asia.

Many people contributed their efforts to this book. My good friends and colleagues Paul James, Heikki Patomaki, Terrell Carver, and Lane Crothers offered important suggestions. Franz Broswimmer provided me with a steady stream of pertinent information, and Jamal Nassar contributed his expertise in the areas of global terrorism and Middle East politics. Their criticisms and suggestions surely made this book better. I would also like to thank Mark Amen, Pierre Atlas, Clyde Barrow, Stephen Eric Bronner, Mike Douglass, Michael Freeden, Jon Goldberg-Hiller, Mary Hawkesworth, Manfred Henningsen, Fumio Iida, Micheline Ishay, John Kautsky, Douglas Kellner, Elizabeth Kelly, Sankaran Krishna, Ramdas Lamb, Tim Luke, Bradley Macdonald, Peter Manicas, Khalil Marrar, Jim Mittelman, Valentine Moghadam, Ken Panfilio, Carlos Parodi, Joe Peschek, Sherri Replogle, Steve Rosow, Saskia Sassen, Nisha Shah, Mike Shapiro, Joe Siracusa, Jim Spencer, Nevi Soguk, and Amentahru Wahlrab for their perceptive comments on my work.

My research assistant, Erin Wilson, did a fantastic job. Susan McEachern, my editor at Rowman & Littlefield Publishers, has been a genuine beacon of support and encouragement. Finally, as always, my deepest expressions of gratitude go to Perle Besserman—thanks for everything.

CHAPTER 1

THE ROOTS OF MARKET GLOBALISM

THE "END OF IDEOLOGY DEBATE"

The defeat of Nazi Germany in 1945 and the collapse of the Soviet Empire in 1991 enticed scores of Western commentators to relegate "ideology" to the dustbin of history. Proclaiming a radically new era in human history, they argued that all political belief systems had converged in a single vision: liberal capitalism. This dream of a universal set of political ideas ruling the world came crashing down with the Twin Towers of the World Trade Center on September 11, 2001. Indeed, the very rationale for the ensuing "Global War on Terror" was built on the notion of ideological diversity and incompatibility.

Let us consider, for example, President George W. Bush's 2007 televised address to the nation in which he unveiled his administration's new "surge" strategy in Iraq by invoking the specter of an expanding "radical Islamic empire" ready to "launch new attacks on the United States at home and abroad." The commander in chief left no doubt that the contest with militant Islamists was much more than a military conflict: "It is the decisive ideological struggle of our time. On one side are those who believe in freedom and moderation. On the other side are extremists who kill the innocent and have declared their intention to destroy our way of life. In the long run, the most realistic way to protect the American people is to provide a hopeful alternative to the hateful ideology of the enemy—by advancing liberty across a troubled region." These sentiments were echoed in Secretary of State Condoleezza Rice's lead article on the "new American realism" published in the August 2008 issue of *Foreign Affairs*: "Ultimately, however, this [struggle] is more than just a struggle of arms; it is a contest of ideas. Al Qaeda's theory of victory is to hijack the legitimate local and national grievances of Muslim societies and twist them into an ideological narrative of endless struggle against Western, especially U.S., oppression."[1] Indeed, the idea that the United States and its "coalition of the willing" were engaged in a "great ideological struggle" with Islamist jihadists around the globe has been at the center of official White House rhetoric since the start of Bush's second term in January 2005.

The president's announcement of a protracted ideological war that, in his opinion, would last well into the twenty-first century, runs counter to a prominent thesis posed by several reputable twentieth-century social thinkers that ideological politics had ended with the defeat of fascism and communism. This controversy over the fate of ideology first erupted in the United States and Europe in the 1950s when political pundits on both sides of the Atlantic found themselves embroiled in what came to be known as "The End of Ideology Debate."[2] The book that set the terms of this controversy bore the suggestive title *The End of Ideology: On the Exhaustion of Political Ideas in the Fifties*. Widely hailed as a landmark in American social thought, the study was authored by Daniel Bell, a rising intellectual star who would eventually establish himself as one of the most influential American sociologists of the twentieth century.

Postulating the utter exhaustion of Marxist socialism and classical liberalism—the two "grand" ideologies of the nineteenth century—Bell argued that old master concepts such as the "inevitability of history" or the "self-regulating market" had lost their power to rally modern constituencies who had witnessed the economic desperation of the Great Depression, the hypocrisy of the Moscow Trials, the treachery of the Hitler–Stalin Pact, the horrors of Nazi concentration camps, and the unleashing of weapons of mass destruction against defenseless civilians in a devastating war of truly global proportions. Most westerners, Bell argued, had abandoned simplistic beliefs in nineteenth-century utopias that projected visions of perfect social harmony—be it the classless society of Marxist socialists or the commercial paradise of laissez-faire liberals. Novel ideological formations had emerged in the newly independent states of Africa and Asia, but their nationalistic messages and politically naïve slogans of "liberation" were too parochial and limited to appeal to post–World War II audiences in Europe and the United States.

In spite of its nostalgic tone, Bell's book showed much appreciation for the virtues of a world without ideological battles. He noted that people in the West had become less prone to pledge their allegiance to dangerous forms of political extremism and more accepting of a pragmatic middle way embodied in the class compromise of the modern welfare state of the 1950s. On one hand, this pragmatic middle way offered the political stability and economic security most people were craving after the traumatic events of the first half of the century. On the other hand, however, its technocratic framework seemed to provide hardly any outlets for political passions and heroic ideals.

Ideology—for Bell largely an emotionally laden and politically dangerous "all-or-none affair"—had become intellectually devitalized and increasingly displaced by a pragmatic reformism built on the virtues of compromise, utility, and scientific objectivity. The preoccupation with administrative solutions for largely technical problems related to the state and national economies had rendered ideology obsolete. Bell cautiously applauded the alleged demise of nineteenth-century ideologies, implying that a deideologized politics of the 1950s was facilitating Western progress toward a more rational and less divisive society.[3]

However, as his detractors were quick to point out, Bell's analysis contained a number of uncritical assumptions. For one, in implying a necessary link between the "ideological" and "totalitarianism," he painted the pragmatic mode of empirical problem solving in overly rosy colors. He made the demise of ideology appear as an attempt to refashion a new age of rational moderation—a natural state lost in nearly a century's worth of irrational attempts to put radically utopian ideas into practice. In particular, some commentators interpreted Bell's assertion of a deideologized climate in the United States as a deeply ideological attempt to reclaim objectivity, compromise, and pragmatism as the essential attributes of a superior Anglo-American culture. They considered The End of Ideology a sophisticated defense of the "free West" that was itself thoroughly pervaded by the ideological imperatives of the Cold War.

Second, several reviewers argued that Bell was unconsciously trying to substitute technocratic guidance by experts for genuine political debate in society. They charged him with evoking a myth of a popular consensus around basic norms and values in order to forestall a potentially divisive discussion on the remaining inequalities in America. Third, the international tensions produced by the Cold War, together with the sudden upsurge of ideological politics in the 1960s and 1970s, seemed to disprove Bell's thesis entirely. The civil rights movement, the numerous protest movements against the Vietnam War, the feminist movement, and the meteoric rise of environmentalism all pointed to the distinct possibility that at least some of the central norms and values contained in radical, Western nineteenth-century ideologies were still alive and well a century later.

Nearly three decades later, the sudden collapse of communist regimes in Eastern Europe and the Soviet Union unexpectedly resurrected the end-of-ideology debate. In a seminal 1989 article he later expanded into a book-length study, Francis Fukuyama, then a deputy director of the U.S. State Department's policy-planning staff, argued that the passing of Marxism-Leninism as a viable political ideology marked nothing less than the "end point of mankind's ideological evolution." This end state was "evident first of all in the total exhaustion of viable systematic alternatives to Western liberalism." Fukuyama also postulated the emergence of a "deideologized world," but he insisted that this new era would not be characterized by the convergence between liberalism and socialism as predicted earlier by Bell. Rather, Fukuyama asserted that it represented the "unabashed victory of economic and political liberalism." Downplaying the significance of rising religious fundamentalism and ethnic nationalism in the "New World Order" of the 1990s, Fukuyama predicted that the global triumph of the "Western idea" and the spread of its consumerist culture to all corners of the earth would prove to be unstoppable. Driven by the logical development of market forces and the unleashing of powerful new technologies, Western capitalist democracy had emerged as the "final form of human government."[4]

Hence, Fukuyama's vision of a deideologized world only partially overlapped with Bell's similar analysis. While Fukuyama agreed with his colleague on the irrevocable demise of socialism, he disagreed with Bell's bleak assessment of free-market liberalism. Indeed, Fukuyama expected a high-tech realization of the old nineteenth-century free-market utopia. Expressing some discomfort at the coming ideological vacuum at the "end of history," he predicted the rapid marketization of most social relations in a globalized world dedicated to self-interested economic calculation, the endless solving of technological problems, and the satisfaction of ceaseless consumer demands.[5]

In more recent articles on the subject, Fukuyama defended and expanded his central idea that the end of ideology would be connected to free-market globalization. He not only reiterated that these developments constitute an "irreversible process" but also added that Anglo-American norms and values would largely underwrite the cultural makeup of the new deideologized world. Indeed, Fukuyama concluded that the current position of the United States as the sole remaining superpower has made it "inevitable that Americanization will accompany globalization."[6]

Looking back from the vantage point of our own post-9/11 world, it appears that any pronouncement of an end of ideology ought to be considered from a more sober historical perspective. Bell's thesis makes sense insofar as it coincided with a major postwar shift away from unregulated capitalism toward the welfare state. Fukuyama's triumphalism constituted a sensible response in the late 1980s because it echoed the central ideas of rising free-market forces. As Fred Dallmayr notes, "Western liberalism and liberalization have emerged as the triumphant ideological panacea, spreading its effects around the globe."[7] Hence, twentieth-century end-of-ideology visions should be seen as historically contingent attempts to universalize the dominant ideological imperatives of their time by presenting them as a natural finality to which history no longer poses an alternative. But in so doing, they reiterate the absolute truth claims of nineteenth-century ideologies.

It should come as no surprise that this study rejects the thesis of a deideologized world. Instead, I will advance the opposite argument: ideology not only is very much with us today but also represents just as powerful a force as it did a century ago. As I see it, far from condemning people to ideological boredom in a world without history, the opening decade of the twenty-first century has become a teeming battlefield of clashing ideologies. The chief protagonist—the dominant ideology I call "market globalism"—has encountered serious resistance from two ideological challengers—justice globalism and jihadist globalism. Seeking to control the conceptual meaning of globalization and, as a result, determine the form and direction of actual social processes of globalization, market-globalist forces will continue to clash with their opponents as each side tries to impress its own ideological agenda on the public mind. As most spectacularly shown by the events of 9/11 and the ensuing Global War on Terror, the ideological contest over the meaning and shape of globalization has deeply impacted the political landscape of the new century. However, before elaborating on these arguments in more detail, let me turn to a brief discussion of the main elements and functions of ideology and clarify their relationship to market globalism.

IDEOLOGY: ELEMENTS AND FUNCTIONS

Ideology can be defined as a system of widely shared ideas, patterned beliefs, guiding norms and values, and lofty ideals accepted as "fact" or "truth" by significant groups in society. Codified by social elites, ideologies offer individuals a more or less coherent picture of the world not only as it is but also as it should be. In doing so, they organize the tremendous complexity of human experience into fairly simple and understandable images that, in turn, provide people with a normative orientation in time and space and in means and ends.

Each ideology is structured around certain concepts and claims that set it apart from other ideologies and endow it with a specific structure or "morphology." As political theorist Michael Freeden puts it, "Central to any analysis of ideologies is the proposition that they are characterized by a morphology that displays core, adjacent, and peripheral concepts."[8] What makes an ideology "political" is that its concepts and claims select, privilege, or constrict social meanings related to the exercise of power in society. In an excellent essay on the historical development of the concept of ideology from the early nineteenth century to the present, political theorist Terrell Carver draws attention to this inescapably political function of ideology. He argues that ideology is neither an abstract template against which something is or is not an ideology nor a recipe stating how to put a system of thought together "correctly." "Rather," Carver writes, "it is an agenda of things to discuss, questions to ask, hypotheses to make. We should be able to use it when considering the interaction between ideas and politics, especially systems of ideas that make claims, whether justificatory or hortatory."[9]

Following both Freeden and Carver, one could say that to explore ideologies is to study the heart of politics understood as the exercise of power with regard to collective decision making and the regulation of social conflict. After all, politics is the public arena where various "agendas of things to discuss" formulated as "claims whether justificatory or hortatory" and connected to the power interests of particular groups and classes are contested and implemented. Thus, ideology is inextricably linked to the many ways in which power is exercised, justified, and altered in society. Ideologists speak to their audiences in stories and narratives whose claims persuade, praise, cajole, decontest, convince, condemn, distinguish "truths" from "falsehoods," and separate the "good" from the "bad." Ideology enables people to act while simultaneously constraining their actions by binding them to a particular set of ideas, norms, and values. Hence, ideology constitutes the glue that binds theory and practice by orienting and organizing political action in accordance with general linguistic rules and cultural codes of ethical conduct.

I contend that market globalism is a political ideology that has achieved dominance in our time. Espousing a hegemonic system of ideas that make normative claims about a set of social processes called "globalization," market globalists seek to limit public discussion on the meaning and character of globalization to an agenda of things to discuss that supports a specific political agenda. The following example provides a first glimpse into the workings of market globalism. The headlines of a *Newsweek* cover story on economic globalization published at the height of the "Roaring Nineties" contained the following phrases: "Like It or Not, You're Married to the Market" and "The Market 'R Us."[10] By equating globalization with marketization, these statements seek to entice their readership to accept a particular representation of social reality as a general truth. A closer analysis of these headlines reveals the following ideological elements and functions.

First, the postulated link between the reader's identity and the impersonal market offers an explanation of economic globalization. It is couched in objective terms that emphasize the "factuality" of the market. Market principles are portrayed as pervading even the most intimate dimensions of our social existence. And there is nothing consumers can do about it. In other words, socially created relations are depicted as exterior, natural forces that are more powerful than human will.

Second, the headlines suggest standards of normative evaluation. Although marketization is portrayed as an objective process, there is the implication that its effects are nonetheless beneficial. After all, the concept of "marriage" resonates on a deeply positive note with most *Newsweek* readers. Who would want to be married to a "bad" person? Who would want to assume the identity of a "bad" person? Thus, the market must be a benign force, after all, worthy of becoming our most intimate partner.

Third, the statements serve as a guide and compass for action. As the stories below the headlines make abundantly clear, markets reflect a natural and superior way of ordering the world. Hence, they ought to command the reader's approval and support. If "free markets" come under attack by hostile forces, the former should be protected and the latter repelled. The implication here is that good citizens should demand from their political regimes that they facilitate and defend globalization as understood in market terms.

Fourth, the headlines offer a simplification of complex social reality. Most importantly, market interests are presented as general interests. After all, the clever permutation of a well-known brand name—Toys 'R Us—

serves as a marker of positive identity. Lack of choice ("like it or not")—a seemingly undesirable condition—is resolved in a marriage of convenience that appears to harbor great financial opportunity for those who know how to treat their (market) spouse. Finally, the gender dynamics at work in these headlines are far from subtle. There is little doubt as to who is the commanding husband in this patriarchal marriage.

In his seminal *Lectures on Ideology and Utopia*, French philosopher Paul Ricoeur integrates these ideological elements and functions into a comprehensive conceptual framework.[11] Drawing on the insights of Marxist thought, Ricoeur characterizes the first functional level of ideology as distortion—that is, the production of contorted and blurred images of social reality. Most importantly, the process of distortion hides the contrast between things as they are envisioned in theory and things as they play themselves out on the plane of material reality. Indeed, all ideologies assemble a picture of the world based on a peculiar mixture that both represents and distorts social processes. Yet Ricoeur disagrees with Karl Marx's notion that distortion explains all there is to ideology. For the French philosopher, distortion is merely one of the three main functions of ideology, representing the surface level of a phenomenon that contains two more functions at progressively deeper levels.

Inspired by the writings of the German sociologist Max Weber, Ricoeur identifies legitimation as the second functional level of ideology. Two main factors are involved here: the claim to legitimacy made by the ruling authority and the belief in the authority's legitimacy granted by its subjects. Accepting large parts of Weber's explanation of social action, Ricoeur highlights ideology's function of mediating the gap between belief and claim. In other words, Ricoeur argues that there will always remain some discrepancy between the popular belief in the authority's right to rule and the authority's claim to the right to rule. It is one of ideology's functions to supply the people with additional justification in order to narrow this credibility gap. Ricoeur's model is completed in his description of integration, the third functional level of ideology.

Drawing on the writings of anthropologist Clifford Geertz, who emphasizes the symbolic structure of social action, Ricoeur claims that, on the deepest level, ideology relies on rich symbolic resources that play a mediating or integrative role. Thus, ideology provides society with stability as it creates, preserves, and protects the social identity of persons and groups. Performing a constructive function, ideology supplies the symbols, norms, and images that go into the process of assembling and holding together individual and collective identity. Yet this also means that ideology assumes a conservative function in both senses of that word. It preserves identity, "but it also wants to conserve what exists and is therefore already a resistance."[12] Such rigid forms of resistance to change often turn beliefs and ideas into a dogmatic defense of dominant power structures.

Ricoeur's model inspires my own view that the study of ideology yields a better understanding of political action as mediated, structured, and integrated by symbolic systems—most importantly language. Ideologies permeate all societies, with different segments of the population holding particular ideas about power and social order. In no case will a given society be so completely dominated by a single ideology as to have no alternatives available within the system. Even in the "totalitarian" regimes of the past century, pockets of ideological resistance remained despite the government's efforts to eliminate all opposition. At the same time, however, it must be emphasized that there are periods in modern history when a particular ideology becomes predominant or "hegemonic."

Made famous by Antonio Gramsci, a leading socialist thinker who died in 1937 in an Italian prison as a victim of Mussolini's fascism, hegemony can be defined as a power relationship between social groups and classes in which one class exercises control by gaining the active consent of subordinate groups. According to Gramsci, this process involves the internalization on the part of the subordinate classes of the moral and cultural values, the codes of practical conduct, and the worldview of the dominant classes. Submerged in a symbolic universe created by the dominant group, the subordinate groups give their spontaneous consent to the social logic of domination that is embedded in hegemonic ideology. This allows dominant groups to maintain a social order favoring their own interests in "informal" ways—that is, largely without having to resort to open coercion.

In his discussion of hegemony, Gramsci also comments on the power of ideology to shape personal and collective identities. Indeed, the two *Newsweek* headlines discussed earlier represent a good example of how ideological integration contributes to hegemony. As Gramsci scholar William I. Robinson notes, "Under a hegemonic social order, embedded in ideology are definitions of key political, economic, and philosophical concepts and the ideological framework establishes the legitimacy or illegitimacy of the demands placed on the social order."[13]

As I interpret the normative claims of hegemonic market globalism and evaluate the responses of justice globalism and jihadist globalism in chapters 3 to 5, I draw on the insights into ideology provided by Ricoeur, Gramsci, Carver, and Freeden. Their respective explanations of the elements and functions of ideology provide a helpful framework for my own discussion of the three globalisms of the twenty-first century.

MARKET GLOBALISM AND NEOLIBERALISM

After the collapse of Soviet-style communism in 1989, Anglo-American proponents of the nineteenth-century utopia of the "self-regulating market" found in the concept of "globalization" a new guiding metaphor for their neoliberal message. The central tenets of neoliberalism include the primacy of economic growth, the importance of free trade to stimulate growth, the unrestricted free market, individual choice, the reduction of government regulation, and the advocacy of an evolutionary model of social development anchored in the Western experience and applicable to the entire world.

Neoliberalism is an economic perspective rooted in the classical liberal ideals of British philosophers such as Adam Smith (1723–1790), David Ricardo (1772–1823), and Herbert Spencer (1820–1903). Smith is often credited with creating the Scottish Enlightenment image of *Homo economicus*—the view that people are isolated individuals whose actions reflect mostly their economic self-interest. In Smith's view, economic and political matters are largely separable, with economics claiming a superior status because it supposedly operates best without government interference under a harmonious system of natural laws. The market is seen as a self-regulating mechanism tending toward equilibrium of supply and demand, thus securing the most efficient allocation of resources. Any constraint on free competition is said to interfere with the natural efficiency of market mechanisms. Composed of small buyers and sellers, the market's "invisible hand" translates individual pursuit of self-interest into optimal public benefit. Attacking the seventeenth-century economic doctrine of mercantilism—absolute control of the economy by a powerful state with the objective of building up large gold reserves—Smith argued vigorously in favor of "liberating" markets from intrusive state regulation. His classical understanding of liberalism defends freedom as a person's right to be "left alone" by social demands so that the individual may act in the market as *Homo economicus* unencumbered by social regulations. This early vision of economic liberty still forms the backbone of contemporary neoliberal doctrine. Smith complemented his laissez-faire market ideal with a defense of free trade and its principles of laissez-passer, most importantly the elimination of tariffs on imports and other barriers to trade and capital flows between nations.

But it was Ricardo's "theory of comparative advantage" that became the gospel of modern free traders. Ricardo argued that free trade amounted to a win–win situation for all trading partners involved because it allowed each country to specialize in the production of those commodities for which it had a comparative advantage. For example, if Italy could produce wine more cheaply than England and England could produce cloth more cheaply than Italy, then both countries would benefit from specialization and trade. In fact, Ricardo even went so far as to suggest that benefits from specialization and trade would accrue even if one country had an absolute advantage in producing all the products traded. Politically, Ricardo's theory amounted to a powerful argument against government interference with trade and was used by later liberals like Richard Cobden as a formidable ideological weapon in the struggle to repeal the protectionist Corn Laws in England.[14]

Perhaps the most influential formulation of classical liberalism appears in Spencer's justification of the "natural dominance" of Western laissez-faire capitalism over the rest of the world by drawing on Charles Darwin's theory of evolution by natural selection. For Spencer, free-market economies constitute the most civilized form of human competition in which the "fittest" would "naturally" rise to the top. Establishing himself as the leading proponent of early industrial capitalism, Spencer did not support imperialist policies but limited the required tasks of the state to protecting individuals against internal and external forms of aggression. Any interference with the workings of private enterprise would inevitably lead to cultural and social stagnation, political corruption, and the creation of large, inefficient state bureaucracies.

Spencer denounced socialism, trade unions, and even rudimentary forms of social regulation such as factory safety laws as examples of "over-regulation" inimical to rational progress and individual freedom. In his early study *Social Statics*, he enshrined laissez-faire capitalism as the final system toward which all societies were evolving under the economic and cultural leadership of Anglo-American countries. Spencer's elevation of free-market competition as the natural source of humankind's freedom and prosperity proved to be extremely influential with the commercial interests of Victorian England. Toward the end of his life, the reported total sales of his books approached 400,000 copies. No doubt, Spencer's theories greatly contributed to the hegemony of free-market economic doctrine in nineteenth-century Britain.[15]

The intensification of European and American imperialism in the 1890s, the collapse of world trade during World War I, and the economic crises and conflicts during the interwar years caused free-market ideas to lose much of their appeal. Virulent forms of nationalism and trade protectionism emerged as extreme reactions to laissez-faire capitalism, and it was not until the end of World War II that modified versions of liberalism reappeared on the political agenda of Western countries. Until the 1970s, even the most promarket political parties in Europe and the United States embraced rather extensive forms of state interventionism propagated by British economist John Maynard Keynes. Culminating in the creation of the modern welfare state, Keynes's advocacy of a "social market" engineered by a pragmatic government represented the impressive attempt to combine some redeemable values of socialism with the virtues of liberalism in a system of mixed economy and political pluralism that balanced capitalist markets with demands for greater social equality.

However, the rise of neoliberal ideas in the late 1970s found a favorable economic context as inflation, high unemployment, and other structural problems plagued Western industrialized countries. Making a strong case for the return to free-market policies of the past, neoliberal politicians drew on the neoclassical laissez-faire economic theories of Anglo-American economists such as Friedrich Hayek and Milton Friedman. In the early 1980s, British Conservatives under the intellectual leadership of Keith Joseph and Margaret Thatcher implemented what some commentators have called "Second-Coming Capitalism" or "Turbo-Capitalism."[16] Their social conservatism combined with neoliberal economic policies to create a strange hybrid often referred to as "neoconservatism"—a position favoring the weakening of the power of labor unions and initiating drastic market-oriented reforms while opting for a hawkish foreign policy, especially toward the Soviet Union. By the late 1980s, British Prime Minister Margaret Thatcher and U.S. President Ronald Reagan were both revered and reviled as the founding figures of a new market paradigm. After the collapse of communism in Eastern Europe, President Bill Clinton and Prime Minister John Major (and later Tony Blair) could afford to drop the tough foreign policy stance of their predecessors and expand the neoliberal project into a full-blown market ideology.

Indeed, the heyday of market globalism occurred in what American Nobel Prize–winning economist Joseph Stiglitz calls the "Roaring Nineties." The public interpretation of globalization fell disproportionately to global power elites enamored with the philosophical and economic principles of the Thatcher–Reagan revolution. This global phalanx consisted mostly of corporate managers, executives of large transnational corporations, corporate lobbyists, prominent journalists and public-relations specialists, cultural elites and entertainment celebrities, academics writing for large audiences, high-level state bureaucrats, and political leaders.[17] They marshaled their considerable material and ideological resources to sell to the public the alleged benefits of the liberalization of trade and the global

My Favorite Prayer Reflection...

A Prayer Companion for
MOMS

Vickie LoPiccolo Jennett
with Paula Hagen

Resource Publications, Inc.
San Jose, California

Editorial director: Kenneth Guentert
Managing editor: Elizabeth J. Asborno
Cover design and production: Huey Lee

Reprint Department
Resource Publications, Inc.
160 E. Virginia Street #290
San Jose, CA 95112-5867

Library of Congress Cataloging in Publication Data
Jennett, Vickie LoPiccolo, 1955-
   A prayer companion for MOMS / Vickie LoPiccolo Jennett with
   Paula Hagen

      p.   cm.
   ISBN 0-89390-265-9
   1. Mothers—Prayer-books and devotions—English.   2. Christian
life—1960-   I. Hagen, Paula, 1937-   . I. Title.
BV283.M7J46   1993
242'.6431—dc20   93-19670

97 96 95 | 5 4 3 2

**Grateful acknowledgment is extended for permission to reprint the
following copyrighted material:**

Verses marked (TLB) are taken from *The Living Bible* © 1971. Used by
permission of Tyndale House Publishers, Inc., Wheaton, IL 60189. All
rights reserved.

Scripture quotations marked (NAB) are taken from *The New American
Bible* Copyright © 1970 by the Confraternity of Christian Doctrine, 3211
Fourth Street, N.E., Washington, DC 20017-1194, and are used with
permission. All rights reserved.

The artwork in this book represents designs rich in tradition that date
back more than 100 years. The designs were inspired by common objects
of everyday life in Early America. These floral renderings largely are
adaptations of 19th-century quilting and embroidery designs. The
illustrations are among hundreds reproduced by Suzanne E. Chapman in
Early American Design Motifs, published and copyright © 1974 Dover
Publications, Inc., for the Dover *Pictorial Archive Series*.

Contents

Preface

This book of prayers and reflections is for moms, from MOMS and about moms. That may sound rather cryptic at first, but it actually is quite simple.

MOMS—the Ministry of Mothers Sharing—is rooted in a parish program that started out as a meeting place where moms could share their ideas, feelings, and needs. Over the years, MOMS was revised, refined, and, eventually, compiled in journal format so that mothers everywhere could benefit from their shared wisdom. Two more books—a complete manual for developing a MOMS ministry and a guide for facilitators—followed.

MOMS has helped many women begin to understand how their daily experiences and reflections (even the ones that seem most mundane) are intimately tied to their relationship with God. They have learned to talk about spirituality in their own, everyday terms rather than seeing it as some distant and formal religious experience.

As a mother and co-author of MOMS, Vickie LoPiccolo Jennett snatched a few minutes when her schedule would allow and wrote down some of the thoughts and prayers that flowed through her mind as she went through her daily tasks. Paula Hagen, creator and co-author of MOMS, then added some reflections, which will help readers apply these very human, heartfelt thoughts to their own lives. The result of their efforts is this book, which is both a companion to the MOMS program and a companion for moms everywhere.

Introduction

Practical Prayer: Everyday Spirituality

Our prayer lives are as varied as our backgrounds. For some, formal prayer fits like a well-worn shoe. We're comfortable with it and have been since our early years. For others, prayer is a spontaneous reflection or request acknowledging God's presence. Still others lift their voices in song, praising creation and the dawning of a new day. Very common are prayers of petition—words asking for help, comfort, or guidance.

There is no set prescription for the perfect prayer. Both by definition and in practice, prayer is a very personal form of communication with God.

1

The form our prayers take is of little consequence. More important is that we *do* pray—that we consciously set aside some space within our day (or night) for our relationship with God. Better yet, we can make our very lives a prayer. And that doesn't imply passing the day with hands folded and head bent.

What appealed so much to me about children's author Dr. Seuss was that he was (and still is through his books) able to make learning fun. His books teach without teaching. When I was growing up, we had a pastor who preached without preaching. His words struck a chord in our hearts without carrying a "holier-than-thou" attitude. I like to think of prayer without praying as a continual awareness of and thankfulness for that which is simply sacred in everyday life.

At times our prayers may be peaceful, quiet and pleasant. Other times, we cry out in exasperation, grief or depression. Sometimes the words just don't seem to come. We're confused, concerned or self-conscious. We must realize it's OK that not all prayer is articulate and awe-

inspiring. We also can rejoice that even silence or the most simple words with God can create treasured and profound moments.

The more comfortable we are with prayer, the more likely we are to make it an integral part of our lives. Too often, we fall into the trap of viewing prayer as a chore or duty to be accomplished along with other mundane tasks on our agendas. Not true! Taking a few moments to reflect on an event or happening can help us see even the most ordinary occurrence as a sacred experience. A three-year-old is the one who unwittingly opened my eyes to the spontaneous, joyful and even frivolous side of prayer. This is what transpired one gloomy morning:

Rain tapped at the windows.

A half-folded newspaper rested next to an empty coffee mug.

The sound of cars splashing by was anything but soothing.

A mile-long "to do" list clamored for attention.

Water—maybe two inches deep—blanketed the porch.

"Mommy," exclaimed a sleepy-eyed toddler with drenched slippers.

The doormat and the carpet were soaked too.

"Mommy," he persisted. "Did you thank Jesus today?"

His warm, wet hands and face made steamy imprints on the windowpanes.

"Well, did you?"

Telltale signs of a dog with sopped paws graced the kitchen floor.

"Did I what?" she called back.

It would mean mopping them up before they dried.

"Thank Jesus," he beamed.

He started tracing animals on the fogged window.

"Oh. Why?" she glanced at the list.

Errands would be no fun on such a miserable, wet day.

"It's raining!"

What a child saw as cause for praising God—the rain—was a nuisance to a parent looking at the practical side of dealing with flooded streets and wet floors. It is in the open spirit of this

4

child that I hope you use this *Prayer Companion*—not as a guidebook or a formula but rather as an inspiration to help you express your unique forms of praise, requests and thanksgiving for God's loving presence.

My Thoughts and Prayers...

I. Praise and Thanksgiving

I.

Praise and Thanksgiving

Some days it's so easy to pass the hours with a grateful heart. The sun is shining in a clear blue sky. Cares and worries are at a minimum. The family is happy. The world seems to be as much at peace as is possible. It's a plain and simple, all-around good day.

Times like this, we willingly thank God for the blessings bestowed upon us. We can find so much for which to be thankful. However, when our world is topsy-turvy, neither the feelings nor words of praise flow as freely.

Especially during trying times, attitude can have a real impact on our lives, the lives of our loved ones, and even the lives of those with whom we come in casual contact. Our hearts

can remain thankful even when adversity strikes—an action that truly is easier said than done.

Being thankful is a tall order to fill when you or someone you love has been hurt or has lost a job or is ill. It's easy to focus on the pain or shortcomings rather than look at the overall picture, which does include the things that are going "right." More important, in the big picture, God's unconditional love is ever-present.

Even when the going gets rough, we can find words of praise and thanksgiving if we remember:

> There is an appointed time for everything,
> and a time for every affair under the heavens.
> A time to be born, and a time to die;
> a time to plant, and a time to uproot the plant.
> A time to kill, and a time to heal;
> a time to tear down, and a time to build.
> A time to weep, and a time to laugh;
> a time to mourn, and a time to dance.
> A time to scatter stones, and a time to gather them;
> a time to embrace, and a time to be far from embraces.
> A time to seek, and a time to lose;

a time to keep, and a time to cast away.
A time to rend, and a time to sew;
a time to be silent, and a time to speak.
A time to love, and a time to hate;
a time of war, and a time of peace.
— Ecclesiastes 3:1-8 (NAB)

A Gift of Words Straight from the Heart

Most Valentine's Days, it's flowers or a card or some country-style token of affection that I find perched next to my bowl of crispy cereal.

This year it was a piece of computer paper folded in thirds.

My initial disappointment quickly vanished as I read:

"Sometimes I get so busy I don't get a chance to do a lot of things I really want to do...such as getting to the store before Valentine's Day.

"I'm so lucky you came along to be my valentine. You have made a beautiful home for the boys and me. They will be able to carry into their adult lives a great moral background and happy memories because of your careful guidance. Thanks for all you are and all you do."

Those are words that couldn't be replaced with a pound of dark-chocolate-covered almonds, or, for that matter, gold!

Thank you, God, for words from the heart. Amen.

To whom do I give heartfelt words?

_____

_____

_____

_____

_____

_____

Take time to write down some heartfelt words:

_____

_____

_____

_____

_____

_____

Wake-Up Call

Some mornings the alarm doesn't have a chance to sound.

My eyes fly open and a song of praise fills my heart.
(It's not on my lips because I can't sing.)

The air is clear, the sun is shining.
Another day awaits. It may be filled with challenges.
Hopefully joys. Maybe even sorrows.

How splendid, I think, if every day were a mirror of this one.
Peaceful, calm, and promising.

Like the words of a song that has survived down through the ages, I truly do "praise God from whom all blessings flow!"

Hand-Me-Downs

"Heaven help you, child," adults used to say when one of us kids managed to pull off some ridiculous stunt that seemed to get us in trouble every time. *"When will you ever learn?"* they would quip as we hung our head in shame, sulking as we left the scene of a broken window, or spilt soda, or a snowball fight gone awry. How we feared those words.

"Have faith. Just have faith," my mother used to say. As teenagers (who *knew* we had all the answers), we thought she was crazy. How could we have faith that we would make the debate team? Or that we would get asked to the Spring Fling Dance? Or even that our geometry teacher really didn't hate us? How we despised those words.

"Be patient." Those two words seemed to flow endlessly out of the mouths of parents and other adults. Be patient that the school year would end and summer vacation would arrive. Be patient until you can get your driver's license. Be patient—you'll find out soon whether or not you got the job. How

we prayed those words would be removed from the English language.

Time has a funny way of imparting wisdom that helps us see those once-abhorred phrases in a new light.
I sure could use some help from heaven today, Lord.

Faith is what sees me through many days, although there always are times I could use a little more.

And patience. Now, there's one I'm struggling to perfect.

As children we questioned the value of these words much the same way that we shied away from hand-me-down clothes. But as adults, we can appreciate the value of hand-me-down clothes, as well as the value of those oft-repeated phrases.

Thanks, Lord, for hand-me-downs!

What are some "hand-me-downs" my children might treasure in years to come?

_____

_____

_____

_____

Magnificent

The red rocks reaching skyward
to a blue forever.

The blue forever mingling with
wisps of white.

The wisps of white bringing
gentle breezes.

The gentle breezes caressing
a tear-stained cheek.

The tear-stained cheek turned skyward
praising God's creation.

Magnificent.

Some of God's creations that I view as magnificent are:

_____

_____

_____

Thank You, God, for Family and Friends

You know, God, sometimes I moan and complain
about members of my family. I even grumble about
my friends. But underlying those thoughts and
words are bonds whose value knows no limits.
Thank you, God, for family and friends!

The comfort of knowing we have them.
   Family and friends.

The security they bring.
   Family and friends.

The simple pleasures we enjoy.
   Family and friends.

The unconditional love they give.
   Family and friends.

The joy we share.
   Family and friends.

The need to say nothing.
   Family and friends.

17

The opportunity to confide.
  Family and friends.

The examples they set.
  Family and friends.

The comfort they provide in times of crisis.
  Family and friends.

Thank you, God, for
  Family and friends.

Spoken Without Words

The closing number was especially inspiring.
The entire cast joined voices and hands
    in a finale that was felt as well as heard.

The performers left the stage
    and filtered through the audience.
Hugs and handshakes mingled with ecstatic
    congratulations.

The emotionally charged atmosphere
    was a perfect backdrop
for the chance meeting between actor and child.

Strangers.
Their eyes met.
He took the child's hands.

Words were superfluous.
The child's gratitude for the inspiring performance
    glistened in her eyes.

"Thanks," he said,
    knowing that a magic bond
    had been created once again.

19

We are blessed, Lord,
   to have such talented individuals
   in Your world.

**When have I observed that special form of communi-
cation that's spoken without words?**

_____

_____

_____

_____

_____

_____

Footnote

The day is done.
The lights are out.
Quiet fills the house.
Weary bones and tired back
climb gently into bed.
A cluttered mind
takes a look
at all that has been done.
Another day
of work and play
and now some time to pray.

My prayer, dear God,
is mostly filled with
thanks and praise and joy and hope.
What I cannot hide (because You know)
is disappointment
about things still left undone.
With Your help
I'll look at them as challenges
that carry over to a new day.

And I will rest now, knowing
that with Your help
all things
will fall into place. Amen.

II. Growth and Challenge

II.

Growth and Challenge

Change is part of the rhythm of life. Just when we've planned the perfect picnic, the weather pulls an unexpected switch from sunshine to rain. A body that used to slide into a sleek size 6 or 8 today is a generous 12 or 14. We finally become comfortable in our neighborhood and we're uprooted due to a job change. At last our children seem to adjust to the rigors of high school and it's time to graduate and move on to jobs or college. The list is endless.

"Why me, God?" and "Why now?" are common reactions to situations that challenge our plans.

These logical questions come to mind because of the frustration and fear that fre-

quently accompany change. We may be frightened by the need to make adjustment in our lives. Or we may resist a change—fighting any adaptations that accompany it. Yet, viewed in a different light, change *is* a terrific opportunity for growth and challenge. God created us to grow for all eternity.

The following pages include some examples of prayerful approaches to growth and challenges. When confronted with challenging situations or opportunities for growth, it may help to open the Bible to the Book of Psalms, which includes religious songs of old, many calling on God for help in time of need.

As we are reminded in Psalm 6:10,

> The Lord has heard my plea;
> the Lord has accepted my prayer (NAB).

Looking in a prayerful light at the challenge brought about by change truly does help lighten the weight of our burdens. It also provides the inner courage and wisdom to keep growing.

25

When Refrigerators Resemble Life

I was puzzled the other day.

I could only laugh when I opened the refrigerator door and realized that the cluttered, crowded shelves closely resembled my cluttered, crowded schedule.

I couldn't decide whether it was time to clean out the refrigerator or time to revamp my life.

Not to worry. They'll both be there when I'm ready to tackle them.

What are some of the "leftovers" I need to get rid of in my life?

_____

_____

_____

_____

_____

Exasperation

Our lives
   are chaos.

Our burdens
   are heavy.

Our minds
   are cluttered.

It *has* been one of those weeks.

We cry
   for help.

We ask
   for guidance.

We look
   for peace.

There must be an answer!

God hears
   our fears.

God feels
  our needs.

God sees
  our pain.

There is cause to rejoice!

The storm
  will quiet.

The rifts
  will heal.

The answers
  will come.

We move forward in faith!

Choices

Thank you, Lord, for helping me understand my
    ability to make choices.

For giving me the insight
that the foundation was laid years ago
when my decisions were whether to pick chocolate
    or vanilla ice cream...
or to sneak over to the neighbors or stay and play
    in our yard...
or to spend my allowance on a card for Granny or
    on some candy
    beckoning from behind the counter.

My choices today are of a different magnitude.
Do I report a children's coach
    who repeatedly uses foul language
    (thus risking the criticism of those who choose
    to overlook it)
or do I remain silent
    and risk having future children subject to the
    profanities?

Do I take the job that will make use of my
professional skills
or do I stay home a little longer and make full use of
my nurturing skills?

Can I afford time out for me?
Time to pray? To exercise? To play? To study
scripture?
Or do I carry on filling my time with chores, duties
and obligations?
What is best for me, God?

Help me make the choices that are right for me
today, Lord.
Choices that will make me a better person and
make our world a better place.

Amen.

Alone

Solitude or loneliness?

Peace or turmoil?

Strength or weakness?

Freedom or burden?

Order or confusion?

Perspective. It makes all the difference.

Please, God, give me a sense of perspective.

The Difference

Complacency is different than contentment.

Contentment brings peace, joy, energy.
Complacency is lackluster, bored, tired.

With contentment, I care.
With complacency, nothing matters.

When I care, those around me feel my peace, joy
   and energy.
When nothing seems to matter, I exude that
   lackluster, bored, tired attitude.

When I am content with myself, I can dream,
   hope and plan for the future.
When complacency rules my spirit, those dreams,
   hopes and plans are smothered.

Contentment is a blessing.
Complacency is a burden.

Help me see the difference, Lord. Amen.

Refueling and Retooling

It's tough sometimes to admit
    that just like our cars,
    we need refueling, maybe even some preventive
    maintenance.

We know when our personal needle
    is nearing the empty mark...
    we're irritable, tired and out of sorts.

We refuse sometimes to make a choice
    to do just what it takes...
    quiet time or read a book or just a little rest.

But like our cars, our fuel runs out
    and we can't take another step.
Help us, God, to refuel before we reach this point.

Amen.

What can I do to retool before I hit the empty mark?

_____

_____

_____

_____

_____

_____

Sometimes

Sometimes...

I am aware

I am wrong,

I am quick to judge,

I am angry.

Yet...

I am sorry,

so sorry, God, oh so sorry.

I ask forgiveness. Amen.

My Thoughts and Prayers...

III. Shortcomings and Requests

Fears

Practice Makes...

Help

Laughter, Lord, I Need More!

Unburdened

Words of Wisdom

III.

Shortcomings and Requests

There are plenty of times when we unnecessarily berate ourselves for perceived shortcomings. We find fault with our appearance, actions or words. An inner voice nags us with "should haves." We look at unrealistic ideals and try to reach them. We set ourselves up for depression, anger and failure.

Rather than look at the down side of shortcomings, I like to accept them as a part of me—a part, that when balanced out with the strengths, doesn't look too bad. It's OK to be less than perfect. It is, after all, human nature.

Turning to God with our shortcomings and requests takes a great burden from our minds. It allows us to tap into our inner strength, our

God-given ability to make healthy choices. Our prayers are heard.

When our children were just toddlers, my husband and I discussed the type of bedtime prayers we would like to teach the boys. We wanted to shy away from verses that would frighten or puzzle them. We opted for a prayer that actually allowed them to enter into a conversation with God. This prayer was part of a handout at a church function and was attributed to an "anonymous" author.

Make me, Dear Lord,
Polite and Kind to Everyone, I pray.
And, may I ask You
How You find Yourself, Dear Lord, today?
Amen.

Fears

Help me, God. My fears are real.

They lie within my soul.

One day they're small.

The next day large.

The fears just seem to grow.

I know You're there to light the way,

Though sometimes I just can't see

That strength and faith and love abound

To ease the fears each day.

Christ showed us how real fears and temptation can be. He also showed us the power of faith and hope. How can I apply Christ's example in my life?

_____

_____

_____

_____

_____

_____

Practice Makes...

Practice makes me a better piano player,
    a better cook,
    a better mother.

Practice improves my tennis game,
    my prayer life,
    my sewing techniques.

Practice helps me become more organized,
    more responsible,
    more compassionate.

Practice leaves room for improvement,
    for mistakes,
    for triumphs.

Some say practice makes perfect.
But, not me.
I'm pleased as can be with practice.

I hope you are too, God.

Where in my life do I choose to practice?

_____

_____

_____

_____

_____

_____

Help

My cries for help, you hear them, Lord.
They come throughout the day.

I may be working furiously
   or just engaged in play.

Yet, when I call, you hear my need.
It may be large or small.

Nothing seems too tedious, God,
   by now you've heard it all!

Amen.

Laughter, Lord, I Need More!

Laughter, Lord, I really do need more.
From within and also from without.

Offices lined with glum-faced workers,
    stores with grouchy clerks.

Newspaper headlines screaming death,
    schools with crying kids.

The world's so great, the world's so grand, yet
    hardly anywhere I turn
is laughter ringing in the streets or in our hearts and
    souls.

Laughter, Lord, free my soul. Amen.

Unburdened

What can I do, God, to lessen the load?

It's not that I want to get out of doing my fair share.

Or that I don't care.

It's just that sometimes I seem to add extra baggage,
   unnecessary worries.

Where can I turn, God, when my mind is a blur?

Sometimes I'm overtaken by this bleak and dreary
   mood.

I'm so unproductive, I just sit around and brood.

There are solutions and answers but none seem to
   fit.

When will I realize that You've given me the power

to let go,

to unburden myself of these woes?

46

Help me, God, to unclutter this mind and to hear
  Your Word.

Amen.

Words of Wisdom

We have words of wisdom
    words to the wise
    words by which to live.

We seek advice.
We get advice.
We take advice to heart.

The words, they touch us.
The advice, it helps us.
Yet, somehow we always know...

It's the voice that lives
    deep within our souls
    that guides our lives each day.

God, give me the courage to listen to that voice.
    Amen.

IV. Hopeful Hearts

Waiting

Visiting Hours

On Hold

Variations on Some Themes

Material Blessings

Hope Rises from the Depths of Despair

IV.

Hopeful Hearts

"I hope," my husband said as I grappled with the right words to start this section, "that you come up with something really profound." My fondest dream at that moment was to stuff a dirty sock in his mouth. "How can I think 'hope'," I wondered, "when we have bills to pay, deadlines to meet, a flooded back yard, a whining preteen, and business paperwork coming out of our ears?" Actually, maintaining hopeful hearts—even when our minds are cluttered with less optimistic thoughts—helps create a positive approach to life.

Can you think of a period in your life when your worries were few? A time when your very fondest hopes and dreams occupied a great deal of your waking hours? For some of us, the

answer is, "Yes." The time may have been during childhood when dreams were as simple as riding a pony or traveling to the beach. For some of us, the answer may be, "No." Our lives have always been in some way burdened by cares, pain, worry, or sadness.

Whatever we answer, it's not too late to start dreaming now, to look to the future with a hopeful heart, to wake up to the limitless possibilities that exist in our lives. Fortunately, there is no formula or equation for the perfect dream.

Our dreams can range from the simple and attainable to the fantastic or, even, impractical (if not impossible). There is no validity scale for dreams. Calorie-less chocolate-covered almonds top my list of frivolities. A friend in Minnesota punctuates the long winter with visions of lazy summer days boating on the lake. One friend who never had the opportunity to prepare for a career longs for the day when she can enroll at the community college. A neighbor caring for her croupy child finds pleasure thinking of leisurely searching out bargains at the flea mar-

ket. Early retirement is at the top of one friend's wish list—it may never come, but the thought of it fuels her through grueling days in a demanding job. Many times we share hopes that carry our children to a future bright with opportunity, harmony and peace.

Dreams can be quite healthy so long as we don't become obsessed with them or despair when real life delivers a different picture. The hope in our hearts is very real and can serve as encouragement and inspiration when kept in balance with reality. (There still are bills to pay. Meanwhile I'm waiting for those no-calorie chocolate-covered almonds! A trip to the beach wouldn't be bad either.)

Waiting

Waiting.

It's a part of motherhood right from the start.

We wait nine months for the miracle of birth.

Then there's waiting for teeth, talking and toddling.

We wait in doctors' offices, at dance lessons and in
    barber shops.

There are lines for photo sittings, carnival rides and
    sporting events.

And then the hours that seem like an eternity when
    curfew's past.

But time waiting need not be time wasted.

It's time for thinking...

Time for praying...

Time for reflecting...

...about our day, our family, our lives.

...in thanksgiving, in sorrow, in praise.

...on our hopes, our dreams, our fears.

Waiting for God's revelations in our lives.

Amen.

Visiting Hours

A single rose
  on a sterile bedside table.

A stark contrast
  to the high-tech beeping, buzzing, ever-vigilant
  monitors
  that assure us he is alive.
  Not well. But alive.

A nervous smile
  on an intimate visitor's face.

A testimony
  to the life that struggles inside
  the once strong body now lying at the mercy of
  modern medicine.

A voice
  on the intercom
  announcing an end to visiting hours.

A moment to remember
  that although we're often separated
  from those we love so much,

God gives us the memories, the hope for a
brighter tomorrow
and the strength of oneness in spirit.

A collection of gifts
that can't be taken away.

Thank you, God. Amen.

On Hold

"Can you hold? All lines are busy now."

Lord, if I hear that one more time, I think I'll
   scream!

Everywhere we turn, life seems to be on hold...
   or detoured...
   or under construction.

Lord, why don't things flow orderly and logically
   and calmly?

What comfort it is to know that the one line always
   open is the line that leads to You, Lord.

Am I sometimes busy when you try to reach me, God?
What can I do to be more responsive to God's call?

_____

_____

_____

Variations on Some Themes

When life seems so serious that nary even a smile
can be found, consider these variations of some
tried-and-true sentiments:

Embroidered on a pillow displayed in a gift shop:
**BLESS OUR HOME, LORD.
WE NEED ALL THE HELP WE CAN GET!**

Painted on a sign above the kitchen door:
THOU SHALT NOT WHINE.

Stitched in a sampler:
**ALL THINGS ARE POSSIBLE WITH FAITH.
THAT DOESN'T MEAN
ALL THINGS WILL BE EASY.**

A word to the wise:
THOU SHALT LEARN TO SAY, "NO!"

Material Blessings

Sometimes shabby. Sometimes splendid.

The roof over our heads.

The food on our plates.

The clothes we wear.

Lord, let us not feel proud or guilty or ashamed.

Help us make the most of our material blessings.

Help us to see the sacred here and now.

We ask this in Your name. Amen.

Hope Rises from the Depths of Despair

History gives us countless women to admire—
　　women who rose up from times of adversity and
　　despair to accomplish great things.

Their lives shine as beacons
　　reminding us there are no dead ends—
　　that the promise of hope continues through the
　　centuries.

We are inspired by their courage.
We stand in awe of their wisdom.
We look to them for inspiration.

In my mind one woman stands out
　　for what she said, for what she did,
　　for who she was.
She is Mary, mother of Jesus.

She was greatly troubled and
　　questioned the angel who came to visit;
　　but she had faith.

Her reaction was one of praise:

"My soul proclaims the greatness of the Lord;
my spirit rejoices in God my Savior."

She raised her Son; taught Him His lessons.
She watched Him die on a cross.
She did not despair.

Her heart was faithful and hope-filled.
May ours be likewise.
Amen.

My Thoughts and Prayers...

V. Living Gospel Values

Peace

Being There

To Forgive and Be Forgiven

Harmony

Humility with a Capital "H"

Gifts Mothers Understand So Well

Time Out for Fun

V.

Living Gospel Values

When we think of Gospel values, certain images come to mind. The Gospel is proclaimed by missionaries, preachers and by the person on the street. It is proclaimed in weekly liturgies and in our homes. In recent years, televangelists have aggressively proclaimed the Gospel via satellite. One of the most shining examples of faith in action is set by Mother Teresa, whose selfless life of charity so vividly exemplifies Gospel values.

As mothers, we too proclaim the Good News. Our actions and words are often subtle and low-key. We live Gospel values when we give a smile to a weary traveler in a crowded bus terminal, or when we taking daily meals to a disabled friend, or when we encourage a spouse

who's down and out. As mothers, we minister to the needs of our families countless times each day. What perfect opportunities to deliver the messages of love and peace to those around us.

We are all called to respect one another, to offer a helping hand when needed (not just when it's convenient for us) and to work toward reconciliation when conflicts arise. At the same time, God intends for us to experience joy—the joy that comes from living Gospel values. Jesus' disciple James reminds us:

> [I]t is best to listen much,
> speak little and not become angry...
> so get rid of all that is wrong in your life,
> both inside and outside,
> and humbly be glad for the
> wonderful message we have received,
> for it is able to save our souls as it
> takes hold of our hearts.
> — James 1:19-21 (TLB)

Peace

So many kinds, so many forms, so many types of
    peace.

...peace of mind

...peace of heart

        ...don't let it go away.

...peace within

...peace without

        ...if only it would stay.

...peace around

...peace about

        ...one more try, it's worth one more try,

        peace shall reign someday.

We know that the peace Christ promised is ever-present. Yet, at times—both personally and globally—we lose touch with this peace. What can I do to stay in touch with my inner peace?

_____

_____

_____

_____

_____

_____

Being There

On a nondescript morning of a nondescript day, an acquaintance of several years came walking through the office door.

His visit was all business; but his face showed much pain.

My temptation was to take care of business and say, "Have a nice day."

But those old Gospel values and words from my past brought forth an image of what Christ might have done.

A few words and a listening heart were all that it cost to let him know that someone did care.

Who walked into my life this week needing my listening heart?

_____

_____

_____

_____

_____

_____

Do I recognize Christ in others?

_____

_____

_____

_____

_____

_____

To Forgive and Be Forgiven

Dear God, there are so many lessons
  we want to pass on to our children.

Be polite, wash your hands, say "Thank you,"
  love your neighbor, get plenty of rest.

There is one lesson, God,
  that I strive each day to grasp.

That lesson
  is forgiveness.

I need Your help when I try to forgive
  the playful hands that decorated the carpet with
  shoe polish,

Or when I strive to forgive
  the teenager who pierced my heart with pain.

You are there when I seek forgiveness
for my quick temper,

Or when I ask pardon
for my forgetfulness that created problems at
home.

Help me, God, to be a living example
of Your forgiving love.

Amen.

Harmony

It's taken me a long time, God,
    to understand
    that we need not always see eye-to-eye
    in order to live in harmony.

And, actually, God,
    differences of opinion and taste
    help open our eyes
    to the vast possibilities that exist
    in the world You created.

My friends and I don't agree
    on the appropriate age for teens to date.
    (But they've got a point.)

I don't like to exercise,
    my doctor says it's a must.
    (She's right.)

My sister's a free-spirited liberal,
    I seem to be getting more conservative with age.
    (We have some interesting discussions!)

The neighbors have a ranch-style house,
　　ours is colonial.
　　(They're both beautiful.)

My husband likes caramel,
　　my favorite is chocolate.
　　(He's crazy.)

Our children prefer sports to homework,
　　we don't let them know that we really agree.
　　(That's life.)

My mother's pet peeves are coloring and perming hair,
　　I say hair's personal—do your own thing.
　　(Does it really matter?)

Agreement on all things at all times?
　　It's just not possible.
　　(Honest.)

Respect, admiration, compassion, understanding.
　　Harmony can exist in all God's creations.
　　(Thanks for the insight, God!)

Humility with a Capital "H"

Those unspeakable (nearly unthinkable) moments
    when fate reminds us of our human frailty.

Those embarrassing, unplanned events
    that derail even the best-laid plans.

Like the time we were an hour or so into a
booked-solid flight and our 10-year-old developed a
sudden, violent case of stomach flu. Our hearts
ached for the child while our minds searched for a
convenient way out. We were there for him.

Or the morning I left the bank with a new box of
1,000 blank business checks on top of my car. The
hitch: I forgot to put the box inside the car before
driving off. By the time I realized the error of my
ways, checks were scattered for blocks and we had
an account that needed to be closed. I felt labored
and burdened.

Thanks, Lord, for seeing us through our very
    vulnerable, very human times.

What was a time when, with God's grace, I was able to muddle through or even laugh at a very trying situation?

_____

_____

_____

_____

_____

_____

Gifts Mothers Understand So Well

Gentle hands help tie a shoe,
    wipe a tear,
    pat an aching back.

Knowing eyes watch with pride,
    see the truth,
    look for signs of grief.

Ever-alert ears hear the cries,
    sense the pain,
    listen for the joy.

Concerned minds ponder problems,
    search for clues,
    answer others' needs.

Loving hearts beat in sympathy,
    fill with love,
    try to understand.

Gifts we give
    throughout the years
    expecting nothing in return.

Time Out for Fun

"Come on, Mom, let's play,"
  you've heard those words before.

"Not now, I'm busy,"
  is a frequent response, though, as the guilt begins
  to grow.

"Laugh! Relax! Have fun!"
  an inner voice does say.

"Sure," you think,
  remembering all that has to be done.

There's a stack of bills,
  a pile of laundry
  and reports to be filled out.

Sometimes amidst the busywork
  and chores and jobs to do,
    God reminds us of our children's words:
    "Come on, Mom, let's play."

"Come to me,
all you who are weary and find life burdensome,
and I will refresh you."
— Matthew 11:28 (NAB)

What application do these words of Christ have in my life?

_____

_____

_____

_____

_____

_____

VI. Simply Sacred

Smiling

Tokens, Trinkets & Treasures

A Coming of Age

Handpainted in Portugal

Love's Touch

Enjoy Today!

Cash In on Daydreams

VI.

Simply Sacred

As mothers, each of us can provide countless examples of memories and moments that hold special places in our hearts. Daily, we experience thoughts and feelings that remind us of the intimate connection we have with God. For me, jotting down those ideas is a concrete way to acknowledge the many blessings life holds.

I laughed when an acquaintance asked if I had some quiet, secluded hideaway where I went to write.

"Well," I said, "my kind of inspiration—if you can call it that—comes in spurts, at odd hours and in even stranger places."

She gave me a puzzled look. So I elaborated.

"Sometimes I'll be in the shower and a thought hits. Since I don't have a waterproof tape recorder, I'm often hard-pressed to remember the brilliant thought by the time I exit the shower.

"Other times, I'm spending what seem like endless hours in the car (we live in the country) commuting from home to school to work to church to the homes of family or friends when another seemingly worthy idea enters my consciousness. I nearly cause an accident searching for a pencil only to find the lead broken.

"Occasionally I will be sitting at the computer when the spirit moves me to write. But times like that, I get a 'Memory Full' message from the machine or we experience a power failure."

She looked even more puzzled by this time. So I explained that what I really do is write about everyday situations that somehow might connect me to the lives of many women who also share the role of motherhood.

"Oh," she said, the light clicking on in her mind, "so you don't spend all kinds of time concentrating and planning. You just sort of tell it like it is. You put your inner voice to paper."

She was right on target. That's because we each have our own practical, everyday, realistic approach to the prayers found deep within our hearts. Dwelling there are prayers that can lift spirits, provide inspiration, move mountains.

Smiling

Just outside the kitchen window...

Green fields highlighted by the afternoon sun...

Children's voices punctuated with squeals of joy...

Their love for life is contagious.

What are some views from my kitchen window?

_____

_____

_____

How might my love for life be more childlike and contagious?

_____

_____

_____

Tokens, Trinkets, & Treasures

Somewhere...
 in a closet, box or drawer...
 I have tokens, trinkets and treasures
 that carry special memories.

A wilted flower.
A faded snapshot.
A note from way-back-when.

Somehow,
 sometimes
 I find these things
 tucked away
 somewhere.

Amazing
 how just a glimpse
 can bring the past to life.

Thanks, God,
 for being there in my memories.
 Amen.

A Coming of Age

Who would ever think
that a peanut butter and jelly sandwich
could mark
the changing
of the generational guards?

She was a marvelous Great Granny.
For years she coddled and cooked,
    comforted and caressed.

"Hey, Mom," came a voice from the kitchen.
"Can I make a peanut butter and jelly sandwich?"
Before Mom could answer,
Great Gran replied:
"Can you make one for me?"

Wasting no time, the eleven-year-old hands set about
    the task
    of creating two insignificant little sandwiches—
    one for Gran and one for him.

The sticky snack was devoured and forgotten.
What will remain forever
   is the memory
   of the pride on their faces
   when he said:
   "Here Gran, I made it just for you."

Lord, thank you for opening our eyes
   to the simple things.

And, thank you for Great Gran who added to the
special moment when she said,
   "You know, not only is that the *best* sandwich I've
   ever had, it's so nice that you care about me."

Lord, thanks, too, for teaching us how to care.

Amen.

Handpainted in Portugal

It's sometimes tough
   to be enthusiastic
   about yet another of those
   quick, unglamorous meals-in-a-box.
They've become
   a sort of necessary convenience
   in our homes today.

The other day
   while cooking one
   I glanced behind the stove.
A tile there looked back at me,
   its colors bright and crisp.
Painted there in simple lines
   was a story often told
   of a woman in much calmer times
   completing her daily chores.

The artist somehow passed on to me
    the sacredness of these tasks—
    whether milking cows or cooking meals
    the story's much the same.
We ask that God be present
    in all we do and say.

Amen.

What thoughts or prayers race through my mind as I scramble to prepare meals?

_____

_____

_____

_____

_____

_____

Love's Touch

There are sonnets, ballads and essays.

Sentiment flows from each.

Words attest to the power, the glory, the joy and
even pain of love.

Love is the greatest gift we can give or receive.

It cannot be contained in a box all tied up with
string,

nor trapped on the printed page.

It flourishes as it flows from God through our hearts

touching those around us.

Where in my life am I touched by love?

_____

_____

_____

_____

_____

_____

Enjoy Today!

Relax.
   Just do it.
   Put your cares aside.
   Just for today.

Smile.
   Just do it.
   Tuck that frown away.
   Just for today.

Play.
   Just do it.
   The work can wait.
   Just for today.

Rejoice.
   Just do it.
   Sorrow need not overwhelm.
   Just for today.

Enjoy.
    Just do it.
    Worry won't help anyhow.
    Just for today.

Praise.
    Just do it.
    For the good times and bad.
    For today and every day.

Amen.

What can I do to let my spirit shine today?

_____

_____

_____

_____

_____

_____

Cash In on Daydreams

Kick back.
Gaze out a window.
Daydream.

Take time.
Look to a bright future.
Frivolous thoughts are free.

Open your eyes.
Be hopeful.
Let your thoughts know no bounds.

Hold fast to dreams.
Keep hope in your heart.
It will do your mind a world of good.

Remember,
God gave you
the world to explore,
and a lifetime in which to do it.